International Political Economy Series

General Editor: **Timothy M. Shaw**, Professor of Commonwealth Governance and Development, and Director of the Institute of Commonwealth Studies, School of Advanced Study, University of London

Titles include:

Hans Abrahamsson
UNDERSTANDING WORLD ORDER AND STRUCTURAL CHANGE
Poverty, Conflict and the Gobal Arena

Morten Bøås, Marianne H. Marchand and Timothy M. Shaw (*editors*)
THE POLITICAL ECONOMY OF REGIONS AND REGIONALISMS

Sandra Braman (*editor*)
THE EMERGENT GLOBAL INFORMATION POLICY REGIME

James Busumtwi-Sam and Laurent Dobuzinskis (*editors*)
TURBULENCE AND NEW DIRECTIONS IN GLOBAL POLITICAL ECONOMY

Martin Doornbos
GLOBAL FORCES AND STATE RESTRUCTURING
Dynamics of State Formation and Collapse

Bill Dunn
GLOBAL RESTRUCTURING AND THE POWER OF LABOUR

Myron J. Frankman
WORLD DEMOCRATIC FEDERALISM
Peace and Justice Indivisible

Barry K. Gills (*editor*)
GLOBALIZATION AND THE POLITICS OF RESISTANCE

Richard Grant and John Rennie Short (*editors*)
GLOBALIZATION AND THE MARGINS

Graham Harrison (*editor*)
GLOBAL ENCOUNTERS
International Political Economy, Development and Globalization

Patrick Hayden and Chamsy el-Ojeili (*editors*)
CONFRONTING GLOBALIZATION
Humanity, Justice and the Renewal of Politics

Axel Hülsemeyer (*editor*)
GLOBALIZATION IN THE TWENTY-FIRST CENTURY
Convergence or Divergence?

Helge Hveem and Kristen Nordhaug (*editors*)
PUBLIC POLICY IN THE AGE OF GLOBALIZATION
Responses to Environmental and Economic Crises

Takashi Inoguchi
GLOBAL CHANGE
A Japanese Perspective

Kanishka Jayasuriya
STATECRAFT, WELFARE, AND THE POLITICS OF INCLUSION

Dominic Kelly and Wyn Grant (*editors*)
THE POLITICS OF INTERNATIONAL TRADE IN THE 21st CENTURY
Actors, Issues and Regional Dynamics

Mathias Koenig-Archibugi and Michael Zürn (*editors*)
NEW MODES OF GOVERNANCE IN THE GLOBAL SYSTEM
Exploring Publicness, Delegation and Inclusiveness

Craig N. Murphy (*editor*)
EGALITARIAN POLITICS IN THE AGE OF GLOBALIZATION

George Myconos
THE GLOBALIZATION OF ORGANIZED LABOUR
1945–2004

John Nauright and Kimberly S. Schimmel (*editors*)
THE POLITICAL ECONOMY OF SPORT

Morten Ougaard
THE GLOBALIZATION OF POLITICS
Power, Social Forces and Governance

Richard Robison (*editor*)
THE NEO-LIBERAL REVOLUTION
Forging the Market State

Leonard Seabrooke
US POWER IN INTERNATIONAL FINANCE
The Victory of Dividends

Timothy J. Sinclair and Kenneth P. Thomas (*editors*)
STRUCTURE AND AGENCY IN INTERNATIONAL CAPITAL MOBILITY

Fredrik Söderbaum and Timothy M. Shaw (*editors*)
THEORIES OF NEW REGIONALISM

Susanne Soederberg, Georg Menz and Philip G. Cerny (*editors*)
INTERNALIZING GLOBALIZATION
The Rise of Neoliberalism and the Decline of National Varieties of Capitalism

International Political Economy Series
Series Standing Order ISBN 0-333-71708-2 hardcover
Series Standing Order ISBN 0-333-71110-6 Paperback
(*outside North America only*)

You can receive future titles in this series as they are published by placing a standing order. Please contact your bookseller or, in case of difficulty, write to us at the address below with your name and address, the title of the series and one of the ISBNs quoted above.

Customer Services Department, Macmillan Distribution Ltd, Houndmills, Basingstoke, Hampshire RG21 6XS, England

Statecraft, Welfare, and the Politics of Inclusion

Kanishka Jayasuriya
Principal Research Fellow
Asia Research Center, Murdoch University, Australia

First published in 2006 by
PALGRAVE MACMILLAN
Houndmills, Basingstoke, Hampshire RG21 6XS and
175 Fifth Avenue, New York, N.Y. 10010
Companies and representatives throughout the world.

PALGRAVE MACMILLAN is the global academic imprint of the Palgrave
Macmillan division of St. Martin's Press, LLC and of Palgrave Macmillan Ltd.
Macmillan® is a registered trademark in the United States, United Kingdom
and other countries. Palgrave is a registered trademark in the European
Union and other countries.

ISBN–13: 978–0230–00211–1 hardback
ISBN–10: 0–230–00211–0 hardback

This book is printed on paper suitable for recycling and made from fully
managed and sustained forest sources.

A catalogue record for this book is available from the British Library.

Library of Congress Cataloging-in-Publication Data

Jayasuriya, Kanishka, 1959–
    Statecraft, welfare, and the politics of inclusion / Kanishka Jayasuriya.
      p. cm.—(International political economy series)
    Includes bibliographical references and index.
    ISBN 0–230–00211–0
     1. Social policy. 2. Neoliberalism. I. Title. II. International political economy
series (Palgrave (Firm))

HN18.3.J38 2006
330.12′6—dc22
                                                2005056372

10 9 8 7 6 5 4 3 2 1
15 14 13 12 11 10 09 08 07 06

Printed and bound in Great Britain by
Antony Rowe Ltd, Chippenham and Eastbourne

To My Parents

Contents

Acknowledgements

Much of the stimulus for this volume came from my work on globalization and social policy at the Asia Research Centre (ARC), Murdoch University, where I am currently located. I am greatly indebted to Garry Rodan, the director, for his generous support for this work. I also wish to acknowledge the intellectual stimulation and collegial atmosphere at the Asia Research Centre. The centre is a rare example of a university – based research institution that enables the pursuit of basic rather than 'applied' social science research, and demonstrates a commitment and capacity to undertake this kind of quality research in the contemporary academic environment.

Some of the ideas and themes on which this volume is based emerged during my earlier work at the South East Asian Research Centre, City University of Hong Kong and for this I thank Kevin Hewison, for promoting my fieldwork and work on Thailand, which has helped me in fashioning the framework developed in this volume. I have also benefited considerably from the ongoing conversations over a number of years with Richard Robison, going back to my tenure in the mid-1990s at the ARC during his stewardship as director.

I remain greatly indebted to a number of colleagues, in particular, Daniel Bell, Mark Beeson, Michael Dowdle, Vedi Hadiz, Richard Higgott, Laksiri Jayasuriya, Khoo Boo Teik, Martin Painter, Pasuk Phongpaichit, M. Ramesh, Andrew Rosser, Vivienne Wee and Anna Yeatman, all of whom have been ever willing to engage in discussions, and assisted me in different ways in completing this work. The usual disclaimer applies.

Finally, I would like to thank my parents for their encouragement and support.

KANISHKA JAYASURIYA
Perth, Australia
September 2005

Introduction

As I write this, the 2005 G8 Summit at Gleneagles – with a supporting cast of ageing rock stars and celebrities – claimed a frontal assault on African poverty. Crocodile tears, or the end of neo liberalism? Stripped to its bare essentials it is this question that prompted this study. The G8 Summit is but one illustration of an intriguing dilemma. On the one hand there is a new social agenda with an enhanced focus – discernable even within the ramparts of neo liberalism such as the World Bank and other international financial institutions – on such issues as poverty and welfare; then, on the other hand, this new ethos, often couched in a new political language of inclusion and cognate governance structures, is framed within the boundaries set by the market model which has dominated politics and policy over the last three decades in advanced industrial as well as newly industrializing countries.

Therefore, the critical problem posed in this volume is: do these new social policies and programmes present a fundamental challenge to the neo liberal model? Or, rather, are they merely an attempt to develop new forms of regulatory governance to entrench programmes of economic reform? It is neither crocodile tears nor the end of neo liberalism. Rather, I argue that these forms of social governance provide a logic and rationale for developing a new social policy agenda arising from core elements of the neo liberal market model. Yet, this cannot be simply written off as a 'warmed-up' version of neo liberalism. The new social politics provide a terrain of engagement for social issues, one which is different from the postwar social democratic model – what we call 'social constitutionalism'. In this sense it provides the language and regulatory space for the socialization of the market, and it is this regulatory space that is the focus of this study.

This volume explores this new social politics through the frameworks of welfare governance that attempt to constitute what Gilbert (2002) calls an 'enabling state'. These forms of social regulation, however, differ from the hard-edged neo liberalism of privatization and the retrenchment of welfare services that marked the first phase of neo liberalism. It is this more recent socialization of the market model and its distinctive political language and institutions – not the programmes of market reform – that is likely to be the distinctive feature of neo liberal politics

1

in the early twenty-first century. This signifies a fundamental transformation of the 'idea of welfare' that underpinned the postwar social settlement in industrial democracies of the western world – a social settlement which framed welfare in terms of its function as a means of compensation or redistribution to redress the vagaries and inequalities created by the operation of market forces. The terms of engagement of the postwar 'social question' which hinged on the negotiation between the competing logic of market and social solidarity has now been replaced by a new emphasis on social policy in the enabling of greater or heightened economic participation. In order to explore the nature of these policy thrusts towards a social politics of inclusion, the study examines its relationship to the market model, scrutinizing some of its justificatory principles and assumptions, and identifying the political forces and coalitions that underpin the strategies of inclusion. But at the same time we need to situate this social politics within the wider context of the transformation of the idea of welfare from earlier social democratic notions of social protection. Third way politics – or, better, strategies of statecraft – represent a move towards the socialization of the neo liberal market model.

Different manifestations of these 'third ways' are identified in the New Labour social policies of the UK as well as in the populist social contracts in Thailand, the welfare programmes in Korea or the social agenda of Lula in Brazil or Kirchner in Argentina. All these statecraft projects seek to reconcile a commitment to market reform with the politics of inclusion.

But the most important outcome of this new socialized neo liberalism is that it delineates new institutional arenas within the state for deliberation and engagement over social policy. Importantly, this argument suggests that the politics of inclusion cannot simply be reduced to the neo liberal model. In fact, as we see in our case studies of Thailand and Korea, it has its own internal political logic that brings it into conflict with various aspects of neo liberalism. But the thread that runs through these variegated third way projects is a reconstruction of citizenship as a 'market citizenship' which, in contrast to the social citizenship of the postwar welfare state, seeks to enable participation and inclusion within the economic order.

In this context a key proposition advanced in this volume is that this emerging form of welfare governance reflects a new constitutional order described as an 'economic constitutionalism' which, unlike social constitutionalism, privileges the pursuit of economic and market order, and fosters a notion of welfare as market citizenship. This form of 'economic constitutionalism' is not confined merely to formal legal practices, but also pertains to the broader set of state–society relations as well as to the guiding normative principles of the political order. In other words, it reconstitutes the state and what sparked my interest in this research project was the recognition that social policy – far from evaporating within this reconstituted state – continued to play a crucial role. But herein lies the challenge. Whilst social policy continues to play a role within economic constitutionalism, a fundamental transformation is occurring in the nature of the social question, that is, the analysis, understanding and response to the social inequalities created by capitalist market in these various forms of 'economic constitutionalism'.

Economic constitutionalism frames the social question in a manner that incorporates the 'social' within the 'economic' realm in the form of a 'market citizenship'. For example, this is illustrated in the development of various 'asset-based' forms of social policy that are seen as strengthening the entrepreneurial endowments and capabilities of citizens for participation within the economic order. Asset-based policies of this kind exemplify a normative framing of welfare, thereby entailing the creation of a very different mode of social association geared towards inclusion and participation within the sphere of the market. At the same time these strategies of inclusion, characteristic of economic constitutionalism, are not mere functional responses to changed economic circumstances; they are also distinctly political projects of statecraft that reshapes the relationship between political community and the state. In this context that social policy becomes a vital instrument of this statecraft of inclusion, and facilitates a social contract that articulates a new relationship between citizen and the state by transforming the means and purposes of public action.

The social policies examined in this book are not aiming to push back the state, but rather the achievement of some measure of internal transformation within the state. Paradoxically, these policies devote as much attention to the economic regulation of markets as they do to social policy concerns. Therefore, insofar as social governance constitutes an essential element of the new regulatory state, neo liberalism reshapes the institutional architecture of the state. Though neo liberalism is often identified in terms of the retreat and withdrawal of the state from the allocation of social and material goods, I propose that its more profound impact lies in the way it entrenches new forms of social and economic regulation of the market.

Finally, a guiding motif in this book is the way in which political liberalism itself is being transformed by the politics of social inclusion. As we argue, a significant consequence of this new social policy rationale is that social institutions and their governance are depoliticized in a way that limits the conflict and negotiation of social interests that formed such a crucial element of social constitutionalism in the earlier era. This earlier model of social constitutionalism was sustained by the politics of negotiation and conflict of social interests that in turn hinged on the dualism between the market and the social sphere. Welfare was at the heart of this often conflictual and contradictory logic of the market and social solidarity. But this politics of social conflict or, more broadly, a politics of interest, is absent in the new economic constitutionalism that has come to dominate both the industrialized and newly industrializing countries.

And this is clearly evident in the fact that by reshaping welfare along the lines of policies of social inclusion, the new welfare governance situates liberal subjects in terms of their capacity for inclusion within the economic mainstream not in terms of the political standing of citizens. Inclusion suggests a very different structure of social claim making because claim making within the new strategies of inclusion is based on the possession and management of those endowments or capacities needed to participate and compete within the productive sphere of the economy. All this serves to reinforce an anti pluralist strand of liberalism that is at the core of economic constitutionalism.

The book is structured as follows. As a preamble to the substantive issues surrounding the new set of social contracts evident in the contemporary phase of neo liberalism, the opening chapter examines the relationship between the new welfare governance and the market. These new ideas of welfare and markets are explored through an analysis of two strands of liberalism: the ordo liberal movement and the early twentieth-century New Liberalism. Both forms of liberalism have one distinctive feature in common with contemporary forms of welfare governance in that they both seek to create liberal subjects who are embedded in the productive sphere of the economy. Equally, both strands of liberalism understand property rights as an inherently social and juridical process, rather than a spontaneous creation of market forces. The market is socialized, but in a manner different from the social democratic logic of social constitutionalism.

In Chapter 2 the study moves on to explore the distinctive normative foundations of the politics of social inclusion. If there is one key word that captures this new socialization of the market in various third way programmes it is 'capability'. Capability, it is argued, becomes a key term within the various forms of social democratic third way programmes because it enables the reconciliation of a liberal conception of individual autonomy with a social commitment to equality. However, the notion of capability as used in the new social democratic literature is presented largely as a descriptive rather than as an analytical category. I use the work of Amartya Sen to explore a more analytical and normative notion of capability that is especially interesting because of its many similarities with some of the philosophical thrust of the New Liberals. Based on Sen's capability paradigm, the study explores how third way programmes reframe equality from a notion of a 'simple equality' to that of 'complex equality' where equality can be mapped through multiple dimensions of capability. In turn, this reframing signifies a normative shift from a resource-oriented perspective, characteristic of old social democracy, to a notion of equality as the enhancement of the capabilities of individuals to pursue diverse ends.

Equally important is the fact that there has been a dramatic change in the delivery and governance of social policy, as well as in changes in the policy and practice of the welfare state in advanced industrial societies. But it is at the level of governance that these changes are most pronounced, and these governance arrangements are subject to critical scrutiny in Chapter 3. At the heart of these governance changes is the organization of social policy around modes of contractual governance. Welfare now becomes an organized set of contractual relationships, and the notion of contractualism itself signifies a restructuring of the relationship between state and citizen, as well as a reshaping of the basis of membership of the political community. From a social policy perspective this amounts to not only a change in delivery mechanisms of benefits or entitlements, but also directs our attention to a more fundamental reshaping of the state and society in the direction of conditional citizenship that ties citizenship to market participation. While this contractual governance subjects citizens to often stringent procedural controls these procedures and the broader governance arrangements are placed outside the framework of democratic control and judicial review. But is neo liberalism contractualism the only alternative? I suggest an alternative of democratic contractualism based on Habermas's work on law and democracy.

Contractualism, an equally significant dimension of the new global social policy, is explored in Chapter 4, which examines the governance of transnational social policy, especially in the emphasis that has come to be placed on the social agenda of poverty reduction. This rediscovery of poverty by the global community differs from the earlier 'Washington Consensus' approach in that it identifies poverty reduction as a primary objective of global public policy. But what is important in these new policy strategies is the contractual framework through which the social agenda is implemented. Contractual governance of global social standards has become a strategy of regulatory governance that seeks to influence the conduct of agents at various levels of governance. The new social standards are premised on meeting certain obligations so that, even at the transnational level, claims associated with welfarism are contingent on the prior and continuing performance of certain obligations and not simply based on the membership of the political community.

But this mode of contractual governance seeks to ensure not only that stakeholders be consulted, but also that their deliberations and participation are seen as vital in establishing the legitimacy of programmes and policies. All forms of contractualism – be it the transnational social policy or New Labour's social programmes in the UK – attempt to enrol clients in deliberative policy making. Indeed, much of welfare contractualism is about setting out the procedures for this participation rather than mandating specific policy outcomes. But the point is this: new forms of participation are 'problem oriented' and located in institutional arenas outside the formal representative structures of political society.

Transnational social policy is one form of 'third way' politics, but equally significant third way trajectories can be discerned in statecraft projects under way in newly industrializing countries because these states confront social issues raised by economic restructuring. Illustrative of this trend is the emergence of the statecraft of the social market in South Korea, the subject of Chapter 5. South Korea, hit hard by the Asian economic crisis of 1997–98, has responded by placing an increased emphasis on social policies and expenditure. It is argued in this chapter that these policies were formulated in the context of a regulatory state that not only established procedures and institutions of economic governance, but also sought to establish forms of social regulation, best understood in terms of the development of an innovative social market model.

The essence of this social market model was the push to establish market imperatives at the heart of social policy. In this way, it sought to establish a form of welfare governance that was different from a notion of welfare as the amelioration of market forces through various redistributive mechanisms characteristic of the postwar European welfare state. At the same time this emerging social market model also differs from the various forms of East Asian productivism that made social policy an ancillary to the operation of economic forces. I argue that the

Korean social market model then, represents a distinctive 'third way' attempt to socialize the market in the context of transition from the developmental to the regulatory state.

Chapter 6 is devoted to an analysis of the dynamics of yet another 'third way' alternative in newly industrializing countries – namely the neo liberal populism manifest in Thailand. This chapter demonstrates how the new welfare governance has come to be reflected in the distinctive populist politics evident with the election of the Thaksin Shinawatra government which has radically transformed the political system in Thailand. There is little doubt that Thaksin fits the populist bill on several counts: he relies on personal leadership, his political message constantly invokes the idea of the Thai people, explicitly appeals to a notion of – albeit soft – Thai nationalism, relies on a broad cross class constituency, and on keeping his coalition together through the introduction of a range of new social contracts. This particular market model of Thaksin denotes a specific form of neo liberal populism similar to that found in Latin American countries. Neo liberal populism, however, is not simply limited to redefining social policy within a broader economic frame. It also illustrates a much more broad-based effort to reshape the internal architecture of the state as well as using welfare to rearticulate the fundamental relationships of state and society. Neo liberal populism is a form of statecraft.

The concluding chapter takes up the key questions of the relationship between the new politics of inclusion and changing forms of statecraft by examining how the new welfare governance fundamentally alters the nature and purpose of public authority or stateness. The broader point is that the idea of state transformation enables a more meaningful and theoretically defensible way of understanding the political dynamics of social policies in a neo liberal context. In particular, the collapse of the social democratic model and the developmental state has altered the context of welfare governance in both advanced industrial and newly industrializing countries. To this end, we examine social inclusion as a particular model of social association defined in terms of access to market participation. This model differs from those models of social association framed in terms of material relations of conflict based on the centrality of class and its struggles for recognition and representation. In contrast to this social democratic grammar of politics the new politics of inclusion exemplifies the 'new social question' of neo liberalism.

'. . . to develop a middle way of economic life which will preserve the liberty, the initiative and (what we are so rich in) the idiosyncrasy of the individual in a framework serving the public good and seeking equality of contentment amongst all . . .'

John Maynard Keynes

1
Economic Constitutionalism and Social Inclusion: Transforming Liberalism

The new welfare governance

At the beginning of the twenty-first century the neo liberal market model[1] that so dominated economic and social policy making during the later decades of the last century is increasingly being called into question. This arises not only from the anti-globalization movements (such as the World Social Forum), but also from the populist politics of elected governments in some of the newly industrializing countries. For example, in Latin America, the election of leaders such as Lula Da Silva of the Brazilian Workers Party, Nestor Kirchner in Argentina, and Hugo Chavez in Venezuela, has, it seems, bucked some of the main tenets of the 'Washington Consensus'. In East Asia, the election of Thaksin Shinawatra was on a platform that championed a form of Thai nationalism against the austerity policies advocated by the IMF. This would suggest that even on the home turf of the Washington Consensus – the 'miracle' economies of East Asia – the neo liberal economic policies that so dominated the 1990s are facing mounting pressures. These trends have been compounded by the development of a raft of policies and programmes that focus on issues such as poverty reduction and social safety nets[2] promoted by international financial institutions (IFI), and, especially, the World Bank. These developments would seem to document clearly a growing concern with, and awareness of, the social dimensions of economic development that were absent in the era of the hard-edged neo liberalism of the Washington Consensus. But to see this new welfare governance as a retreat from economic to social policy is to miss the essential point that this new policy strategy seeks to entrench a form of 'market citizenship' that differs from that reflected in the political grammar of postwar social democracy.

This chapter explores the nature and dimension of this emerging policy framework, particularly in its relationship to the neo liberal market model. As we shall argue, the social policies underlying this framework arise out of – but are not reducible to – neo liberalism. Public policy here is broadly defined as social

> when they deal with the allocation of resources and opportunities between potentially competing groups, and – as a consequence which may be more distant but equally important – with relations between groups in society, their status and self respect, their powers and their access to broader social opportunities. (Donnison 1976: 9)

But these social policies are organized around a certain understanding of public purpose, which are the proper and legitimate ends of policy, and within a technology of public action[3] – that is, the instruments, organization and concepts that mobilize social policy. The central argument of this volume is based on an analysis of the transition from the postwar social settlement in industrial democracies reflected – albeit in different ways – as a notion of welfare seen as a means of compensation or redistribution, to redress the vagaries and inequalities produced by the working of market forces, to an understanding of welfare as involving the enabling of participation within the sphere of the market. These changing notions of welfare reflect a deeper shift from what I have previously described as 'social constitutionalism', to a form of 'economic constitutionalism' (Jayasuriya 2005). This new constitutional order is not confined merely to formal legal practices, but also pertains to the broader set of state–society relations as well as the guiding normative principles of the political order. Importantly, this reorientation to a new form of constitutionalism favours the pursuit of an economic and market order which fosters a notion of welfare as market citizenship. The crux of the argument being advanced here is that social policy continues to play a crucial role in these new forms of economic constitutionalism, but that it is today designed and shaped so as to enhance inclusion within the market rather than having its earlier emphasis on the redistribution of income.

One of the consequences of this location of welfare and social policy within the market is a reinforcement of a new language of liberalism that contrasts with the negotiation of conflict of social interests within the postwar social constitutionalism. There is here a crucial shift in the language of liberalism away from political pluralism and towards the regulation and imposition of standards that are congruent with the larger objectives of the economic order. This chapter explores the language of liberalism that is associated with the new welfare governance. Arguing along these lines, it is suggested that this governance reflects a transformed liberalism that seeks to create new liberal subjects and institutions whose purpose and ends are shaped by economic imperatives that are seen to be inimical to pluralist politics of interest. Running counter to the thrust of much of the literature on the effects of globalization on the scope of the welfare state, this chapter explores how different ideas of 'welfare' have come to replace the postwar social democratic project of the welfare state. Of course, these shifts in ideas of welfare are not simply ideational; they come to be embodied in governmental routines, practices, and organization or are simply put in strategies of statecraft.

Framed in these terms the policies and programmes instituted by the political leaders drawn from countries such as Brazil (Lula) or Thailand (Thaksin) represent a kind of 'third way' politics that bears comparison with the policies of New Labour in the UK. Like New Labour, it could be argued that both Brazil and Thailand reflect a move that attempts to reconcile fidelity to market imperatives with policies dealing with issues of social disadvantage. In fact, in Brazil, Cardoso,[4] and, subsequently, Lula, have been active participants in the third way progressive governance conferences. The enrolment of Lula in the third way enterprise is noteworthy because Lula's Workers Party had previously been cast very much in the mould of a traditional socialist party. What this would appear to indicate is that Lula's programme is in many ways a continuation of Cardoso's policies and programmes.

Cardoso's Party of Brazilian Social Democracy (PSDB) initially presented a fairly standard Western European social democratic programme. Yet his party very quickly embraced neo liberal policies, but sought to supplement these policies with a commitment to dealing with the social fallout of these economic programmes (Powers 2001). As Powers rightly observes

> the inclusion of Cardoso and his government in the evolving Third way debate points up some important ways in which his experiment differs from others, above and beyond the obvious fact that Cardoso

governs a developing country and the third way has mostly been debated in Europe. (Powers 2001: 612–13)

Cardoso was replaced by Lula Da Silva representing the left-wing Workers Party which seems to promise a much more radical social agenda. Yet, this more left-oriented programme has in fact exhibited a significant continuity with the policies of the earlier Cardoso administration. Some analysts, such as Petras and Veltmeyer (2003), regard Lula's programme as a deepening of some of the key third way elements of Cardoso's programme. However, a simplistic dismissal of this as merely neo liberalism wrapped in radical rhetoric misses the crucial point that Lula's political project differs substantially from the policies advocated under the Washington Consensus. The crucial point is that Lula seeks to develop a significant social agenda while still being committed to neo liberal economic reform. Similarly, the populist government in Thailand, led by Thaksin Shinawatra, has introduced several substantial social policies the broad thrust of which have been to promote the entrepreneurial capacities of its citizens and to extend participation in the economic sphere. All of these different political projects have to be seen and understood neither as a 'warmed up' neo liberalism nor as a traditional social democracy, but rather as the development of a new neo liberal mode of sociability in the form of market citizenship.

Even at the transnational level poverty reduction strategies such as the World Bank's Poverty Reduction Strategy Paper (PRSP) have come to occupy a prominent role in transnational aid policy (see Chapter 3). The OECD sums up this new role for Development Assistance Cooperation (DAC) in the following terms:

> The DAC has embarked upon a complex of task of developing guidelines for donor support for poverty reduction, closely associating the developing partners in its deliberations. Lastly the donor countries and international financial institutions have stepped up debt forgiveness for the most heavily indebted poor countries, tying their efforts directly into poverty reduction strategies. This will be crucial for the reinforcement of those strategies, which have now become, in a practical way the accepted approach to development cooperation. (OECD 1999b: 3)

It is apparent from this that international financial institutions have shifted from purely financial or economic restructuring towards placing a higher priority on social goals such as poverty reduction. These trends have led some to fear – and others to hope – that the neo liberal market model may be on the wane. Although each of these views has a degree of truth they do not tell the whole story. Clearly, the market model or neo liberalism is being modified; but these new governments in Latin America and East Asia exhibit a continuing commitment to economic liberalization, albeit one which now places a strong emphasis on a whole new set of social contracts between the citizenry and the state.

These new social contracts and associated social policy agendas are being harnessed towards creating and facilitating active participation within the world of work. In this sense they seek to create new liberal subjects imbued with market or entrepreneurial capacities. Social inclusion and asset building have become the new watchwords for the new welfare governance. For this reason, these new social programmes call for a more activist role of the state that stands in contrast to earlier more economically oriented neo liberal strategies that sought to hollow out the state. Instead of hollowing out the state, these new social policy frameworks seek to create new forms of social regulation that actively foster market participation by individuals. This regulatory neo liberalism stands out more as a political rather than an economic project.

These new social forms and arrangements promoted in countries such as Brazil and Thailand, and also by the World Bank through its new social policy agenda, point to a neo liberal sociability which may be understood as a 'socialization of neo liberalism'. This understanding of sociability frames social issues or the 'social question' not in the language of social democracy, but in economic constitutionalism in a manner that makes it compatible with market efficiency. Hence, insofar as this brings back the 'social' it seeks to reframe the social or economic problems within – rather than in opposition or in contestation to – the market. And, crucially, it rejects the social democratic argument central to 'social citizenship', namely that the market, if left unhindered, will produce inequalities of income which can only be corrected through public intervention. The expectation is that these new social policies will in the long term work to include citizens within the sphere of the market rather than seeking – as in the more orthodox models of welfare – to insure against the vagaries of market misfortunes. Moving away from the conventional insurance model of welfare towards a more inclusive model constitutes an understanding of 'social citizenship' very different from that contained in the Marshallian sense of citizenship and welfare (Marshall 1964). By contrast, economic constitutionalism promotes an inclusive or a productivist version of welfare in which issues of poverty and inequality are 'identified with individual trajectories of social exclusion and the idea of shared social risk as the basis for organising solidarity is rejected' (Procacci 2001: 51). These social contracts allow for the promotion of a market citizenship, which above all, is consistent with neo liberal projects of economic reform. Neo liberalism then on this view is more than a set of economic prescriptions but is increasingly about the creation of social forms that promote enterprising subjects and values.

The argument here is not so much about the shift of expenditure or the retreat from the welfare state, but a fundamental reformulation of the idea of welfare. Much of the literature on the welfare state has remained exclusively concerned with distinguishing regimes and patterns of welfare to the exclusion of any normative practices that came to be embodied in welfare policy programmes and policies (Esping-Andersen 1990). As Pinker (1979) notes in his prescient book written just before the Thatcher era, there have always been competing traditions or ideas of welfare and these ideas, in turn, have reflected different understandings of the relationship between the market and welfare. In fact, Pinker (1979) draws pointed attention to – and implicitly advocates – the varying currents of what Levitas (1996, 1998) has elsewhere called a 'social integrationist' model of social policy. The 'integrationist' model envisages a relationship between market and social policy different from that implied in the then dominant social democratic framework of social policy. Thus, Pinker (1979: 241) advocates what he calls a model of welfare 'which sees no fundamental incompatibility between the enhancement of social welfare and the values of the mixed economy and pluralist social order'.

In tracing this productivist tradition in Britain to both Keynes and Beveridge,[5] Pinker implicitly appears to be contrasting this with Titmuss's (1974) notion of the welfare state as an 'institutional redistributive model'. In fact, during the last decade this social integrationist perspective has become much more influential, as evidenced in the increased popularity of terms such as 'social exclusion' and 'social capital'. Welfare, as the thrust of Pinker's argument suggests, is by no means a static concept. Significantly, he draws attention to the fact that competing forms of welfarism represent a version of a preferred model of social association and a relationship with the market. The implication of what Pinker is suggesting is that citizenship, or rather the normative grounding of citizenship – seen as the decisive link between welfare and the market – has always been historically variable. This is no less true of the postwar model of social citizenship so well articulated by Marshall.

But 'ideas of welfare' are not a free-floating set of traditions that can be cherry-picked. Rather, they remain tied to various political projects of citizenship and statecraft and the real question is: how and why are certain ideas of welfare replaced by others? Market citizenship carries with it a distinctive model of welfare that fundamentally changes the relationship between welfare and the market. And it is this shift towards 'market citizenship' which makes the new social policy a political project that is more than a simple amalgam of public policies. It also entails changes in the patterns and routines of statecraft as well as providing a distinctive model of social organization and association that is based less on class relations than on a consideration of promoting access to and participation within the economic sphere.

In other words, market citizenship is as much about statecraft as it is about welfare. Using this statecraft perspective allows us to understand, for example, that the much-discussed 'third way' is not so much a set of political beliefs or ideology as a set of governance arrangements, or a project of statecraft that seeks to reshape the relationship between state and citizen through the internal governance of the state. To the extent that the third way is a political ideology its central concern is with governance itself. It is within the interstices of this developing new statecraft that we need to identify and locate political projects such as British Labour's third way or Thaksin's new populist politics and even transnational programs such as the World Bank's Poverty Reduction Program (see Chapter 4).

Market citizenship, welfare, and economic constitutionalism

Citizenship, or, rather, the changing regimes of citizenship, lies at the heart of new frameworks of social policy. Citizenship, we know, can be defined either as a status or a practice: as a status, citizenship is defined by its legal attributes and conditions of access to various entitlements; as a practice, it is constituted through the way it is exercised by individuals in various social and political domains. In reality, any citizenship regime will be a combination of both 'legal status' and political practice, and, as Lister (1997: 41) argues,

citizenship is thus conceptualized here both as a status, carrying a wide range of rights, and as a practice, involving both obligations and political participation, broadly defined. Both as a practice and in the relationship between that practice and rights, citizenship can be understood as a dynamic process.

Lister's insight here about citizenship as a dynamic process provides us with the starting point for an understanding of citizenship as a fundamentally political process that reshapes state practices and institutions.

This understanding of citizenship as being tied to various statecraft projects underlines the fact that regimes of citizenship serve to define the form of citizens – i.e., how citizenship is understood in a given context. This has traditionally been at the centre of the burgeoning citizenship studies literature, but at the same time helps to define what we call 'stateness', which essentially concerns setting the boundaries and powers of public authority. In this sense projects of citizenship are at one and the same time creating new forms of public power and authority that serve to constitute these forms of citizenship practices. Recent studies of immigration policy in Western Europe (e.g., Joppke 1999) provide a rich illustration of how conceptions of 'stateness' have served to reinforce different practices of citizenship, especially as they relate to immigrant settlers in otherwise liberal states such as Germany, Holland, and the United Kingdom in the post-Second World War period. Using the concept of 'stateness' rather than the 'state' as a conceptual framework makes possible an analysis of how 'state transformation', or, indeed, 'state building', is an evolving political process. Or, worded differently, citizenship has to be understood as a socially constituted relationship between state and society and through which new forms of statehood or stateness are created. 'Stateness' is not a static property but a dynamic process; the statecraft project attempts – bearing in mind its contested nature – to shift conceptions of stateness through a notion of market citizenship.

White (2004), in formulating his own version of asset-based welfare, points out that there are various strands of economic citizenship – ranging from the libertarian to the new workfare programmes of the US. White is keen to distinguish between some of these market strands of economic citizenship from the substance of what in his view are potentially progressive policies such as widening asset ownership within the community. White is correct to point out the range of positions that can be found within the framework of economic citizenship, but the problem with this argument is that it fails to identify what links together these various notions of economic or market citizenship. We can identify five fundamental elements that link market citizenship. These are that:

i. citizenship is framed within the market rather than in opposition to, or in compensation for the effects of market activity;

ii. social policy within the market citizenship is designed so as to make a productive contribution or enhance greater participation within the economy;

iii. participation is individualized in terms of the ability to mobilize individual endowments of capacities and assets;

iv. social policy moves from a rights-based to a contractual version of welfare that makes social policy claims conditional on the performance of specified obligations or duties; and,

v. market citizenship tends to define social association in terms of access to, and participation within, the market.

In this sense third way programmes of all shapes and hues can be considered as programmes that give effect to forms of market citizenship. Instead of being in tension with the market, key ideas such as equality and redistribution have become reframed in a way that promotes inclusion within the productive sphere of the economy. Most crucially, in third way programmes such as that in New Labour in the UK, equality is understood as an 'equality of opportunity' where fairness is assessed in terms of participation within the market. It is a formulation that moves equality – as an issue of the redistribution of income – to a notion of equality as inclusion and participation within the market economy. For Cammack, commenting specifically on the work of Giddens, this does not mean either a marginalization of the role of the state or indeed of social policy; rather it

> reflects the 'second phase' neo liberal approach which moves on from initial short term 'shock treatment', aimed at dismantling structures hostile to the operations of markets, to the construction for the longer term of enduring institutions which will sustain markets and capitalist disciplines into the future. (Cammack 2004: 165)

These third way ideas therefore resonate with those traditions of welfare that seek to combine welfare with a productive market economy. Importantly, this goes well beyond the specifics of the third way programme to encompass a whole range of new social policy approaches – from the World Bank's social capital approach to the European Union's social exclusion policy. The common thread running through these otherwise different conceptions is a reworking of the 'social question' as one of market rather than social citizenship.

What this implies, as Rosanvallon (2000: 5) notes, is that 'in both cases the philosophical crisis of the welfare state indicates a decisive change in the perception of society that has prevailed for more than a century'. Rosanvallon, like Giddens, looks upon this transformation as driven by a new form of modernization that works to undermine the assumption around which the modern welfare state was built and con-solidated. New forms of economic complexity and risk, it is argued, demand that social policy be directed at furthering the risk management capacities of individuals. Along these lines the new social policy frame-works seek to place a high premium on the identification and prudential management of risk. This is a distinctive understanding of risk, that is, risk as precaution (Ewald 2000) or preventive governance (Shearing 1996) or prudentialism (O'Malley 1992) that emerges in these regulatory frameworks. What Ewald calls the 'notion of precaution' replaces the dominant notion of solidarity and compensation which formed the basis of much of the insurance programmes of the twentieth century. Indeed, as Ewald points out, this new emphasis on 'prevention' takes us back to dominant nineteenth- and twentieth-century notions of risk that were:

> obsessed with the problem of accidents (work or car); we are now rediscovering the existence of disaster, but with the difference that disasters are no longer, as before, attributed to God and his provi-dence, but to human responsibilities. It is in this deeply disrupted context that the notion of precaution now appears. (Ewald 2000: 59)

Similarly this principle of precaution or 'prudentialism', to use O'Malley's (1992) term, is most evident in the design of new neo liberal forms of social policy.

The predominant view that tends to cast these new social policy frameworks as a product of an inexorable process of modernization is limited in that it elides the political context in which these new frame-works now thrive. Overlooked in these sociological accounts is the fact that what we call the social democratic logic of the social question rested on a particular political grammar around which issues of equality and welfare were framed. In contrast, the third way frames the new social question in terms of how welfare governance enables or embeds market processes within the social process. The new welfare governance seeks to develop those capacities and endowments of individuals that will enable them to compete more effectively in the productive mainstream of society. The workfare programmes which have characterized Anglo-American social policy over the last decade demonstrate a vivid example of this mode of thinking. In fact,

> as western economies struggle with permanent mass unemployment, problems of productivity and pressures of global competition, and as states strive to hold back the level of public expenditure, it is demanded of social policies that they meet new criteria of economic rationality. (Walters 1997: 226)

But the underlying rationale of this market citizenship is evident across a broad domain of social policy initiatives, ranging from the World Bank's PRSP to participatory budgeting in Brazil (Jayasuriya 2003; Cammack 2001; see also Chapter 4). The new economic constitutionalism does not so much contract the welfare state as activate an idea of welfare that sits in tension with the redistributive and compensatory notions of social citizenship which defined the social constitutionalism of the earlier era of the welfare state.

Of course, some of these proposals are not entirely new. Recall, for example, that it was Beveridge (1942), in his path-finding report which led to the foundation of the welfare state, who recommended that unemployment benefit be made conditional on attendance at a training or work centre. Whatever the particular history of this tradition of welfare, there is no doubt that the direction of the new social policy paradigm is towards the constitution of welfare as a form of social investment combining economic efficiency with social welfare. In this sense, an inclusive society means furthering various forms of entrepreneurial governance that are intended to regulate the social conduct of citizens. In locating the social within the market the new social policy marginalizes issues of class and class conflict while at the same time enhancing a model of social association that is based on access to participation within the market.

Linking markets to welfare

Central to our argument is that this shift from social to market citizenship is expressive of a deeper transformation in the liberal order. Social citizenship was organized around the negotiation and conflict of interest which originated in the dualism between the market and the social sphere. In contrast, market citizenship reflects a more anti-pluralist understanding of politics that seeks to subordinate social policy to market imperatives. It marginalizes those social relations that arise in conflict with the market in favour of modes of social association based on access to, and participation within, the market. Consequently, notions such as *social capital* and *community* have come to replace class and social conflict; and, importantly, this reflects a deeper transformation in the language of liberalism towards the inculcation of certain standards of behaviour or values rather than the mediation and negotiation of social conflict. We explore two earlier liberal traditions – the ordo liberals and the New Liberalism – as a way of putting some flesh on the liberal language of market citizenship.

At the core of this market citizenship and the new welfare governance are two key liberal concepts of welfare: one is the idea of 'inclusion' within the economic mainstream of all citizens, and the other is that of economic independence to enable individuals to compete more effectively within a globalized market economy. But this language of liberalism moves away from the politics or pluralism of social interests sustained by the competing ontologies of the market and social solidarity, towards a liberalism that is increasingly anti-political. The new welfare governance therefore needs to be understood in terms of this more fundamental reconstitution of the language of a pluralist liberalism. Social contracts, then, somewhat surprisingly become the leading edge through which these new liberal subjects are being created.

The notion of inclusion occupies a key role in the justification for welfare couched in terms of including individuals in the mainstream of social and economic life, and finds expression in those policies that are designed to promote a social market economy. An important precursor to this understanding of the social within regulatory neo liberalism can be found in the ordo liberal tradition that seeks to marry a strong state to a commitment to maintaining economic order within a competitive market economy. In particular, as I have argued elsewhere (Jayasuriya 2001a, 2001b, 2005), this is consistent with an understanding of economic and social intervention as a way of 'constitutionalizing' economic processes. Economic constitutionalism refers to the attempt to treat the market as a constitutional order with its own rules, procedures, and institutions operating to protect the market order from political interference. I trace these ideas through an exploration of the social market traditions of ordo liberalism, especially the argument that social conduct needs to be market conforming.

A cognate notion that drives new welfare governance is the desire to improve the economic independence of individuals by enhancing the asset holdings of the poor and the socially disadvantaged. In this particular strand of the new welfare governance greater inclusion within the economic mainstream is to be accomplished through policies that enhance the capacities and endowment of individuals to compete within a globalized economy. These ideas are explored through an analysis of the British New Liberal tradition whose members include theorists such as Hobhouse and Hobson. These ideas are similar to the economic constitutionalism of the ordo liberals which locates welfare within the ontology of the market order. But in these versions liberal subjects are located within a moralized or 'ethical' market economy.

Ordo liberalism and the social market

The guiding idea of the ordo liberal tradition is that the construction of economic order cannot be left to the spontaneous actions of the market, and needs to be created through a consistent order-based policy (*ordnungspolitik*) of the state (Peacock and Willgerodt 1989). For the ordo liberals the 'various economic, political, legal, and other social processes are interrelated. Each act of government intervention must therefore be seen in connection with the total processes and overall economic order so as to ensure the 'system conformity of measures' (Petersmann 1991: 63). Accordingly, the state should not attempt to conduct the economy; rather, it should provide a system of juridical institutions that would facilitate the construction of the market. In fact, in its emphasis on the role of economic institutions in creating market order it presages the new institutional economics. The point here is that the purpose of the state is to protect the underlying values and traits ('the economic constitution') of the economic order.

Hence the central characteristic of this 'economic constitutionalism' is the attempt to insulate social and economic institutions from the assumed debilitating effects of political bargaining (Jayasuriya 1999a, 2000a, 2001a, 2001b), so much so that the

> economic constitution distinguishes between those actions that are consistent with the economic freedom-based logic of that choice and those that are not. The former represents 'conforming' conduct, the latter is politically based regulatory discretion. Economic constitutionalism thus represents a cognitive map or template for evaluating governmental action. (Gerber 1994: 17)

But the point here is that this economic constitutionalism, as Gerber observes, encompasses much more than a shift towards a rule-based rather discretionary economic policy; it is equally concerned with enabling 'conforming conduct' within the sphere of civil society. From this perspective, economic constitutionalism seeks to institute processes and structures of governance that activate modes of conduct appropriate to a competitive market economy.

Running through the ordo liberal movement, it is possible to discern a distinctive political dimension to notions of economic constitutionalism. In essence the ordo liberals develop a political conception of market order where institutions are designed to protect it from the corrosive influence of politics; it is a politics of anti-politics. Those concerned about the anti-competitive effects of society on the economy, for example, as Eucken (1950), argued that by the end of the nineteenth century the state was increasingly captured by private interest groups leading to the politicization of the economy, which, in turn, weakened the state. Economic constitutionalism was not merely designed to protect economic institutions of the market from 'political interference', but also to facilitate the creation of the kind of social order that is consistent with the market economy. What is crucial here is the fact that the purpose of the state is defined in terms of pursuing the ends of economic order articulated within a language of liberalism which itself is counterposed to the pluralism of social interests.

The economic constitutionalism of the kind promoted here has two important features: first, it sees markets as a product of state or political intervention. In this view, properly functioning and effective markets require systematic state intervention. This view of state intervention is a significant departure from those public choice conceptions of state intervention – so influential in the early development of neo liberalism – that reduce any form of state intervention in the marketplace to unhealthy predatory impulses. The ordo liberal tradition of capitalism was conceptualized as a system that was intrinsically juridical in form, and, therefore, government or statecraft in our terminology, must seek to consciously provide economic order and security (Lemke 2001).[6] The difference here is that for the ordo liberals a strong state is essential for the protection and furthering of market forms. To use Oakeshott's terminology, the state becomes an enterprise association whose purpose it is to promote economic order.

But economic order goes beyond the governance of economic institutions; it also seeks to regulate those elements in society that are deemed to be uncompetitive. For the ordo liberals, society itself can become an obstacle to an efficient and competitive market, so much so that it becomes an object of governance, particularly to those economic institutions that are considered vital for the maintenance of economic order.

Economic constitutionalism as envisaged in ordo liberal accounts encompasses much more than a move towards a rule-based economic policy; it is equally concerned with directing 'conforming conduct' within the sphere of civil society. What this amounts to is that social order is inextricably tied to the reproduction of economic order. Thus, programmes that seek to maintain economic order must seek to institute processes and structures of governance that activate modes of entrepreneurial conduct appropriate to an efficient market economy. Not only does the state become an 'enterprise association', but society itself is seen as a site that can further entrepreneurial forms of action.

These perceptions of economic and social order that came to be embodied in the notion of the social market economy formed an important aspect of ordo liberal thinking. Importantly, for our purposes these strands of liberalism exemplify a neo liberal understanding of welfare which can be clearly distinguished from earlier formulations of social citizenship. Ordo liberalism justifies state intervention in the social realm only to the extent that it promotes those entrepreneurial forms considered to be vital for the effective functioning of the market economy. The economy and society, though acknowledged as separate realms, only serve to reinforce the fundamentals of the economic order of society; hence social intervention can be justified if it has a substantial impact on the reproduction of economic order.

The origin of the term 'social market economy' is to be found in the work of Alfred Muller-Armack who was associated with the Freiburg School.[7] His contribution to ordo liberalism was expanding the legalistic focus of the ordo liberal programme to encompass a range of social measures that were thought to be essential for the maintenance of economic order. Not surprisingly, some of these social market ideas proved to be an especially important element in the formation of the postwar German economy. As Joerges and Rödl (2004: 15) point out:

> The political function of the term 'social market economy' was basically to present an alternative to the socialist or at least interventionist ('mixed economy') spirit of the era dominating public opinion and the conforming to the practical predominance of planning elements in Germany's economy during the occupation period.

But what is a social market economy? Muller-Armack discussed a number of ways in which market and societal spheres mutually reinforced each other (Joerges and Rödl 2004). The first way was through the mutually beneficial social effects of the market through lower prices or the range of products available in the market. However, societal intervention was justified to the extent that it performed two functions which we might call an order and legitimacy function. Muller-Armack (1966) argues for those policies such as full employment which serve to maintain whatever social order was considered essential to market order. But more interesting was his expansion of the notion of the social market economy. It was framed in a way that social problems were related to more basic

> concerns about the stable pertinence of liberal society under – as he perceived them 'modern' conditions. The most threatening factors were 'mass society' as a whole and its general tendency towards proletarianisation, as well as specific institutions of mass society, namely large business concerns and mass organizations. (Joerges & Rödl 2004: 17)

However, we need to bear in mind that this justified state intervention only to the extent that it promoted and furthered market and economic order. As a result, various innovative institutional schemes to enable greater individual participation within the economic sphere become tethered to a broader pattern of economic constitutionalism. Accordingly, social policy becomes an integral element in the management of an efficient economic programme. What is critical here is that social policy rather than 'lessening the anti-social consequences of competition ... had to block the anti-competitive mechanisms which society can spawn' (Lemke 2001: 195). Within this tradition of economic constitutionalism, welfare was not compensatory, but was perceived largely as an instrument of economic reform to create more competitive and entrepreneurial forms of conduct within social institutions.

However, considering that in the social market model societal institutions were seen as subordinate to the demands of economic order, this did not necessarily rule out extensive intervention in the social sphere. Rather, it implicitly embodied the 'anti-pluralist' liberalism of economic constitutionalism by seeking to mould societal interest to the values of the market order. In fact, the very pluralism of politics was seen to be a potential source of anti-competitive values and behaviour. Therefore social interests and conflict were seen to be fundamentally at odds with the institutions of economic order (Joerges and Rödl 2004). In this sense, the social market economy, at least as conceptualized by the ordo liberals, has markedly anti-pluralist and had authoritarian elements. Market citizenship embodies some of these anti-pluralist elements and it is in this language of liberalism that we can identify a major dividing line between the new welfare governance and the social constitutionalism of the postwar period.

From this vantage point various versions of the third way can be seen as constituting the basis for a new framework of the social question that attempts to justify public intervention in the social order in terms of the imperative of the market order itself. Pivotal to this approach to social policy is the 'legitimacy function' that Muller-Armack identified with the social market economy. Of course, the kinds of legitimacy issues that he faced in postwar Germany were quite different from those faced by present-day neo liberal modes of statecraft such as those associated with the third way. Third way programmes are more likely to focus on issues of legitimacy through the active promotion of entrepreneurial forms of action and institutions. Similarly, many transnational social policy programmes – such as social funds and micro credit policies – are directed at the promotion of legitimacy through entrepreneurial activity. This is a point well made in Weber's (2001) perceptive paper on the global development architecture and micro credit strategies where she analyses the role of social safety nets as mechanisms of political crisis management. Therefore, building on such notions as social capital or community empowerment, social programmes had the effect of turning unemployment from a social issue or a social problem to one of 'social conduct' while at the same time dealing with the issues of legitimacy created by policies of market reform.

A further striking convergence between the ordo liberals and this social policy ethos is that both tend to exemplify a kind of institution-alism that tends to view the capitalist economy not as a set of social relations but as an ensemble of institutions.[8] In this way, social institutions, and by implication the welfare system, are shaped by the imperatives of the capitalist economic order. But this social policy orientation and statecraft such as those associated with the third way are similarly directed at enabling those institutional forms of capitalism that are thought to be essential for the reproduction of market order. Clearly, the new welfare governance places great store on developing partnerships between civil society and the state in the pursuance of various social projects. So, for example, the poverty reduction strategy of the World Bank (see Chapter 4) seeks to further what it calls 'pro-poor strategies' by encouraging individuals and groups to participate in the formulation of social policies, strategies, and programmes.

Similarly, Bevir notes that many of the policies adopted by the New Labour government in the UK seek to implement a broad range of governance programmes that are based implicitly on an institutionalist understanding of networks and partnerships to activate 'stable relationships characterized by trust, social participation, voluntary associations, and friendship, at least as much as from markets and competition' (Bevir 2003: 459). But what is missing in Bevir's account is the point that this new governance privileges certain forms of social association and community primarily by marginalizing the conflicts of class and social relations, and serves to reinforce the anti-pluralism of economic constitutionalism. And to the extent that it succeeds in this form of statecraft it manages to depoliticize social and economic governance.

New Liberalism, property and liberal subjects

Whereas ordo liberals seek to link markets and welfare by creating and strengthening social institutions to reflect market priorities, an earlier British tradition of New Liberalism associated with theorists such as Hobhouse,[9] Green[10] and Hobson[11] sought to elaborate a utilitarian justification for welfare and economic efficiency. These theorists, writing at the turn of the twentieth century, sought to reconcile classical liberal ideas of individualism and economic freedom with mounting social problems of unemployment and poverty resulting from rapid industrialization. They did this by developing a notion of welfarism that was compatible with economic efficiency. Hobhouse, in particular, argued that public policy should be directed at removing obstacles to individual self-reliance. He recognised that this justifies public intervention only insofar as it was deemed to be crucial for the operation of an efficient and legitimate market system. This justification of a role for government in protecting and securing what might be called the 'social requisites' of the market economy was mainly made on the grounds that this would lead to higher levels of overall civic welfare.

The New Liberals regarded it as crucial that there should be a broadening of the ownership of property within the community. Hence the 'right of an individual to hold property was an expression of his membership in the community and its justification was to be found in welfare and will of the community' (Freeden 1978: 220). Property ownership was an essential component of a liberal society, as theorists such as Green, Hobhouse, Bosanquet, and Hobson argued, it permitted citizens to become full members of a liberal community. In other words, as Morrow (2001) notes, the assumption was that liberal subjects could exercise their full moral capacities only through the ownership of property.

Unlike the libertarian notions, these ideas of property rights sought to emphasise the way possession of property was constitutive of liberal subjects with a stake in the community. For Hobhouse (1922: 155): 'property is the common basis of the freedom and self dependence, the possession of some property is desirable for individuals and for any corporate body that has to direct its own affairs'.

Property rights then – unlike for the libertarians – were a means towards creating the moral capacities of liberal individuals. One of the consequences of this was that New Liberals such as Hobhouse and Hobson were willing to justify an expansive range of intervention strategies 'for systems of state regulation that fostered efficiency, and promoted justice by ensuring that all members of population were able to possess the amount and type of property necessary for full membership of the community' (Morrow 2001: 108). What distinguishes this early-twentieth-century understanding of market citizenship is the way it relates the exercise of liberal capacities to the possession of a stake in the productive economy.

The relevance of New Liberal arguments for market citizenship lies in the fact that they sought, as observed by Vincent (2001), to combine an ethical understanding of rights with a commitment to the liberal market. Property for these theorists had a strong ethical component in that it provided an instrument for creating liberal subjects with the ethical capacities to contribute to the common good. In this way New Liberalism transformed the notion of poverty from material 'misery and insufficient spending-power and into the realm of the negation of human status, participation, self control and opportunity' (Freedan 2004: 77). Social intervention was then directed at producing these self-reliant and economically independent individuals who were to be found within the realms of an ethical market order. What this view has in common with third way ideologies is the marriage of communitarianism with market ontology, but this marriage is only possible by locating citizenship within the realms of an ethical market order. And this comes at the cost of displacing those competing social interests within the market, which underpinned the pluralist politics of social constitutionalism. New Liberalism and the contemporary welfare governance converge around a language of liberalism that is hostile to the pluralism of social interests within the market economy.

These ethical imperatives were equally evident in the way the New Liberals sought to link market citizenship and welfare by grounding social rights in the form of reciprocal obligations. As Freeden (1978: 219) notes, for the New Liberals rights were

> a benefit conferred by society for mutual advantage of the recipient and the conceder. What they were not prepared to accept was the idea of an unconditional right, irrespective of whether it was feasible or merited – which was what an absolute right is.

Market citizenship in its various modern incarnations is characterized by this valorization of social integration through policies that enhance participation and stakeholding in the economic sphere and the individual liability for reciprocal obligation in return for social claims on the state.[12]

An echo of this New Liberal emphasis on broadening participation within the market can be found not just in programmes for social inclusion (which belong to the social market category), but also in various programmes introduced to enhance the endowment of individual assets – be it income, training, or social capital – to enhance active participation within the market. Whereas social citizenship of the postwar period was directed towards income replacement these market citizenship policies are directed towards enhancing individual assets in order to compete within a market economy. It follows that in contrast to social citizenship this view of citizenship not only decommodifies welfare – that is, social policy is individualized – but market imperatives are at the heart of the justification for welfare, thereby helping to create new liberal subjects. In this way recent social policy initiatives have turned towards the development of asset-based social policies as an 'integral part of an overall development strategy that seeks to raise incomes and standards of living for all' (Midgley 2003: 10) and endeavouring to situate asset-based policies within a framework of 'developmentalism' which strongly echoes the New Liberal justification of welfare in terms of enhanced economic independence. It points to the way in which citizenship is defined within the capitalist market economy, and at the same time precludes the pluralism of interests so vital to social constitutionalism.

Arguing along these lines, one of the main objectives of these asset-based policies is the broadening of asset ownership in the economic sphere. So, for example, the Singapore Central Provident Fund (CPF) – a retirement insurance scheme – allows for individual accounts for health, education, and specified investments (Sherraden 1997; Low and Choon 2004). The CPF model, it should be recalled, had a considerable influence on early third way thinking on the stakeholder economy. More recently, these asset-based ideas have been expressed through the concept of individual development accounts for a whole range of welfare and education needs. Be they stakeholding or individual development accounts, these asset-based programmes individualize welfare in a manner which contrasts sharply with the collectivist insurance model of the postwar welfare state. Equally illustrative of these property-based policies in developing countries in the NICs such as Thailand, are the so-called 'asset conversion programmes' that encourage poor farmers or the urban poor without property rights to convert their assets into legal title (Jayasuriya and Hewison 2004). The assumption here is that the individuals will then be able to convert these property rights into an asset which can be used to participate more actively in the economy.

These New Liberal ideas of property and self-reliance are also echoed in recent World Bank approaches to poverty reduction that explicitly target policies to improve the assets of poor people. One of the consequences of this approach to poverty has been lowering the emphasis placed on income and expenditure levels – let alone distribution of income – and a shift towards an assessment of the opportunities of social advancement. This approach to welfare places great store on the exclusion of the poor from participation in the economic mainstream. Such views found expression in the World Bank Development Report of 2001 which argued that: 'lacking assets is both a cause and an outcome of poverty. Poor health, deficient skills, scant access to basic services, and the humiliations of social exclusion reflect deprivations in personal, public and natural assets' (World Bank 2000: 22). The report then goes on to suggest that this focus on asset ownership is in three main areas: first, in the use of public power to redistribute public resources such as health and education towards the 'poor'; second, in the implementation of those policy and institutional reforms that provides effective delivery of services; third, in engaging the poor in the policy-making process so that they have a stake not just in the economy but in the actual process of policy making. The implicit assumption in this approach is that enhancing the assets of the poor will make them more self-reliant within the productive sphere of the economy, resonating with the strong echo of the New Liberal emphasis on property ownership as the key to creating self-reliant individuals.

Another equally significant strand of the new social policy is its aim to enhance the learning capacities of individuals. For example, British New Labour has sought to develop programmes of training and continuous learning – in what has sometimes been called a 'learning society' – to enable people to actively participate in the market stream (Department for Education and Employment 1998). Again, here the justification for these policies is to be found in the higher levels of efficiency and competitiveness that is produced by strategic social investments. In the new knowledge economy assets lie not in the 'skill set' that individuals possess, but rather in their ability to learn and upgrade skills over their working lifetime.

New Liberalism – as with the ordo liberals – allows us to examine the normative foundations of market citizenship and welfare by underlining the new social contracts which aim to inculcate individual self-reliance and responsibility in attempting to create liberal subjects operating within an 'ethical' market order. Individual self-reliance and economic independence – which was especially important in enhancing community membership – were to be achieved through the ownership and possession of property. It is the possession of property that serves to bind liberal subjects to the broader community and the common good. But this ideological hybrid of communitarianism and markets is only possible by locating liberal subjects within – as with the New Liberalism – an 'ethical' market economy. But this moralised economy diminishes the contestation of politics in favour of anti-political liberalism.

Welfare, inclusion and economic constitutionalism

Welfare, for both the New Liberals and the ordo liberals alike, was framed within the market; the bond between welfare and market order is clearly a defining feature of forms of market citizenship in economic constitutionalism. And the common thread that links the ordo liberals and the New Liberals is that both seek to create liberal subjects whose capacities and purposes are shaped by the productive economy. In turn, an efficient market economy depends upon the creation of these liberal subjects. For the ordo liberals such liberal subjects were created through enabling societal institutions that would enhance the entrepreneurial capacities of individuals as well as furnishing the foundations for legitimate market order. For the New Liberals such as Hobhouse the possession of property was a means of creating self-reliant individuals who would have a stake in the community.

Both forms of liberalism have this in common with contemporary forms of welfare governance: they seek to create liberal subjects who are embedded in the productive sphere of the economy. There is another point at which the ordo liberal and the New Liberals converge; both groups see property rights as inherently social and juridical processes rather than a spontaneous creation of market forces. For Green, property rights had to be socially recognised and enforced; there was no natural right to property. Hence, both strands of liberalism made property central to their understanding of economic and ethical order in a way that clearly distinguished it from postwar social democracy. But this was based on a particular understanding of property rights as a product of juridical and social processes.

This is not to say there are no important differences. For Hobhouse and other New Liberals like Hobson, market order was just one purpose of public action, whereas what is distinctive about the ordo liberals – which creates a striking affinity between them and the new policy frameworks – is the overwhelming importance they attached to the pursuit of market order. More especially for the New Liberals property itself was a claim on social resources, and not a 'liberty right' in the sense used by Hohfield (1946). Hobson, in particular, articulated a notion of rights 'as claims to elicit beneficial conduct from others, claims to reciprocate with duties arising out of the nature of the social relationship' (Freedan 2004: 103). Intriguingly, these notions of property rights as 'claim rights' may well furnish the foundations for a more radical and progressive notion of a social market within economic constitutionalism than that currently envisaged by the defenders of the 'third way'.[13]

Another motif running through these liberal traditions of market citizenship is a conception of welfare as a component of a well-ordered and efficient market system. But the point at issue for both the New Liberals and the ordo liberals is not social intervention per se but the type and form of intervention. Understanding welfare in this way – unlike early forms of neo liberalism – makes a 'strong state' an important dimension of a properly functioning market system. Hence there has been a proliferation of programmes and policies of welfare governance – the new social policy ethos – that have sought to reshape the relationship between state and citizen in order to foster forms of market citizenship. These social entitlements may be quite generous and expansive. But that is not the point. What matters is the fact that these entitlements are justified in terms of their capacity to enable the greater participation of individuals within the economic mainstream.

Market citizenship, whether formulated in terms of the social market economy, the New Liberal idea of community, the World Bank, or the EU, focuses on social inclusion and justifies welfarism in terms of its capacity to create an inclusive society, placing a high value on economic participation. This differs from the idea of welfare as compensation or redistribution that was such an influential element of the social democratic 'grammar' of politics that defined the postwar welfare state.

This shift from an insurance paradigm – the collective indemnification of the risks of the market economy – to an understanding of social policy, and, more broadly, the social sphere, as the furthering or rein- forcing of an inclusive and participatory market economy constitutes a significant transformation in the very language of liberalism.

But its most significant consequence is that social institutions and their governance are depoliticized in a way that limits the conflict and negotiation of social interests that formed such a crucial element of social constitutionalism. Sustaining this social constitutionalism was the politics of negotiation and conflict of social interests that, in turn, hinged on the dualism between the market and the social sphere. Welfare was at the heart of this often conflictual and contradictory logic of the market and social solidarity. But it is this politics of social conflict, or, more broadly, a politics of interest, that is absent in the new eco- nomic constitutionalism which has come to dominate the industrial- ized as well as the newly industrializing countries. By reshaping welfare along productivist lines the new welfare governance creates liberal sub- jects who are defined not on the basis of membership of interest or class communities, but in terms of the possession and attributes of those endowments or capacities to participate and compete within the pro- ductive sphere of the economy. Moreover, the new welfare governance, as well as the broader governance structure in which these policy alter- natives take shape, embodies a particular conception of politics as one of management and consensus. This serves to reinforce an anti-pluralist strand of liberalism that is at the core of the new market citizenship and it is this reconstitution of liberalism that is the most significant aspect of the emerging structures of economic constitutionalism.

Finally, what underpins much of the new welfare governance is an elaboration of what one might term a neo liberal statecraft. Malloy (1991) provides a useful definition of statecraft in the following terms:

> statecraft is viewed first as one aspect of an essential mediating process in which 'public policies' (the concept of the public is core to any historical notion of the state) gives form and substance to the phenomenon of citizenship. Specifically, statecraft is viewed as the initiation of public policies by 'agents' (in legal terms fiduciary agents) empowered to act in the name of the state which elaborate and regularize fundamental relationships between of state and society. (Malloy 1991: 4)

What is attractive in Malloy's definition of statecraft is that it makes social policy the pivotal set of policy arrangements working to elaborate the 'fundamental relationships between state and society'. Boundaries between state and society are not fixed and immutable, but are themselves the product of various statecraft projects. And in the final analysis the new welfare governance provides an element of a putative statecraft that reshapes the boundaries between state and society.

Neo liberalism cannot be reduced to a set of policy prescriptions for economic liberalization and deregulation. In fact, as programmes of market reform faced significant challenges there has been an appreciable shift in thinking from a predatory view of the state that characterized the initial move towards projects of neo liberal reform in the US and the UK as well as World Bank structural adjustment programmes. We argue that recent neo liberal programmes are more focused on developing new forms and practices of social and economic regulation. These new regulatory practices call for a more interventionist and activist state that would enable those forms of social conduct that promote market norms and practices.

Hence neo liberalism is transformed into a political project which will be able to regulate the social in a way that is compatible with the market. Therefore, the kind of new social policy rationale currently promoted aims not at pushing back the state but rather at achieving some measure of internal transformation *within* the state. In this respect, Peck and Tickell (2002) have suggested that neo liberalism be seen as an ongoing process of economic and political change. They propose a useful dividing line between what they call 'rollback' and 'rollout' neo liberalism. 'Rollback' neo liberalism represents the early deregulationist thrust of Thatcher and Reagan, while 'rollout' neo liberalism represents a new political project that leads to a re-regulation of newly deregulated markets. The fact is that the issue is not so much as to whether state intervention diminishes or is less marginal to the regulation of economic and social life, but that intervention within this new regulatory economic order – economic constitutionalism – takes an ideological character and tone that is different from that of the social constitutionalism of the postwar period.

2
Capability, Freedom and the Third Way

Introduction

Although there has been a great deal of interest, both scholarly and public, in the 'third way', there is little analysis that suggests why the third way constitutes a distinctive approach to ideas such as liberty and equality. There is a tendency to see the third way or the new social democracy as merely old wine in new bottles. This chapter will explore some of the normative presuppositions of the third way, that may be more appropriately labelled the 'new social democracy'.[1] More especially, the new welfare governance which the third way exemplifies is, as we have suggested, a form of economic constitutionalism that can be viewed as a conceptual framework seeking to reorient social democratic[2] ideas of equality and freedom. What is distinctive here is that these ideas of freedom and equality are situated within the framework of the market. As such, we explore how and why the third way can be described as a social democratic response within the parameters of the new economic constitutionalism.

Teasing out the normative rationale that is often implicit in the policy repertoire of the new social democracy is a difficult task. Most practitioners of the third way are not only dismissive of any ideological commitment in their political programmes, but also tend to emphasize both its pragmatism and its absence of a defining commitment to social democratic values as two of its major political attractions. Nevertheless, it is possible to distinguish some of the key normative underpinnings in the political programme of the third way from the work of some of its most prominent theorists, such as Anthony Giddens, who do provide a rationale for the third way, but it is a distinctive kind of normative reasoning, framed in sociological terms of responsible social conduct. In this context, a distinguishing feature of the third way is the fact that 'policy is legitimated not by ethical principles but by the truth of certain social facts' (Finlayson 1999: 271).

Finlayson's observation[3] here is perceptive; third way theory is not a political theory in the conventional sense, but rather an attempt to think through the emerging social complexity of contemporary society ('reflexive modernization' to use Giddens's term) and consequent changes in forms of sociability. For example, there is an emphasis on the increased amplification of 'risk' in late modern society and the correlative obligation of responsible social conduct this imposes on individuals. But the point is that this description of these modes of social conduct substitutes for the ethical and political reasoning found in most political programmes. Third way accounts provide a very distinctive kind of moral sociology that has its origins in a particular understanding of social reality. Finlayson observes that 'the third way derives its justification from a claim to access to a certain kind of "truth" about the present' (Finlayson 1999: 272).

There are three main dimensions to this moral sociology. First, it confuses an emphasis on legitimacy – or, more specifically, a concern with social cohesion and solidarity – with the justification of social arrangements and institutions. It is simply a logical error to proceed from a description of social reality to the justification of a set of institutions. Second, the moral sociology that is produced by third way theories has a disturbing streak of moral authoritarianism; perhaps this is seen most clearly in the area of social policy, where there is a strong accent on moral paternalism. Finally, and in some tension with its moral sociology, third way approaches to social governance seek to enhance individual autonomy and choice in the face of an increasingly complex society. In fact, the key aim of the revisionist social democracy is to reconcile social commitment to equality with the liberal virtue of individual autonomy. The role of, and justification for, individual autonomy within the framework of economic constitutionalism, particularly within the third way experiment of New Labour in the UK, will be examined in the rest of this chapter.

Within economic constitutionalism individual autonomy is cashed out in terms of the notion of the capability. Capability is a pivotal normative principle that underpins many of these new social democratic programmes, especially that of New Labour in the UK; it also figures prominently in recent OECD policies and strategies designed to deal with problems of social exclusion. What is more, it is integral to the European Social Charter and figures prominently in World Bank governance programs.[4] But what is capability? It is a term that implies a view of 'complex equality' – to borrow Walzer's (1983) phrase – which, in contrast to the traditional egalitarian notion, places great score on the fact that equality needs to take into account the differing circumstances, institutional locations, and the diversity of individual ends. For this reason, no simple egalitarian standard will suffice. Instead, there is a need to adopt a metric that takes into account the complexity of circumstances, and, in this context, capability provides one such metric that can be used to shift our political horizons from the domain of 'simple' to 'complex' equality.

Capability – particularly as articulated in the work of Amartya Sen (to be discussed below) – also suggests a normative commitment to a notion of freedom defined in terms of the capability of people to make effective choices. As will be argued, this standpoint casts doubt on Berlin's (1958) classic distinction between positive and negative freedom on which much of the debate on liberty and equality has been framed. The notion of capability, pivotal to the new social democracy, construes negative and positive liberty as inextricably linked; therefore, the trade-off between liberty and equality is much more problematic than is commonly assumed. Capability provides a normative framework through which this trade-off takes place and helps to shape a social democratic response within economic constitutionalism.[5]

In articulating this normative rationale of new social democracy, this chapter is structured in four main parts:

(i) Analysis of how the notion of capability is central to many of the programmes and policies championed by new social democrats or proponents of the third way. However, it is argued that the notion of capability as used in the new social democratic literature is – in part as a consequence of the sociological reasoning of the third way – presented largely as a descriptive rather than an analytical category.

(ii) Overview of the normative assumptions of the capability paradigm drawing on the work of Amartya Sen (1985, 1992). Capability allows the reframing of some of the central values of social constitutionalism such as freedom and equality in terms of the capabilities to function within a market order.

(iii) A new rationale for a social democracy within the structures of economic constitutionalism. In particular we examine the possibilities and limitations of socializing the market model in terms of capability equality. In this new socialized neo liberalism equality is reframed in terms of enabling the capacity to participate within the economic mainstream rather than in the redistribution of resources.

(iv) Linking these notions of equality and freedom within a specific republican understanding of freedom as non-domination (Pettit 1993, 1997). These notions of freedom permit more expansive and progressive pathways and yet remain within the parameters of the new politics of social inclusion.

The new social democracy: risk or capability?

Proponents of the 'third way', for instance Giddens (1994, 1998), have been greatly concerned with redesigning the welfare state in response to the new forms of risk as well as the complexity of the economic structures which have served to undermine traditional notions of welfare. These arguments about the role of social policy in the 'third way' are of critical importance because, more than any other set of policies and institutions, the welfare state stands out as the single most important contribution of social democracy in the twentieth century.

Giddens (1998), in an analysis of the welfare state in the post-Second World War period, makes a critical distinction between what he terms 'negative' and 'positive' welfare. Whereas negative welfare is concerned with the provision for security, in reality a form of risk insurance, positive welfare is concerned with not only providing for risk but also for the *capacity* for risk-taking and integrating welfare institutions within the broader economic system. It is this mix of negative and positive welfare which created what Giddens terms the 'social investment state'.[6] One of the constituent elements of positive welfare pertains to the processes of inclusion and exclusion of groups of people in participating in the wider economic system. The contention here is that the new global economy – particularly because it is so technologically driven – creates the potential risk that certain groups (e.g., the unskilled) may be permanently excluded from participating in the wider economy. Accordingly, it is suggested that traditional forms of welfare, e.g., welfare dependency (although here Giddens is ambiguous as to exactly what these are), may exacerbate this social exclusion. An emphasis on positive welfare and capability, it is argued, would offset this possibility and make the process of inclusion in the wider economy one of its dominant concerns. Therefore, for Giddens, 'inclusion and exclusion have become important concepts for analysing and responding to inequality because of changes affecting the class structure of industrial countries' (1998: 103). Hence, the claim is that the emergence of the new global economy creates forms of complexity requiring welfare strategies which seek to develop the capabilities of persons to effectively participate in the economic mainstream of society. Some of this new emphasis on welfare is well reflected in the recent OECD emphasis (OECD 1989, 1994, 1999a, 1999b) on the 'active society'. The OECD (as well as the EU social policy programmes)[7] has articulated a justification for welfare as social inclusion rather than in terms of social protection which, after all, was the hallmark of the normative frame of welfare within social constitutionalism. In these new formulations of 'welfare', the goal of social policy is to:

> welcome into active life all those who wish to take part, and to enable them to do so. The aim is thus not to 'define away' unemployment by assigning those seeking work to some other status, but rather to recognise that realisation of the full human potential of the population involves the employment not only of the unemployed, but of all those who wish to participate – whether working full time, part time, or in casual employment. (OECD 1989: 9)

This approach to welfare sits comfortably with the emergence of new flexible employment patterns as well as a recognition that the service sector has a different structure of employment (more part-time and casual) than that traditionally associated with the manufacturing sector in the more conventional welfare theorizing. Furthermore, the social policy agenda of the new social democracy (also of organizations such as the OECD) reflects the decline of the Keynesian model of full employment that underpinned the orthodox welfare state model, especially in the UK and Europe. In the new global economy, employment is likely to be transitory, and, therefore, the new social welfare is designed to facilitate the re-inclusion of the unemployed into the economic mainstream.

No doubt, at one level these efforts serve to rationalize a continuing effort to retrench welfare programmes, and, more problematically, to seek 'a displacement of the category of the officially unemployed' (Walters 1997: 225).[8] More importantly, these new approaches signal a shift away from regarding welfare primarily as a set of social practices that help to integrate society by reinforcing social solidarity (Titmuss 1950; Marshall 1981). The 'social investment' perspective appears to move away from this orthodox view and objective, and promotes a conception of welfare more as a set of practices that are complementary to the operation of market economies (Walters 1997); welfare is reconfigured within a form of economic constitutionalism.

However, this is not entirely new. In the 1960s Scandinavian social programmes operated in close connection with economic and industrial policy.[9] But what is distinctive about this social investment conceptualization is the particular emphasis placed on the role of the state in strengthening the capability of individuals to participate in the economy. In short, welfare is viewed not as an end in itself, but as an instrument by which people's capacity and choices can be enlarged; in other words, this version of welfare places more emphasis on the positive role of welfare in helping individuals deal with risk rather than playing a passive role as an instrument to provide security. No doubt social protection is an important dimension of the social investment state, but it is subordinate to the more encompassing category of capability.

Some proponents of this new view of welfare regard it as an instrument to retrench welfare expenditure or welfare entitlements. Others see it as a means of redesigning the welfare state to better enable it to confront the new opportunities and risks posed by the global economy. However, from a social democratic perspective this is not merely a question of policy redesign, but more critically one of re-theorizing the understanding of the notions of equality and freedom in a context where welfare programmes are entangled in complex interdependencies with other social and economic structures. Put simply, the new social democracy has a distinctive normative orientation, one which is markedly different from the utilitarian standpoint of conventional welfare theorizing. But the adoption of this newer approach requires not merely the moral sociology championed by third way theorists, but the more strongly normative basis furnished by the notion of capability.[10]

Within the contours of this economic constitutionalism the role of 'social' capability is complemented by the notion of 'economic' capability that finds strong resonance within the new social democracy. Central to its economic policies is a shift from Keynesian strategies of demand and income management to a Schumpeterian state which places emphasis on the policies of innovation, skill management, and training (Jessop 1993; Thompson 1996). Greatly influenced by the new growth theory, this new social democratic approach views the state in terms of its function as an indirect facilitator and regulator of the market rather than emphasizing its distributive and demand management role (Buckler and Dolowitz 2004). At the core of this shift in the strategy of the new social democracy is an understanding that an increasingly globalized economy circumscribes the capacity of the state to directly influence the economy.

If globalization in the form of capital mobility has closed off the capability of the state to pursue demand-side policies, revisionists would argue that one of the key features of the new global economy – the increased skill intensity of trade – has opened new avenues for state intervention (Scharpf 1996).[11] But these new policy repertoires are oriented to the development and consolidation of policies which improve technological innovation and economic competitiveness. Supply-side policies require a kind of investor state, not in the sense of directly investing in the market, but in the form of an investment in infrastructure, innovation and competitiveness. In concrete policy terms, one area where this supply-side emphasis is manifested is in the priority attached to training and education policies. This is a constant refrain in social democratic campaigns; its argument is that human capital formation is the key contributor to economic growth, and that governments need to invest in a skilled workforce.

This emphasis on education and training highlights the key role assigned to the notion of capability within the new economic constitutionalism. Considered from this perspective, capability is concerned with the acquisition of skill and training as well as the provision of public infrastructure for innovation. In the new technologically driven economy these are seen as crucial capital assets, the ownership of which can be influenced by state intervention. For example, Hodgson (1999) argues that the growth of the knowledge intensity of production results in a redrawing of the traditional boundaries between capital and labour. For instance, he notes that:

> As the boundary between manager and employee breaks down, and formal control is eroded, a kind of quasi self-employment will develop ... By owning part of the intangible means of production, in the form of specialist knowledge, and having a considerable degree of control over his or her work process, in some respects the employee self-employed worker (Hodgson 1999: 208).

This argument helps to draw our attention to the fact that acceptance of the new growth theory inevitably sets limits on the traditional income redistribution objectives of social democrats. At the same time, it has the potential to open up the redistribution of the economic opportunities through a redistribution of capabilities. Hence the capability argument shifts the emphasis away from the redistribution of income or resources to that of assets or endowments that individuals bring to the marketplace.[12]

From the foregoing, one may reasonably conclude that the notion of capability is central to understanding the rationale of the new social democracy. Enhancing capability provides one important means by which social democrats can respond to new complexities of economic and social structures. But capability is a concept that is more than just a descriptive category. It is fundamentally about the creation of liberal subjects who, through the possession of various capabilities, are able to exercise freedom and choice within the political community. For example, within this framework equality is defined not in terms of the possession of a certain amount of resources, but in terms of reinforcing individual capabilities. In this context, there is strong convergence between capabilities and the New Liberal ideas of the role of property in the exercise of liberal freedoms. But in order to articulate such a normative foundation for the new social democracy we need to move beyond the moral sociology that so dominates third way theory. For example, Giddens (1998) argues that the emphasis placed on what he calls 'positive risk management' in the new social democracy is a distinctive response to new forms of modernity.[13] The crux of his argument is that globalization as well as the increasing complexity of economic and social life create greater potential risks for both individuals and society – risks that cannot be insured through the traditional welfare state. Hence, Giddens makes a distinction between two kinds of risks: one 'external', and the other, a 'manufactured risk'. External risk is a passive form of risk that can be planned for, while manufactured risk is a new form of risk 'created by the very progression of human development, especially by the progression of science and technology' (Giddens 1994: 4).[14] The point he makes is that the increasing prevalence of manufactured risk requires a different form of risk management that connects risk to individual responsibility. But what is missing here is a recognition of the fact that the analysis of this new world of manufactured risk obscures the more fundamental normative question of how risk management is related to the way egalitarian objectives of the traditional social democracy are pursued within the new framework of economic constitutionalism, the creation of new liberal subjects.

Capability paradigm

To develop a comprehensive account of how the notion of capability is employed in the various formulations of social democratic programmes we need to reconstruct the normative rationale for the concept of capability. Perhaps the most clearly articulated account of the notion of capability is found in the work of Amartya Sen.[15] In exploring the capability approach we focus on the work of Sen because of the way it fits in with the 'socialization of neo liberalism' which is the focus of this volume. Sen's work is especially interesting because of its many similarities with the concerns of the New Liberals explored in Chapter 1. Just as the New Liberals sought to ground public intervention within the context of liberal freedom, Sen, through the notion of capability equality, seeks to reconcile a commitment to individual autonomy with social intervention. However, there are other variants of the capability paradigm and especially important here is the work of Nussbaum (2000) who has developed a version of the capability paradigm in a distinctly Aristotelian direction which focuses less on the market as a site of ethical contestation than on a concern with individual flourishing.

Sen's work developed from his critique of welfarism, particularly those ideas which buttressed many of the claims for the traditional welfare state. Indeed, in this sense, this critique bears similarities with third way arguments against postwar egalitarian notions of social welfare. Sen's achievement lies in going beyond simple models of egalitarianism to provide the foundations for what he calls 'capability equality'. This is a framework for the understanding of equality that enables a serious consideration of the divergent conditions, opportunities and goals of individual agents.

Central to Sen's project – and it is this very fact that raises important implications for the new social democracy – is an attempt to disentangle our understanding of equality from resource-based or utilitarian perspectives. In this context, Sen (1992) makes the important point that equality can be mapped into different spaces or variables, each of which differs from the other. For example, we may choose to focus on income, wealth, or utility, and indeed even libertarians have an implicit focus on the equality of liberties. In short, different theories endorse different favoured baselines against which equality can be mapped. But, the choice of space has significant implications for inequality in other spaces. As Sen (1992: 21) notes:

> the answer we give to 'equality of what?' will not only endorse equality in the chosen space (the focal variable being related to the demands of basal equality), but will have far-reaching consequences on the distributional patterns including necessary *inequalities* in the other spaces.

In brief, debates about equality are more appropriately viewed as being about the reasonableness or validity of the metric by which equality is measured. And in fact what these debates over equality underline is the diversity of views over how individual advantage is to be compared. Indeed any resultant inequality in one 'space' will have to be justified in terms of an equality in another space.[16]

For Sen – and this is a critical aspect of his theory – the plurality of spaces through which equality can be mapped reflects a profound diversity of views regarding the appropriate measure of individual advantage in social comparisons. As he points out, 'the plurality of spaces reflects diversities in substantive approaches to individual advantage, and in the informational base of interpersonal comparisons' (Sen 1992: 26). This plurality of individual circumstances and ends is a critical part of Sen's thesis because he argues that most theories, by focusing on a baseline of equality, tend to assume away other substantial inequalities in, say, well-being and freedom. In this sense, Sen is concerned with acknowledging and incorporating the facts of diversity and pluralism into a theory of equality rather than dismissing these facts through a kind of analytical sleight of hand.

The more substantive point here is that traditional social democratic approaches to equality overlook the complexity and plurality of modern society. Though Sen's theory is not couched in these terms, his approach would suggest that we need to shift from a model of 'simple equality' which focuses on one particular favoured baseline to a notion of – to use Walzer's (1983) rather than Sen's terms – 'complex equality' that takes account of the plurality of spaces by which equality can be mapped. The only way to deal with this complexity is by a focus on the equality of capability. Capability is defined in terms of an individual's ability to choose different forms of life; it is through such a capability perspective that the plurality of human diversity can be taken into account. Capabilities are determined by the space of possibilities open to an individual. It is not defined in terms of some prior end such as utility or initial conditions such as equality of resources, income, or primary goods. It is suggested that instead of concentrating on the resources that people have, it is more useful to focus on the actual lives that people can choose to lead, which, in turn, are constituted by various combinations of human functionings. It is this implicit understanding of the link between pluralism and equality that makes Sen's work an important part of any normative reconstruction of the idea of capability in social democratic versions of economic constitutionalism.

But what is meant by capability?

Capability must be understood in terms of a trinity of concepts: functionings, capability, and agency freedom. Functionings are states of 'being' or 'doings'. Sen points out that 'living may be seen as consisting of a set of interrelated "functionings", consisting of being and doings. A person's achievements in this respect can be seen as the vector of his or her functionings' (Sen 1992: 39). In this context, 'human functionings' could range from the most basic functioning such as nutrition, shelter, or health to even more complex forms of functioning such as self-respect, participation. The 'claim is that functionings are constitutive of a person's being, and an evaluation of well-being has to take the form of an assessment of these constitutive elements' (Sen 1992: 39). Of course, individuals may differ in the weight or attachment they place on various functionings and, it is argued that any normative account of freedom must be sensitive to the differential weights attached to 'functionings'.

The freedom to lead different lives – in other words, 'capability' – is determined by the various sets of human functionings that an individual can choose.[17] Capability is determined by the forms of life that are possible, and these in turn depend on the availability of various functionings. Stated differently, capability is the set of the various sets of functionings that make it possible for a person to choose one kind of life as against another. The capability set is analogous to the budget set in economics which reflects someone's ability to buy a commodity; the capability set refers to the person's freedom to choose from forms of life that are possible.[18]

Within this perspective, capability really lies somewhere 'causally, between income or primary goods or resources on the one hand, and utility and welfare on the other' (Cohen 1994: 119). In other words, capability refers to what it is possible for a person to be able to do and achieve valued objectives which in turn depend on the different forms of life that are possible. It is the achievement of these capabilities which defines the opportunities for well-being; and these opportunities influence the effective freedom that individuals possess. A significant feature of this approach is the recognition that freedom depends not just on personal characteristics but also on more 'social' factors such as, for example, the extent of self-respect which may constrain an individual's 'functioning', and therefore his or her capability.

But capability constitutes the real freedom that individuals need to exercise their chosen ends. For Sen, freedom is defined by the fact that the 'capability to achieve functionings (i.e., all the alternatives combinations of functionings a person can choose to have) will constitute the person's freedom – the real opportunities – to have well being' (Sen 1992: 40). Freedom is defined here in terms of the opportunities that individuals have for well-being, which in turn is intimately connected to the capacity to choose between possible forms of living. In short, real freedom to choose (a form of negative freedom) needs a dose of positive freedom in order to enable individuals to achieve certain kinds of capabilities.

This notion of freedom is central to the new social democracy, as well as to Sen's account of capability. Its distinguishing feature is its identification of the interconnection between negative and positive freedom – that is, to have negative freedom you may need to act positively. In this regard, one of the valuable insights of this perspective is the acknowledgement that freedom depends not just on the personal characteristics but also on the structure of social arrangements (e.g., insofar as social arrangement shapes bases of self respect) which may constrain an individual's 'functioning', and thereby his or her capability.

Further, what is particularly noteworthy in this conception, in contrast to traditional egalitarian theories, is that what matters is the distribution of capabilities rather than distribution of income, primary goods or utilities. The clear implication of this perspective is that it places great weight on our ability to do or to be; choice of social arrangements must be justified by their ability to promote human capabilities, and therefore agency freedom. In this way Sen's notion of capability converges with the approach of the New Liberalism associated with theorists such as Green and Hobhouse (see Chapter 1). The New Liberals, like Sen, sought to reconcile the exercise of real freedom with the possession of capabilities or the access to property within the market order. Both the New Liberal and capability approaches converge in identifying material disadvantage as flowing from the lack of status, participation and resources for development of individual potential.

Complex equality and the new welfare governance

At the core of the normative architecture of the capability paradigm is the philosophical commitment to a notion of freedom that attempts to reconcile the primacy of individual autonomy with the egalitarian distribution of individual capacities. In stark contrast to the concept of equality in conventional theorizing, the capability perspective explicitly acknowledges the pluralism inherent in modern complex societies. It is a pluralism that can be identified in term of: a pluralism of circumstances; an institutional pluralism; and a pluralism of ends.

Pluralism of circumstances: equality and difference

The most important implication of the adoption of the capability paradigm for the new social democracy is that it underscores the importance of the pluralism of circumstances in the assessment of the structure of individual advantage. This is perhaps one of the most significant features of this mode of theorizing as it signals a major departure from conventional notions of equality because in contrast to most standard accounts of equality, the capability paradigm underlines the essential complexity of the notion of equality. The capability approach suggests that equality is multidimensional, and, therefore, achieving equality on one particular dimension creates inequality in another. It differs from welfare egalitarianism where its approach to equality seeks to equalize the distribution of one unique commodity (Crocker 1992) – be it utility, income, primary goods (Rawls 1971) or resources (Dworkin 1981).

From a capability perspective, the problem with this approach is that it confuses means and ends. The critical dilemma with a metric of goods and resources is that due to variations in peoples' circumstances – physical as well as social – there are significant differences in what people could do with a given bundle of commodities. For example, a disabled personal relative of an able-bodied individual may require more of the bundle of commodities to enable this person to achieve valued ends. Moreover, each individual may require different packages of commodity bundles to achieve certain levels of human functioning. For instance, for some individuals being in good health may require greater levels of self-respect than income; for others, the weighting of the commodities may be reversed. Given these intra-personal differences – pluralism of circumstances – no single metric of commodities can be a suitable guide to the range of choices available to the individual. Much better, then, would be to look at the range of choices open to the individual rather the initial endowment of resources.

Perhaps the most pointed differences in this regard are between Rawls's (1971) primary goods argument and Sen's capabilities perspective. As Sen (1990, 1992) admits, the Rawlsian perspective has a close affinity to the capability perspective. It is anti-perfectionist in that primary goods are seen as instruments by which individuals can pursue their freely chosen objectives; its anti-utilitarian bias is in keeping with the scepticism of Sen towards any metric of freedom that depends on utility. However, a comparison of the primary goods that individuals possess is not quite the same as a comparison of the effective freedom to pursue freely chosen ends. This is because: 'primary goods are a *means* to freedom, but they cannot represent the *extent* of freedom, given the diversity of human beings converting primary goods into the freedom to pursue respective objectives' (Sen 1990: 52; author's emphasis).

The crux of the argument here is about the appropriate metric of individual freedom because central to the capability perspective is the view that the wide diversity of human circumstances will result in different bundles of primary goods enabling different levels of effective freedom or the capability to pursue freely chosen ends.

If the individual resources, primary goods, and incomes, are unsuitable as measures of equality, the same problem bedevils those that attempt to measure individual well-being or utility. Utility, it is argued, may be a valued individual objective, but it may not be the only – or even the most important – end in a person's life. The main problem with a utility approach is that, like the commodities approach, it fails to take into account differences in individual circumstances. For example, two individuals – one disabled and one able bodied – who have the same levels of utility, are therefore entitled to similar shares of the total, but this outcome may well be because the disabled person has less expensive tastes or a better temperament than the able-bodied person.[19] There is a further problem with the utility approach to distribution in that a person's low level of utility may itself be a product of an oppressive or repressive social environment. It is not just the ability to achieve certain valued ends that is important; we need to be equally sensitive to the space of possibilities open to an individual.

For the new social democracy this approach to equality raises fundamental questions about the purposes and rationale of income redistribution because an important feature of the capability paradigm is the argument that these primary commodities have no intrinsic value except in relation to the ends they make possible. Of course, this does not rule out redistribution as an objective, although this aspect is often forgotten in some of the new social democratic writing. It remains an element in building individual capability. But the important point is that redistribution becomes a means to an end. In economic constitutionalism the onus on welfare is placed on the degree to which social programs are sensitive to individual differences in the conversion of a given bundle of primary commodities – income, resources, self-respect – into individual capabilities.

Hence welfare programmes redesigned to focus on social inclusion or participation reflect a step in the direction of the capability paradigm because the objective of these programmes is to link welfare programmes with wider social and economic ends that are instrumental to people's functioning. Similarly, the aim of industry policy programmes becomes one of enhancing the training and skill levels of the workforce in order to enable the achievement of certain levels of functioning, and, therefore, capability. State intervention is not an end in itself; it is a means to achieving effective freedom, but this is within the economic sphere; assets, not income, become the driving engine of the new welfare governance.

It might be useful to distinguish between theories of simple and complex equality. The phrase 'complex equality' comes from Walzer's (1983) notion of multiple spheres of justice, but it can be usefully applied to the understanding of the capability paradigm. At the heart of the new social democratic critique of traditional theories of egalitarianism is the idea that the measurement of equality can be reduced to a single commodity or even a group of commodities – be they resources, utilities, or primary goods. In contrast, a complex notion of equality suggests that equality is always multidimensional in that the 'plurality of circumstances' requires us to take account of the different distributions of goods needed by a given individual to ensure effective levels of functioning and capability. These distributions not only include material resources but also a range of other 'goods' such as self-respect, social norms, access to public goods[20] which are instrumental in giving people the capability to achieve effective freedom. While Walzer coined the term 'complex equality' to denote the differentially constituted spheres for the distribution of social goods, the notion of complex equality is used here specifically to denote the complex and multiple ways in which individual capabilities are affected by different individual circumstances. Implicit in this conception of equality is an acknowledgement of the pluralism of modern society – a pluralism that requires responses to issues of inequality that may vary with each specific social and historical circumstance confronting individuals.

Pluralism of ends

However, the most important dimension of the capability paradigm for the new social democracy is the way it allows the reconciliation of individual freedom and justice within the sphere of the market by way of the notion of a pluralism of 'ends'. In our earlier discussion of the 'commodity' or the income perspective, we noted the way these approaches underscored the initial endowments of resources to the detriment of individual circumstances in the measurement of individual advantage. Similarly, welfare or utility approaches underline individual well-being at the expense of other more individual goals or ends. In all of this the capability paradigm is distinguished by a concern with the differential capacity of individuals to use a bundle of commodities to pursue certain valued ends. Indeed, Sen makes an even stronger argument that the main advantage of the capability perspective is its recognition of the importance of a diversity of goods pursued by individuals. As Crocker (1992) points out, the capability perspective attempts to incorporate the variations in conversion of resources to fulfil individual goals as well as the diversity of individual ends; in other words, people are diverse both in their circumstances and in their aspirations.

This commitment to a 'pluralism' of ends is a major normative commitment of the capability approach to freedom. In short, capability is a kind of freedom and the capacity to choose a particular set of goals is itself a good; effective freedom means the expansion of the opportunity for choice. As Cohen (1994: 120) points out, 'capability is good not only, then, as space of choice, but also because free choosing, a process that requires such a space, is itself a good'. This is important. It takes seriously the argument that a theory of justice must not only accommodate a plurality of the conception of the good, but must also value this plurality as a good in itself. This is a critical argument because it takes on board the crucial role of choice, but makes this – in a way similar to the New Liberals – a component of social welfare. Once we acknowledge that choice is itself a good, the argument moves on to judge the extent of what is called 'agency freedom', which can be assessed on the basis of the shortfall between what individuals have succeeded in achieving and the ends to which they are committed. As Hacking (1996) observes, by looking negatively at shortfalls rather than positively at what has been achieved, it is possible to move away from a set of assumptions about individual choice to an argument for social intervention to enable the effective exercise of the capacity of choice.

This is an important line of argument that theorists such as Sen and Cohen have utilized to move away from assumptions about agent autonomy towards justifications for positive intervention to enable individual access or capacity to achieve their goals. However, for this case to properly hold it seems that there is a principal assumption to be made about the importance of defining a liberal conception of the good. For the equality of the shortfall argument to work it is essential to have something like a conception that freedom and the capability to choose a range of ends needs to be actively promoted by the state. This is implicit in Sen's argument when he claims that freedom to choose is an intrinsically important good. Hacking (1996: 42) underlines this point when he notes that from the perspective of the capability paradigm:

> men and women should be truly free in their choices what to value, of what to do with their rights and liberties. Many, he argues, are so

ground down by disease, or the customs of race, gender disability, or all three, that they cannot see their own horizons. Hence they are not free to choose their aims.

It is this reconciliation of the liberal conception of the good and the idea of effective freedom that distinguishes the capability perspective from the equally strong emphasis placed by Rawls on respecting the diversity of individual goals and objectives. The key difference here between Rawls and Sen – though, of course, their theories have much common ground – is that for the capability approach, negative and positive liberties are intertwined; therefore, the pursuit of individual ends may require positive intervention to adjust deficiencies in shortfalls between effective and actual freedom. Like the New Liberals, the capability paradigm sees poverty and material disadvantage as an 'assault both on individual and on community; and an undermining of the possibility of optimising human capacities and recognising the full range of human needs' (Freedan 2004: 77). It is an understanding of social disadvantage that moves away from income management – so central to the postwar social constitutionalism – to a version of welfare as the creation of liberal subjects with capacity to pursue their own choices within the market.

For the new social democracy, this has important implications because it demonstrates that it is possible to simultaneously develop a defence of the welfare programmes as well as a cooperative system of economic production that respects agent autonomy. However – and this is where the argument bites for most traditional social democratic programmes – the design of intervention will need to take into account an agent-centred theory of justice. The point remains that for the new social democracy the capability paradigm enables one to respect the diversity of human goods or ends as well as to advocate positive intervention to make up for shortfalls in the capability of persons to achieve their ends. In short, pluralism of ends becomes an important normative commitment for social democrats.

Freedom and republicanism

Running through the capability paradigm is a distinctive notion of freedom. This, perhaps more than any other element, distinguishes the new social democracy from traditional conceptions of social democracy. Freedom is a central value in the capability paradigm which departs significantly from other approaches such as utilitarianism that focus not on the freedom to achieve but on achieved results. There is no doubt that normative frameworks like utilitarianism have informed much social democratic thinking throughout the twentieth century. In contrast, implicit in many of the programmes of the new social democracy is an attempt to rethink the relationship between freedom and intervention without totally subscribing to a notion of positive freedom.

The emergence of 'liberal socialism' must be based on a recognition of the interconnection between negative and positive freedom. The exercise of negative freedom requires the presence of positive freedom. Sen (1990: 49) presents a telling example as follows:

> I am unable to walk freely in the park because I am disabled, then that is a failure of my positive freedom to take that walk, but there is nothing here to suggest a violation of my negative freedom. On the other hand, if I am unable to walk in that park not because I am disabled, but because some thugs would beat me up if I were to visit the park, then that is a violation of my negative freedom (and not just of my freedom in the positive sense).

The point here is that positive and negative freedoms are interconnected. To quote Sen again: 'while there is real distinction between the positive and negative aspects of freedom, the different aspects can be thoroughly interrelated and intertwined. To concentrate only one or the other is not only ethically incomplete but socially disjointed' (Sen 1990: 50).

As Cohen argues, the importance of this line of argument is that freedom can be exercised not only through direct influence or action of the agent; 'effective freedom' can also exist when the levers of control are set to produce a set of conditions which would have been chosen by an individual, even though he or she does not directly exercise control or influence. For example, living in an environment without malaria is in itself a form of freedom, even though the agent cannot control whether there is malaria in the environment. What should be noted here is that effective freedom can only be exercised in the absence of malaria. Hence the deeper argument here is that the exercise of freedom can be achieved not only through the direct actions of the agent but through other indirect means. It is at this juncture that we find that negative and positive freedom are directly interconnected, and consequently the clear implication here is that effective freedom can be secured by state intervention. This idea of effective freedom has more than a resonance with T.H. Green's (1906) notion of positive liberty as the removal of obstacles to the pursuit of a common good.

There is no doubt that this capability perspective on freedom has many strengths, especially in its identification of the interconnection between negative and positive freedom. However, it concedes far too much to proponents of negative freedom and leads to the tenuous claim that intervention in some indirect way has been willed by the agent. But the more serious difficulty lies in the fact that it is a freedom that conflates two different approaches: freedom from interference (negative vs positive freedom) and freedom from domination. The notions of negative and positive freedom are, in terms of Isaiah Berlin's (1958) distinction, critically concerned with issues of interference, not domination. On the other hand, the notion of effective freedom, developed by Sen, is at root concerned with issues of domination. For agents to exercise capability they need to be free of domination, not free of interference.

Pettit has recently developed a concept of republican liberty that is properly conjoined with notions of capability which have been already discussed here. Republican freedom, he argues, consists of the absence of mastery by others, but not necessarily the absence of intervention. In his words: 'the republican tradition is associated with precisely this conception of freedom as non mastery or, as I prefer to say, non-domination' (Pettit 1997: 22). This view of freedom clearly identifies two distinct political ideals – interference and domination – and the proponents of negative and republican freedom disagree in two sets of cases: first, where there is interference but no domination, and second, where there is no interference but domination. For capability theorists the former is a case of effective freedom while the latter diminishes the effective freedom of individuals.

This is a critical point because if the argument is valid the new social democracy is distinctive in that it articulates a view of freedom which is distinct from both neo liberalism and classical social democracy. It is a conception of freedom as the 'freedom to do' rather than freedom from (negative freedom), or freedom to 'be able to'. And it is this 'freedom to do' that is crucial to the new politics of inclusion. It is a republican understanding of freedom related to the pluralism of circumstance, institutions, and ends, that defines complex equality. From this standpoint, it follows that 'new social democracy' is in part a 'republican' response to the increasing complexity of political and economic life. Central to this complexity is the acknowledgement that the exercise of 'effective freedom' requires a recognition of the institutional constraints and limits on individual choice.

What this tells us is that any account of capability and effective freedom must recognise the underlying structural arrangements that may limit the exercise of freedom. These structural arrangements have to deal with structures of advantage confronting individuals in making choices. It is these structures of advantages that define and delimit domination. Interference in these structures of domination acts to expand freedom. One of the strengths of this perspective is that freedom is located within the context of institutional structures of power, thereby allowing us to understand, for example, the way class, gender or ethnicity may function to constrain the choices that individuals can or cannot make. This formulation of liberty points to a more complex institutional, and indeed, 'political' conception of freedom than that found in the conventional distinction between negative and positive freedom.

The importance of conceiving capability as a form of domination is that it recognizes that capability is an explicitly political concept. Much of the 'resources perspective' on justice – of whatever variety – overlooks the political nature of many distributive issues. As Anderson (1999) points out, the predominant concern of traditional egalitarian theories is with the initial role of luck and chance in the allocation of distributive share. She observes that: 'Luck egalitarianism relies on two moral premises: that people should be compensated for undeserved misfortunes and that the compensation should come only from that part of others' good fortune that is undeserved' (Anderson 1999: 290). But this perspective overlooks the fact that institutional structures of domination help to shape people's choices.[21] However, in order to formulate this more properly we need to move to something like a notion of freedom as domination rather than interference. Certainly, it is possible to develop a radical version of social inclusion along these republican lines, but it is a moot point as to whether such a version would remain within the framework of economic constitutionalism.

Capability, inclusion and equality

This chapter has attempted to identify the basic elements of a normative architecture of the third way as it is embodied in the capability paradigm. There have, of course, been a number of attempts to delineate the contours of the third way, but these have been largely unsatisfactory for several reasons. There are those such as Le Grand (1998) who articulate the main elements of the new social democracy as in essence a blend of neo liberal, conservative and classical social democratic elements. For Le Grand, the third way, in contrast to neo-liberalism, 'is not libertarian or individualistic. Individual rights do not have primacy; community responsibility has at least an equal status and in some areas takes precedence' (Le Grand 1998: 27). But this account fails to pinpoint the distinctiveness of the new social democratic approaches to values such as equality and freedom. The work of Giddens exemplifies a more sociological approach to these problems and endeavours to locate the new social democracy theorizing in the context of changes in the nature of risk which follow more generally from changes in the structure of modernity. This line of reasoning in turn produces a form of moral sociology that serves as a guide to appropriate modes of social conduct and behaviour. It is a moral sociology that often tips over into a form of moral authoritarianism. Moreover, it is a standpoint, which, regrettably, side-steps the key ethical values raised by the new social democracy. In short, the key question is: What makes the third way social democratic?

We have argued that the underlying normative foundation of the new social democracy is the concept of capability. In welfare, the new language of social exclusion enlarges the capacity of individuals to freely pursue chosen ends. Similarly, the emphasis on skill and training enhances the capacity of individuals to participate in the new technologically driven economy. Capability, in the sense used by Sen, allows us to recognise the diversity of individual circumstances, institutions, and plurality of ends that individuals encounter. There is, within this economic constitutionalism, a clear shift away from welfare as income management to a notion of welfare as capability to function within the market sphere. Now these ideas may take a range of forms – as we have seen with republican variants of social inclusion – but they still remain within the framework of economic constitutionalism.

This distinction between the idea of welfare in the new and old social democracy is best recognised in terms of the shift from the notion of simple to complex equality. Simple equality entails a resource-oriented perspective on equality that simply ignores much of the diversity of individual ends and circumstances. On the other hand, the notion of complex equality presumes that equality cannot be reduced to just one dimension, but needs to recognise that there are multiple dimensions by which equality can be mapped. For example, it allows us to acknowledge the fact that for many individuals full capability requires not only redistribution of resources, but also appropriate levels of self-respect or recognition. In short, equality in this case means recognising the interaction of what Fraser (1997) calls the 'politics of distribution and identity'. What this does is to reframe equality in terms of recognition and the 'freedom to do' rather than in terms of the redistribution of income. In framing equality in these terms the capability paradigm converges with both the New Liberal and ordo liberal tradition in situating social functioning within the imperatives of economic constitutionalism. In particular, the capability paradigm as articulated by Sen has a strong affinity with the New Liberalism in that both justify public intervention in social governance in terms of the enabling and enhancing economic participation and autonomy. Capability, then, provides a basis for reconciling individual autonomy with a programme that socializes neo liberalism. As we have seen, this social market may take a form that merely affirms the inequalities of the market, as in current third way accounts, but it may also permit a more progressive 'socialization of the market' (Elson 1988). In either case, there is normative reframing of equality in terms of the equalities of capabilities rather than the distribution of income. It is exactly this understanding of equality that provides an important distinction between the new and old social democracy.

3
The Illiberal Politics of Neo Liberal Welfare Contractualism

Welfare contractualism and the new welfare governance

Conditional citizenship, mutual obligation, and contractualism have become the common policy currency of welfare reform in North America, the UK, and Australia. This new currency signals a major reevaluation of the policy and practice of the welfare state in advanced industrial societies. In the previous chapter we examined the normative architecture of welfare within economic constitutionalism through the lens of the capability paradigm. An important dimension of the new welfare governance is the carving out of modes of contractual governance through which social policies are formulated and implemented. But it is much more than that. This new contractualism seeks to shape subjects in a way that is consistent with the imperatives of the market order. This chapter focuses on the normative implications of this reordering of welfare and the consequent reshaping of the basis of membership of the political community through the new coinage of conditional citizenship and contractualism. In this view, contractualism represents a significant restructuring of the relationship between state and citizen, and reflects much more than simple changes to the administration of the benefit or entitlement programmes.

The argument advanced in this chapter has three central elements. First, following King (1999), the liberal virtues of contractualism stand, rather paradoxically, alongside a fundamentally illiberal and paternalistic set of outcomes; second, the resolution of this apparent paradox is to be found in the broadly anti-political and privatized understanding of individual autonomy which not only informs much of the recent work on contractualism but also has important continuities with the early Beveridge (Beveridge 1942) traditions of social policy; finally, it explores the possibility of a more public or democratic view of autonomy incorporating a defence of welfare as the key component of a broader project of democratic citizenship.

The notion of autonomy implicit in most of the recent work on contractualism remains deeply problematic. This is because it fails to recognise that individual autonomy requires an understanding that individuals make choices within the context of institutional arrangements or structures, some of which may work to inhibit the exercise of choice. Contractualist welfare programmes, through their insistence on economic independence as the defining attribute of individual autonomy, fail to acknowledge how a system of domination or subordination – which cuts across the public/private divide – influences the shape of individual autonomy. This failure to account for the impact of coercive practices on individual autonomy is symptomatic of the anti-political conception which underpins the new contractualism. This mode of analysis, incidentally, fits in neatly with Yeatman's (Yeatman 1998; Yeatman and Owler 2001) more political approach to the autonomy. She argues for a

> model of participation brings to light the dependence of the participation of all individuals on particular social processes, protocols and orientations. In particular this model illuminates the range of skills and learning involved in an individual's participation. (Yeatman 1998: 22)

Stated differently, the claim being made here is that individual autonomy is a political notion that sits at odds with a privatized concept of individual autonomy as economic independence. Of course, this is not to valorize a conception of public autonomy as against private autonomy, but to make the point – which, in fact, underpins Habermas's (1996a, 1996b) work on law and democracy – that public and private autonomy are linked.

In this context, public autonomy and politics more generally refer to public contestation and engagement. Public autonomy is not simply a guarantee of:

> freedom from external compulsion but the possibility of participation in a common praxis, they want to be – politically autonomous authors of a community of free and equal persons. To this extent, the

political process does not just serve to keep government activity under the surveillance of citizens who have already acquired a prior social autonomy in the exercise of their private rights and pre-political liberties. (Habermas 1996b: 22)

Further, the notion of the political is employed in the sense that structures and arrangements that shape individual agency are influenced by political relationships of inequality and domination. The model of responsible agency that underlies the 'new contractualism' uncouples individual agents from structures of systemic coercion which inhibit the exercise of individual autonomy.

Responsible agency and a model of autonomy as economic independence or economic participation are at the heart of recent developments in the thinking about welfare. For instance, the Wisconsin experiment in workfare has in its programmatic charter the clear goal of shifting the individual from welfare to work (Mead 1997a; King 1999; Powell 2000). In addition, the more recent welfare reforms implemented by New Labour in the UK have been built around enhancing the participation of welfare recipients in the labour market. In articulating this perspective, Chancellor Brown observes that:

New Labour is adopting a 'more demanding view of equality of opportunity', an updated version of Crosland's 'democratic equality' or 'real equality of life changes' which means employment opportunities for all and lifetime education opportunity for all – second, third and even fourth changes. (Brown quoted in Powell 2000: 45)

These sentiments are echoed in the Australian government's report on welfare reform in Australia. This report places great emphasis on economic participation and argues that:

Central to our vision for the future is a belief that the nation's social support system must be judged by its capacity to help people access opportunities for economic and social participation, as well as by the adequacy of its income arrangements. The Reference Group considers that a broad concept of economic and social participation can provide for a positive underpinning of the social system. (Department of Family and Community Services 2000: 4)

Admittedly, the report does seek to locate the parameters of participation in broad terms but the overall thrust of the report is geared towards using social policy to move people from welfare to work. Stated simply, economic independence is set in stark contrast to public dependency on welfare. These 'ideas of welfare' have also been reiterated by third way theorists such as Giddens (1998) who advocate a move from negative or reactive welfare, i.e., from a system in which citizens are seen as clients of an inflexible welfare bureaucracy, to a more positive conception of welfare in which social policy is used to enhance the capacity of individuals to respond to the more complex 'risk' environment faced by most post-industrial societies. In short, the goal of social policy is to develop economic independence.

But in parallel with this emphasis on economic participation is a contractualist form of governance that shaped a new social policy regulatory space in the UK, the USA and Australia. Allowing for the substantive differences, such as those between workfare in Wisconsin and New Labour social programmes, there are nevertheless some notable common elements that characterize this contractualist governance. These commonalties pertain to:

 (i) an emphasis on the participation of the individual in determining a form of service delivery which seeks to promote a more active involvement of the individual in satisfying his or her needs (*the autonomy condition*);
 (ii) the need for a more individualized and less bureaucratic form of service delivery enabling a number of innovations such as case management, which would permit a more individualized form of service delivery (*individualized service delivery condition*); and,
(iii) an implicit or explicit contract which specifies the conditional nature of welfare entitlements requiring the performance of a range of duties or meeting of certain expectations (*the contractual condition*).

This broad contractualist agenda swings on a very specific understanding of the 'autonomy condition' which subordinates all other elements of the contractualist agenda. Autonomy is defined here as economic participation and independence and consequently it forecloses a more political understanding of autonomy and agency. This understanding of autonomy, as I shall argue, is particularly problematic and one which leads to troubling illiberal consequences. Nonetheless, this does not rule out other specifications of autonomy which lead to less paternalistic and more democratic outcomes.

Liberal foundations of illiberal social policies

The nature of some of these puzzles can be usefully identified through a consideration of the perceptive study, by King (1999), of recent Anglo-American developments in contractual social policy. Contractualist language resonates with liberal echoes in that it is premised on the active participation of the individual in his or her welfare through a negotiated set of arrangements with public officials. King (1999: 21) argues that:

> Workfare (the requirement of a work activity in exchange for state benefits) is a classic expression of the contractual obligation entailed by liberalism ... Workfare now enjoys political support from the political left and right, and is defended as consistent with liberal democracy. The justification rests upon claims both about 'improving' or removing aspects of individuals' behaviour judged morally unacceptable and about the duties incumbent upon citizens. Designing welfare institutions which avoid moral hazards and disincentives are commonly allied with claims about the obligations of citizens in a liberal polity.

The point that needs to be underscored here is that contractualism is justified in terms of the obligation that members of a liberal polity incur by virtue of exercising certain rights to the use of public goods. According to King, within certain boundaries of obligation, liberal polities constantly need to legitimize the rights they grant, and, in a contractualist model of welfare, these obligations are primarily couched in terms of changing attitudes and behaviour through an array of rewards or sanctions.

But here is the intriguing paradox that King so well identifies. Contractualist policies framed in the name of liberalism have often produced deeply illiberal consequences. First, they have resulted in coercive social policies that fundamentally infringe individual freedom. Nothing illustrates this more than workfare-type schemes where welfare recipients are compulsorily required to undergo work training or perform designated tasks such as community service or enrol in training programmes. For proponents of the new contractualism, such as Mead (1997c), the coercive enforcement of obligations is one of the defining characteristics of the new welfare contract; these analysts make no bones about the fact that punitive sanctions imposed on certain categories of welfare recipients are the real objective of schemes such as workfare or the Australian policy of mutual obligation. Indeed, in the Australian context one writer has aptly termed this a form of 'civil conscription' (Bessant 1999); it is a fundamentally coercive practice.

Second, most workfare programmes violate one of the cardinal principles of a liberal polity – the right to equal treatment (Holmes 1995). Welfare contractualism, by targeting a specific group for punitive treatment, breaches the notion of equal treatment. How do we explain this puzzling accommodation of liberal and illiberal policies[1] within liberal polities? King's answer is that:

> illiberal policies are intrinsic to liberal democracy itself and their adoption reflects an internal contradiction in these polities: policies adopted democratically conflict with expectations about the role of the state in such a policy but governments use them, from time to time, to promote liberal democratic ends under the stimulus of electoral pressures. ... [Illiberal measures reflect two issues]. First, that allegedly liberal democratic governments undertake, from time to time, illiberal policies and assume or proclaim their compatibility with liberal values, exercises which are relatively unsurprising politically; and second that these measures are undertaken, paradoxically, to advance liberal ends. (King 1999: 26)

This explanation underlines the paradox of promoting such liberal virtues as rationality or autonomy, but yet producing illiberal outcomes. For example, the notion of a competent and rational agent as a precondition for citizenship played an important role in justifying a eugenics policy which was given a serious hearing in both the United States and the United Kingdom in the interwar period. King's explanation for these illiberal outcomes of policies is in terms that identify the political dynamics, such as electoral pressure or the pressure placed on solving urgent social problems, which prompt liberal polities to implement illiberal policies. King's work proposes the more general thesis that liberal polities frequently often to engage in shifting the balance between rights and obligations which, as with the current workfare regime, often produces deeply illiberal outcomes.

While this is an attractive and plausible account of the politics underlying these illiberal measures, the answers to the puzzle of liberal intent and illiberal outcomes are entrenched more deeply in the way liberal polities seek to justify and legitimize the provision of public goods. In the final analysis the explanation of the liberal/illiberal paradox is to be found in the problematic understanding of agency in liberal theory. Katznelson (1996) whose approach to these questions was a major influence on King's analysis, has suggested that:

> liberalism also remains vulnerable to illiberal temptations by virtue
> of its principled thinness. Precisely those features many of us con-
> sider liberal virtues – its low-key approach to patriotism, its reticence
> in officially sanctioning communal origins, its commitments to indi-
> vidual autonomy – deprive liberalism of the resources with which to
> construct satisfying political and communal identities or normatively
> grounded guides to public policy. (Katznelson 1996: 51)

But contrary to what Katznelson refers to as the 'thinness' of liberalism, the
illiberal outcomes of liberal contractualism reflect a failure to construct a
justification of public or, collectively provided, goods within the political
foundations of democratic citizenship. As a result, there is a tendency to
rely on justifying public good through 'thick' nonpolitical constructions of
community and agency, all of which may more often than not involve the
implementation of illiberal policies. In brief, the argument being advanced
here is that because liberal policies and practices often lack a foundation in
politically constituted modes of citizenship and agency, liberalism tends to
rely on explicit or implicit notions of community. And this is especially
marked in new forms of market citizenship that are now emerging within
the structures of economic constitutionalism.

In fact, the 'thinness' of liberalism which Katznelson (1996) refers to
demonstrates a failure to construct a political notion of agency – in
terms of democratic citizenship – to justify the provision of collective
goods. Instead, illiberal politics depend on embedding individuals in
'thick' constructions of community that often involve the marginalization of the public status of the agency, which in turn serves to legitimize
a range of illiberal policies. Therefore, the resolution of the paradox of
liberal intent and illiberal outcomes is to be found not so much in the
shifting balance of rights and responsibilities, as King would suggest, but
rather in the periodic displacement of politics by notions of community.

A number of recent writers in political theory (see, for example, Honig
1993; Bellamy 1999) have pointed out that liberal theories of various
hues avoid or seek to displace politics understood as the process of
negotiation and debate. As Bellamy remarks:

> The upshot is much the same, in formal terms at least, namely, a con-
> stitutional restriction of politics that severely circumscribes both the
> sphere within which the state may legitimately exercise its coercive
> power and the kinds of considerations voters can invoke and

legislators ought to take into account when making policy. (Bellamy 1999: 42)

However, the problem is more serious than suggested by these arguments because, as with the new contractualists, it is not merely a question of displacing or avoiding politics, but the active constitution of anti-political actions of agency that intertwine liberalism with a set of illiberal practices.[2] The crucial shift here is in the language of liberalism – from a pluralist understanding of politics as the conflict and negotiation of social interests to an anti-pluralist notion couched in terms of values. In the following section, we explore in more detail the way individual agency is constituted within the new contractualism.

Neo liberal contractualism and anti-politics: the role of active agency

What has accentuated this tension between liberal justification and illiberal practice within the new welfare contractualism is the notion of the welfare recipient as an active agent in the determination of his or her welfare future. What distinguishes the notion of agency within the new welfare contractualism is its location within a rather distinctive context of moral sociology which seeks to lay out proper modes of social conduct. It is at this point that the link between illiberal practices and liberal models of social policy becomes most evident: social policy is seen as the means through which individuals can achieve responsible social conduct; it is a peculiar moralized form of agency that lies at the heart of the new contractualism.

These ideas of active agency are constantly reiterated in various government reports and documents that underpin the new welfare contractualism. For example, the British Green Paper (The Field Report) (DSS 1998) on welfare reform which gives a sketchy history of social policy – although perhaps dubious as history – serves nevertheless to highlight the importance of the notion of agency in the new contractual social policy articulated in the Report. The Field Report (DSS 1998: 17) identifies 'four ages' of welfare as follows: (i) 'the poor law – stopping outright destitution (ii) the beginnings of the welfare state – alleviating poverty (iii) preventing poverty – the stage on which we are now embarked; and (iv) the promoting opportunity and developing potential – the stage to which we aspire'.

Similarly, the Australian interim report on social welfare points out that 'there needs to be a shift in focus from simply meeting people's

immediate needs to help them maximize social and economic participation over the long term' (Department of Family and Community
Services 2000: 12). Contractual governance of welfare, then, leads to an
individualization of welfare so that the needs of the welfare recipient
become paramount in the design of social policy. Individualization, in
the contractual practice of social policy, is buttressed by an arsenal of
agency-centred theories that are now used to understand both welfare
outcomes and behaviour.

Modifying the useful typology of Deacon and Mann (1999), these new
agent-centred theories can be classified into three main subtypes that
they focus on: (i) the emergence of the new risk culture and environment
(ii) the role of incentives in altering behaviour framed within a rational
choice framework; and (iii) changing the moral psychology of individuals,
which is seen to be the mainspring of individual conduct.

The first subtype underscores the nature of the very different risk
environments created by the growing complexity of modern society.
Theorists such as Beck et al. (1994) and Giddens (1994, 1998) argue that
modern – or, rather, late modern – social development results in the
emergence of various forms of manufactured, as opposed to external,
risk, that requires individuals to reflexively respond to this new environment of risk. Risk society, to use Beck's phrase, imposes new functions of risk management on social policy so that it acts as a mechanism
for what Giddens terms 'positive', rather than negative, welfare; and in
this framework 'positive welfare' is about enhancing the capacity of
individuals to deal with risk. Welfare governance is designed to produce
individuals who become responsible risk takers, not passive welfare
recipients or welfare dependants.

The second agent-centred perspective originates from the rational
choice paradigm and is premised on the role of self-interest in motivating and shaping the behaviour of welfare claimants. This point of view
maintains that behaviour can only be altered through a cocktail of incentives and sanctions; otherwise, rational individuals have no motivating
interest in altering their social behaviour. Much of the recent developments in so-called case management are underpinned by rational choice
calculus of sanctions and incentives. But this rational choice calculus
depends on a prior specification of the criteria for responsible behaviour,
which is at root dependent on the working of a moral sociology. In short,
this model of agency, though framed in a highly pragmatic language, is
reliant on a theory of motivation, which is inherently moralistic.

The third perspective, perhaps the most pervasive notion of agency
within the new contractualism, is that social policy needs to have at its

core the regulation of social conduct (see Mead 1997b). For this regulatory notion of agency, welfare policy needs to be directed at the sources of social disorder that are seen to be causally connected to social problems. It is a policy lexicon that resonates with terms such as 'responsible conduct' and 'social disorder', and is premised on a distinctive 'moral sociology' that places great store on the failure of welfare claimants to properly internalize the norms and practices of dominant social practices. Moral sociology, in this sense, is largely concerned with the 'role which welfare can play in the regeneration of moral infrastructure of contemporary Western societies. This regeneration is in turn a precondition of the achievement of a proper balance of autonomy and order, of individual rights and communal obligations' (Deacon and Mann 1999: 426). It reflects a fundamentally illiberal understanding of agency.

Running through each of these notions of agency that underpins the new contractualism are three important elements: first, that social policy should be directed at fostering responsible behaviour; second, that this responsible agency can be modified through a combination of sanctions and incentives; and third, that responsible agency lies in the inculcation of new modes of social conduct. Welfare contractualism is premised on a model of active and individual agency, and 'moral' conduct that works through stripping away the 'public' or political character of individual autonomy.

Within the new contractualism three central features highlight this anti-political notion of autonomy. These refer to: (i) economic dependency and the new paternalism (ii) civil society and the dispersal of public governance; and (iii) de-formalization of law.

(i) Economic dependency and the new paternalism

Social policies within the structures of economic constitutionalism seek to enhance the capacity of individuals to compete within open and free markets. For proponents of the new welfare governance the postwar welfare structures of social constitutionalism promoted welfare dependency rather than economic independence. For this reason the notions of economic independence and autonomy have become central normative elements of the new welfare contractualism. The idea of dependency has, of course, a long and rather complicated genealogy that predates the influence of the new contractualism. Indeed, its enduring influence in social policy highlights our thesis that the liberal justification of collective goods constantly strives to invoke thick nonpolitical conceptions of community and economic order. Nevertheless, the language of dependency within this new contractualism is more sharply defined and highlights clearly the contradiction between the pursuit of liberal qualities and the often illiberal outcomes.

Fraser (1997) provides one of the best accounts of the genealogy of economic dependency, distinguishing between variegated usage in the pre-industrial, industrial, and post-industrial periods. It is the last phase, i.e., the post-industrial, which coincides with the development of welfare contractualism. In this context Fraser notes that dependency has taken a more distinctively negative and individualistic colouring which leads directly to the kind of illiberal paternalistic policies characteristic of new contractualism. Fraser notes astutely that although some forms of dependency (during what she terms the industrial era) were seen as appropriate and natural (consider, for example, the gendered forms of dependency that were the hallmarks of the 'wage earners' welfare state'), this significantly changed in the post-industrial era where dependency is seen in a largely pejorative and negative light.[3] As she observes:

> No longer moderated by any positive countercurrents, the term's pejorative connotations are being strengthened. Industrial usage has recognized some forms of dependency to be rooted in relations of subordination; post industrial usage, in contrast, focuses more intensely on the traits of individuals. (Fraser 1997: 134)

No doubt this is more than a discursive shift in the vocabulary of social policy. It reflects far more significant structural shifts in the economic and social institutions of contemporary capitalism. While a detailed analysis of these shifts is not possible here it is pertinent to note aspects of three key structural changes.

First, these changes reflect the consequences of the more broad-based participation of new groups (for example, women and migrants) in the post-industrial economy. Indeed, the attribution of positive connotations to certain types of dependency in 'the industrial era' can be explained by the exclusion of these groups – particularly women – from economic participation. Changes in the notions of dependency reflect the extent of far-reaching changes in the organization and structure of labour markets in contemporary capitalism.

The second aspect of these structural changes – and one bearing a sharp focus on dependency – reflects a significant shift from the fordist industrial system of regulated labour markets to a more flexible post-fordist industrial organization where labour markets are much more deregulated and flexible. One of the important consequences of this shift has been to eliminate the boundary that existed between the labour market and the social security benefit system. As the boundary lines became blurred and indistinct, structural pressures to move social security beneficiaries into the labour market increased considerably. Work to welfare programmes demonstrate some of the new pressures that emanate from deregulated labour markets particularly in the UK, US and Australia.

Thirdly, as Giddens (1994, 1998) has pointed out, these changing ideas of dependency reflect a changing conception of risk in a complex society. The rapidly changing economy has produced new forms of risk for individuals, which demands a shift from the previously dominant notions of risk in the industrial era. For example, periods of unemployment and continuous training for workers is an imperative in the new economic conditions of the post-industrial era, but this requires a more proactive effort by individuals to combat these new forms of risk. Changes in the notions of dependency then reflect more broad structural changes in the organization of contemporary capitalism.

For these reasons the new language of 'welfare dependency' has been accompanied by an emphasis on economic participation as the main objective of welfare programs (see Chapters 1 and 2). One of the most distinctive features of the social policy initiatives of New Labour in the UK has been its attempt to make economic participation the cornerstone of its welfare policy. This is clearly evident in the Field Report which maintains that:

> The Government's biggest investment since taking office has been in a large-scale welfare to work programme. Our ambition is nothing less than a change of culture among benefit claimants, employers and public servants – with rights and responsibilities on all sides. Those making the shift from welfare into work will be provided with positive assistance, not just a benefit payment. (DSS 1998: 24)

To this end these 'welfare to work' programmes provide a range of 'carrot and stick' measures: the coercive ('stick') part of the programme is the attempt to identify and eliminate the work shy while the 'carrot' comes in the form of a fusion of welfare and tax system designed to ensure that those who move from welfare to work are not financially worse off. To this end the Working Families Tax Credit Scheme will offer increased support to working families (Powell 2000).[4] In the US and Australia the programmes have been much more coercive with tough work tests.

But what needs to be underlined here is the normative underpinnings – the ideas of welfare that underpin these social policy initiatives. Public goods are not justified in political terms as enhancing participation in the public spheres or as enhancing democratic citizenship, but only so far as they enable economic participation. Economic participation may well enhance greater public autonomy for individuals, but the relentless underscoring of dependency in the welfare contractualism highlights the role of welfare in enhancing private autonomy within the structures of economic constitutionalism. Nothing more starkly illustrates this anti-political notion of agency than the contrast constantly made between economic independence within the market system and the debilitating effects of dependence on public goods such as welfare – a contrast that leads inevitably to large doses of illiberal policies.

A further distinctive facet of this recent emphasis on dependency has been its increasingly individualized character. As Fraser (1997) highlights, some forms of dependency within the industrial era were seen to be 'social facts', but dependency is now viewed as a function of individual traits and characteristics. Welfare contractualism is seen to be a method through which these individual pathologies can be challenged. Dependency, then, is related to a particularly troubling view of the nature of agency in terms of competence and a moralized notion of responsibility that marginalizes the structures and institutions of subordination that constrain the exercise of individual autonomy. Driving this anti-political view of agency, then, is a notion that dependency diminishes the competency of welfare recipients; dependence is counterpoised not just to economic independence but to a deeper set of assumptions as to the prerequisites of responsible agency.

For the proponents of new paternalism, welfare governance within this framework of responsible agency is designed to encourage and reward competence and responsible behaviour, always judged in terms of the imperatives of the market economy (Mead 1997b). Implicit in this reasoning is that while traditional welfare policies assumed that welfare clients were responsible, the new contractual governance is explicitly premised on the fact that these clients are unable to exercise responsible choice; consequently, this is seen as justification for a range of paternalist policies that aim to foster responsible agency. In so doing it makes possible the stripping of various public attributes of agency such as the right to equal treatment and, even more seriously, allows for the denial of 'voice' in the determination of contractual arrangements. For the new paternalists like Mead an important cause of these illiberal policies is that long-term poverty or disadvantage is seen to stem from the failure of individuals to inculcate proper norms or values. In fact, the logic of Mead's argument may well be applied to a range of other coercive programmes such as eugenics schemes and racist assimilation[5] policies. In essence, the assumptions of responsible agency lead inevitably to illiberal policies because they shift the causes of social disadvantage to the deficient cultural attributes of individuals, and this in turn licences a range of illiberal policies (Mead 1997c). The new welfare governance in this way implies a form of moral sociology which proposes that social disadvantage results not from structural problems but from a culture of poverty 'where poverty is explained in terms of a cultural and environmental milieu rather than inherited attributes that incapacitates the poor' (Gilbert and Specht 1974: 97).[6]

Responsible agency as articulated by the proponents of the new welfare governance actively diminishes the capacity of individuals to act in the public sphere. By constituting the responsible agent in terms of economic independence rather than political participation, it relegates the importance of 'public' attributes of citizenship. The location of the sources of individual culpability in the failure to inculcate so-called community norms and practices – best seen in the Blair government's punitive anti-social behaviour policies – justifies a whole range of illiberal policies. Welfare contractualism relies on a particular understanding of what constitutes responsible agency which contrasts economic independence to the pathological dependence on public goods; it is an anti-political understanding of individual agency used to justify a broad spectrum of illiberal policies.

(ii) Civil society and the dispersal of public governance

These strategies of depoliticization are further reinforced by examining the role of civil society in systems of contractual governance. One of the features of new welfare contractualism is a mode of service delivery that places a premium on techniques such as case management and individual service delivery. However, in some approaches to the new contractualism this re-specification of service delivery goes much further by assigning a leading policy role to civil society. This understanding of civil society needs to be seen as the diminution of democratic citizenship rather than as a reinforcement of public participation.

Not all proponents of the new contractualisms are supporters of an active civil society; Mead (1997c), for one, is both cautious and sceptical about the civil society; or what he calls privatization, arguing that it detracts from the main issues of reciprocity and the enforcement of obligations. Nevertheless, it remains the case that most advocates of the obligation-based welfare have been keen enthusiasts of civil society. In Australia, the Prime Minister John Howard has advanced the notion of 'social coalition' to parallel his notion of mutual obligation. The Howard government's welfare reform proposals give support to mutual obligation by noting that: 'the social support system will be stronger and more sustainable if governments, business, not-for-profit organisations and communities work together to maximise opportunities for economic and social participation' (Reference Group on Welfare Reform 2000: 47).

These ideas find a strong resonance within much of the third way thinking.[7] For example, the UK Field Report (DSS 1998) identifies public and private partnerships between state and community organizations as an integral element of welfare reform. These policy directions have been given support by third way theorists such as Giddens (1994, 1998) who have identified public/private partnerships between government and civil society as a way of transcending state/market boundaries.

Relatedly, there has been a resurgence of interest in the role of charitable organizations and Friendly Societies[8] as mechanisms through which welfare can be delivered. The preference for these organizations is on the grounds that they will foster greater responsibility amongst individuals since they will be direct contributors to the provision of their own welfare services; and also on the grounds that these organizations will reflect community-based norms. For the advocates of these partnerships there is direct relationship between fostering responsible agency and various modes of public and private partnerships because this form of partnership in service provision effectively removes the rights of individuals in the public sphere.

These new mechanisms create a form of managerial civil society for the effective implementation and control of services. There are three central elements to this managerial civil society. First, civil society is often framed in terms of civic virtue and values. For these proponents of civil society take on an explicitly anti-political stance and in place of rights and political struggles they: 'talk about the virtue and ethics, institutionalise the right values, and foster strong civil institutions that will help integrate people into what will be, in effect, a refurbished American civil religion' (Cohen 1999: 230).

Hand in hand with this civic virtue model there has been what Cohen aptly calls a 're-traditionalizing' of civil society with an accent on institutions such as the family. Again, this civic virtue aspect of managerial civil society reinforces the anti-political understanding of responsible agency because it shifts the emphasis from the rights and entitlements to the cultivation of appropriate values.

Second, the emphasis on these partnership models of state–civil society relationships is very much on the effective management of government-defined goals or objectives. There is little in this model to suggest a civil society that would enable individuals to contest and challenge relations of domination. In other words, managerial civil society disengages individuals from active political participation.

Finally – and crucially for the argument advanced in this chapter – the new managerial roles accorded to civil society does not displace governments, but disperses governmental powers to new agencies and networks. This redistribution of governmental powers is most apparent in the Australian government's Job Network program. In this instance, previous public functions are now being performed by employment agencies in both the public and private sectors (Considine 2001). Dispersing governmental powers in this way does not lead to the diminishing of government, but rather to the removal of a range of governmental functions from public purview, the effect of which is to diminish the rights and entitlements of individuals.

(iii) Deformalization of law

The marginalization of the legal status of welfare recipients is a striking illustration of our argument that the underlying assumption of agency within the framework of welfare contractualisms diminishes the public or citizenship status of the individual. It exemplifies the fact that private autonomy does not necessarily imply public autonomy, that is, the capacity to participate in judgement and deliberation as equal members of the political community. In fact, while the language of welfare contractualism suggests that welfare recipients have some degree of legal right, the reality is that in most cases these recipients are denied the kinds of review rights that existed under administrative law within the 'protectionist' welfare systems. Under the new forms of welfare contractualism individuals are increasingly subject to administrative discretion that is often exercised outside formal administrative channels. Individuals end up in a grey world between the administrative law and the private law of contract. In fact, the marginalization of rights is built into the very obligation-based structure of welfare contractualism which, in turn, as we have argued, is premised on a problematic nonpolitical conception of responsible agency. Erosion of these rights is underlined by the fact that obligation-based welfare contractualism is premised squarely on a punitive sanctions-based regime which further attenuates the legal status of the individual (Mead 1997c). Despite the legal language of welfare contractualism, an obligation-based welfare regime results in the creation of a legal structure that has significantly less legal formality.

Contractual governance serves to significantly weaken the formal legal character of the system. In particular, 'case management' – so beloved of welfare contractualism – explicitly gives officials a high level of discretion that brings with it differential treatment of welfare clients (King 1999). Inequality of treatment strikes at the ideal of formal legal equality.

Furthermore, the highly ambiguous and subjective legal standards of many contractual agreements add to the lack of legal formality within the new contractualism. As Carney and Ramia point out, the standards that apply to case management 'are more diffuse and more subjective. Significant levels of professional judgement and discretion on the part of case managers are entailed' (Carney and Ramia 1999: 134). In the Australian context Carney and Ramia (1999) argue that the welfare contractualism turns welfare administration into a relationship between welfare officials and recipients, but an administrative relationship that is both narrow and which serves to limit the bargaining power of welfare beneficiaries.

And this is the paradox: despite the language of contract and bargaining employed by the new contractualism its net effect is to erode the (always limited) legal formality and rights of welfare recipients. It is a contractual relationship that depends on a high degree of punitive sanction, and, as such, it makes problematic any idea of a bargaining relationship. Such a coercive relationship can only be understood in terms of the ideal of a responsible and competent agent that underpins much of the normative rationale of contractualism. To move beyond this neo liberal understanding of contractualism whilst at the same time retaining the liberal virtues of individual autonomy requires us to develop a political notion of agency.

Towards a democratic contractualism

Welfare contractualism as currently constituted in both policy and practice in the USA, UK, and Australia is based on a high degree of coercion and discretionary executive power that is simply incompatible with a concept of individual autonomy (see Plant 1985). The match between the liberal virtue of autonomy and the illiberal coercive practices is woven into the very fabric of the anti-political notion of autonomy and independence which lies at the heart of current practice of welfare contractualism. As the public rights and status of individuals become marginal, there is a correlative increase in the degree of coercion as well as in the likelihood of paternalist and illiberal outcomes.

Coercion acts to distort individual autonomy in two ways. First, it reduces the availability of options that are open to individuals. An autonomous individual must not only be given a choice, but he or she also needs an adequate range of options to choose from: not just a number of options, but also, as Raz (1986) argues cogently, a variety of options and these options must relate in one way or another to individual projects and goals. Paternalist welfare contractualism limits the number as well as the variety of options open to individuals. On this basis, welfare recipients are subjected to a coercion that is quite incompatible with individual autonomy. It is essential that the criterion of 'adequacy of options' be incorporated in a more democratic contractualism which is non-coercive and takes seriously the concept of individual autonomy.

An adequate range of options for the individual in systems of contractual governance points us towards a more political notion of autonomy. For one, it allows the justification of public goods to be framed in terms of enabling individual autonomy. Obviously, welfare in general can be seen as a public good and as an instrument for generating a range of options for individuals; but it can also bring into consideration the active role of government in giving individuals greater options and choices in welfare arrangements. These, in turn, are vital to exercising their individual autonomy and, as Raz succinctly observes, 'public goods lie at the foundation of most options' (Raz 1994: 121).

But options, as Raz goes on to suggest, are socially defined because the range of choices open to individuals are determined by the kind of social structures and institutions in which they are situated. Hence, any move to widen the range of options open to individuals will inevitably engage in the task of assessing these arrangements in terms of the degree to which they constrain the ability of the agent to exercise choice. We shall return to these issues, but the argument that needs to be underlined here is that the consequence of adopting an 'adequacy of option' standard is to give a more political understanding of individual autonomy than that provided by welfare paternalists.

The coercive character of the relationship within welfare contractualism can also be illustrated in the highly limited bargaining capacity of individual agents. One of the means through which coercion limits autonomy is by distorting the way individuals form goals and reach preferences, or by the extent to which procedures shaping preferences are subject to coercion, thereby constricting the capacity of individuals

to make their own choices. In essence, the autonomy condition of contractualism requires the presence of what may be termed 'procedural
autonomy',[9] that is, the absence of coercion in the process through
which an individual determines his or her preferences. Welfare
contractualism – by limiting the bargaining capacity of individuals –
severely limits the procedural autonomy of individuals. More pertinently,
these restrictions on procedural autonomy reflect the broad hostility of
proponents of welfare contractualism to any notions of rights or public
participation in the determination of individual preferences; procedural
autonomy requires a more public and political understanding of
individual agency than that found in welfare contractualism.

Any noncoercive welfare contract must at the minimum involve a significant broadening of the bargaining relationship. It must be conceived
as a political relationship that places a premium on the political capacity of an individual to bargain with an availability of adequate range of
choice and options. Yeatman's (1998, 2000) work on contractualism[10]
suggests ways in which a focus on the active participation of individuals
can contribute to a more democratic set of contractual arrangements.
For example, in the area of workplace bargaining, Yeatman argues that
contractualism could lead to 'the presumption of employer prerogative
in the employment relationship be statutorily disestablished, and that
contractual capacities of both employees and employers be socially
developed and resourced' (Yeatman 1998: 240). In effect, we have here
an example of a more democratic contract which, rather than being a
device to smuggle in paternalistic and coercive relationships, has the
potential to significantly enhance the rights and capacities of contracting parties. But this democratic emphasis is not a simple matter of modifying this or that element in the current contractualism; it needs a more
radical reconstitution of agency in the direction of a 'public' and political notion of autonomy.

Systemic coercion and the capability approach

Even granting that contractualism is able to deal with the problems of
direct coercion we still face the more fundamental problem of indirect
coercion. Options and choices open to any one person depend in part
on the kind of structural arrangements that confront the individual.
Choices that are intrinsic to individual autonomy may be subject to the
constraining influence of social institutions. Therefore, it is possible that
coercive influences may be more structural than individual; coercion is
indirect and systemic. This idea of systemic coercion leads us to a vastly

different understanding of individual autonomy and one which has significant implications for the design of a democratic contractualism.

One way of dealing with this critical issue is by examining some recent discussions of the legal notion of responsibility in criminal law, particularly in the work of Lacey (1998) and Norrie (1993), with a view to bringing out relevance in addressing the problematic issues of welfare contractualism. According to Lacey (1998: 198), the idea of the responsible subject is one who is deemed to be: 'accountable for his actions as one who has standard cognitive and volitional capacities: only if he understands the nature of his action, and had a fair opportunity to act otherwise than he did, will it be appropriate to hold him responsible for it'. A 'responsible' subject in these terms is defined by familiar terms such as 'intention', 'voluntariness', and 'rationality' (Norrie 1993). However, this notion of the legally responsible individual constitutes the subject in an abstract way resulting in discounting the specific social and political context of individual action. Norrie (1993: 1) points out that in this model, 'legal responsibility abstracts the issue of "intention" from its twin concept of "motive" '. Motives, he suggests, are socially constituted and their incorporation into a notion of agency would lead to a more contextualized account of agency.

Additionally, this notion of a responsible agency is not free from tension or contradiction; legal doctrine constantly needs to legitimize itself by making concessions to the importance of context (Lacey 1998). As Lacey's work points out, this fluidity of conceptual categories makes problematic the notion of the legally responsible subject, which surely lies at the centre of the criminal law. Neo liberal contractualism – like the criminal law or feminist arguments about the legal subject, the target of Lacey's analysis – works within a framework of a responsible agent, one disembedded from its social and political context. But welfare contractualism seeks to explain deviation from the model of the responsible subject as a failure of community norms. A moral sociology lies at the foundation of many punitive and paternalistic policies that are so identified with policies of contractualism.

Models of 'responsible agency' function by excluding those contexts that force us to acknowledge the political relations of domination in which agents are located. In essence, the problem is not so much the absence of context, but rather the failure to address the issues of systemic or indirect coercion in shaping individual autonomy and choice. The failure to acknowledge the role of coercive structure reflects the more general absence of a notion of politics in the idea of responsible agency because it requires – whether in criminal law or welfare contractualism – the exclusion of systemic sources of coercion in shaping individual choices. Recognising the sources of indirect coercion directs us towards a model of individual autonomy that is more embedded and acknowledges the connectedness[11] of individuals.

Raz's (1986) work on individual autonomy provides some important clues as to how we could conceive of a political understanding of individual autonomy. Autonomy, he argues, needs to be understood not just in terms of leading an autonomous life, but also in terms of the conditions and the capacities for such life. Capacity for autonomy provides the second order conditions that sustain an autonomous life. And this is what is most valuable in Raz's argument because the development of the capacities for autonomous life depends on attending to – though this is not the language he uses – the indirect coercive structures and arrangements that influence peoples' lives. Employing the notion of autonomy as capacity:

> yields duties which go far beyond the negative duties of non interference, which are the only ones recognised by some defenders of autonomy. If the duties of non interference are autonomy-based then the principle of autonomy provides reason for holding that there are other autonomy based reasons as well. (Raz 1986: 408)

By implication, adopting the standard of individual autonomy requires us to attend to the condition that impedes or constrains autonomy; it requires us to discard the model of responsible agent with its problematic assumptions about the causal influences on autonomy.

There is a close similarity between these ideas and the capability argument developed by Sen (see Chapter 2). Sen makes the important point that the capability for autonomy depends not just on the choices, but on the very capability to make choices. Again, what is evident in the capabilities approach is the emphasis placed on the second order condition – conditions of choice – for the full achievement of capability; for people to make choices there has to be a range of options or choices. Sen, like Raz, makes explicit the background conditions that enable the exercise of autonomy. The point here is that if choice is an end in itself then we have to direct our attention to those structures and institutions that constrain autonomy or enable these choices. The ramification of these arguments for our understanding of individual autonomy is twofold: first, it means that autonomy can only be understood in terms of the kind of connections and relations that people have. These relationships can influence the kind of options or choices that people have. In Sen's terms, it either enables or disables the achievement of certain capabilities, or, in Raz's terms, the capacity to lead autonomous lives. Much of this argument has a strong resonance with recent feminist writings on relational autonomy, which, despite a number of significant internal differences between various theorists of relational autonomy, tend to emphasise the influence of an oppressive social context (Mackenzie and Stoljar 2000).[12] Brison has noted the affinities between Sen's notion of capability and relational autonomy, and strongly argues for the adoption of a historical approach to autonomy. Hence, to:

> determine whether or not someone is autonomous or is choosing autonomously *now*, we need to know how that person came to have her preferences, including those leading her to the present choice. We need to know whether she developed the competencies necessary for autonomous preferences formation and ranking. (Brison 2000: 284)

This interpretation for a causal model of individual autonomy differs markedly from the privatized notion of autonomy that lies behind the idea of the responsible individual; it is not just historical, it is a political model of agency.

The second implication of adopting the notion of systemic or indirect coercion is that it allows us recontexualize the model of the responsible agent. Recall that a key element of the responsible agency was its decontexualization of the agent's social and political context. Using the idea of systemic coercion enables us to now recontexualize the agent in the context of his or her social and political context. From the viewpoint of democratic contractualism what this entails is the development of legal strategies that permit this kind of contextualization of agency.[13] But again, what needs to be underscored is the fact that this recontexualization forces us to adopt a political conception of agency that contrasts sharply with that of the responsible agency model of the paternalistic welfare contractualism. These considerations point to the need to develop a legal framework that accommodates a model of both public and private autonomy.

Democratic foundation of law and contractualism

The foregoing considerations would imply that a shift towards a democratic structure for welfare governance would need to pay more attention to the legalization of the relationship between the contractual parties – not merely legalization, but a legal structure that would enhance the 'rights' of welfare recipients. Certainly, this would be a move in the right direction. For one thing, it would reverse the process of deformalization of law so evident in the new contractualism. A process of legalization would serve to broaden the contractual relationship, and, more importantly, a rights-based approach to a democratic contractualism would serve to enhance the bargaining capacity of individuals. But even this form of 'legalization of contractualism' would not meet some of the problems raised by issues of systematic or indirect coercion. More especially, this form of legalization would need to incorporate the kind of 'public autonomy' required by a properly functioning democratic welfare governance. We need to develop a jurisprudence and a legal framework that provide a nexus between public and private autonomy. The critical analysis of law developed by Habermas (1996a) provides an important approach to these issues.

It has not been possible in this chapter to consider Habermas's (1996a) theory of law and politics. But some comments may be illuminating. The main challenge for Habermas was to account for the relationship between law and legitimacy in a way which enables one to move beyond the tension between law and legitimacy evident in most accounts of this issue. For Weber, the formality of law – the formal content which defines what constitutes a legal norm – is distinct from what he felt was the irrational foundation of politics. Pivotal to this view is the latent conflict in the dualism between formal legal rationality and politics, and this was, in fact, a point identified by many critics of liberal legalism such as Carl Schmitt (Jayasuriya 2005). Habermas's singular contribution to jurisprudence has been to show that politics and law are not separate, but constitutive. In short, legal procedures are intrinsic to the public autonomy of each of its citizens; democratic ideas are immanent in the very procedures of law.

The distinctive element of the Habermas argument is that there is an internal relationship between private autonomy (or the private rights) of individuals and the public autonomy of the citizenry, which reflects the democratic self-constitution of society. For Habermas, this relationship is intrinsic to the very conditions of formal legal procedures. But unlike the formal legalism of liberal jurisprudence it is radical proceduralism that is intrinsically democratic. It is this constitutive model of democracy and law that is the distinctive feature of a republican jurisprudence.[14] Habermas develops an argument which suggests that public and private autonomy are linked or arise together. Public and private autonomy mutually constitute – the co-originality thesis – each other and what is relevant in this argument is his insistence that our private rights are rights about which a collective agreement is necessary; in short, private rights depend on the exercise of public autonomy, that is, rights of public participation. Similarly, our right of public autonomy must also be determined collectively. A legal order is:

> legitimate to the extent that it equally secures the co-original private and public autonomy of its citizens; at the same time, however, it owes its legitimacy to the forms of communication in which alone this autonomy can express and prove itself. In the final analysis, the legitimacy of law depends on the undistorted forms of public communication and indirectly on the communicational infrastructure of private sphere as well. (Habermas 1996a: 409)

In essence, this democratic proceduralism allows us to ground rights in the public autonomy of the citizenry. There are three major inferences to be drawn from this discussion.

First, it suggests that the very criteria of the adequacy of options discussed above must be open to public engagement and debate. There is no magic formula for determining what significant options are valuable for individual autonomy. This needs to be subject to public deliberation. In short, we need to move towards a conception of democratic equality which permits a rights-oriented legal model for welfare contractualism. Second, it implies that in determining the capacity to take part in this deliberative process, we need to take account of systemic coercive practices that constrain the exercise of public autonomy.

Finally, the democratic proceduralism proposed by Habermas alerts us to the need to pay more attention to those procedural rights which need to be developed if there is to be any possibility of democratic contractualism. These rights, for example, may entail greater collective representation as well as access to information denied to welfare clients under various forms of neo liberal contractualism. Accepting these arguments compels us to confront the fact that any shift to a more rights-oriented legalistic model – albeit of a republican hue – reverses the legal deformalization of the new welfare governance.

Too often critics – barring some notable exceptions – have let the new contractualism 'off the theoretical hook' by conceding too readily to its prevailing notion of what constitutes individual autonomy. In contrast, as we have argued here, the core of welfare contractualism is the problematic notion of responsible agency. It is an understanding of responsible agency that operates to marginalise the 'public' or the political attributes of agency, and in particular, one which elides the direct as well as indirect coercive context of individual action. In other words, it presents a deeply anti political understanding of the nature of agency.

This anti-political notion of agency finds expression in the way liberal virtues of choice and autonomy result, paradoxically, in an arrangement of broadly illiberal practices. It is important to realize that these arguments have a broader significance beyond the parameters of social policy. It is clear that a great many recent changes in the governance and management of policy confront a similar troubling question in relation to issues of agency and autonomy. Even more seriously, the new contractualism leads to the significant marginalization of formal law, allowing bureaucratic and often non-state actors considerable discretionary power. It further accelerates the deformalization of the legal system apparent in the 'old welfare state' (Habermas 1996a). In this sense at one level, this neo liberal contractualism leads to ever-increasing forms of procedural controls, but these procedures themselves are outside the framework of democratic control and judicial review. In this context law not only becomes less formal, but, in a sense, is privatized.

One of the strengths of the democratic proceduralist paradigm of law is that it enables us to legalize welfare arrangements, but in a context where those procedures enable both public and private autonomy for individuals; it is a legal procedure that is intrinsically democratic. It allows us to ground the rule of law in democratic processes. But such a democratic proceduralism requires us to develop a notion of individual autonomy that enhances, rather than narrows, the range of options open to individuals.[15] In short, this model enables us to contextualize individual agency in political terms. The attraction of such a model is that it permits the use of a republican model of agency that makes explicit the criterion of non domination in its account of freedom (Pettit 1997). Neo liberal contractualism is not the only path that is available to those wishing to pursue notions of individual autonomy within the new structures of economic constitutionalism. To develop a social democratic version of socialized markets we need to clearly distinguish between neo liberal and democratic contractualism.

4
Contractualism and Transnational Welfare Governance

Transnational welfare governance and contractualism

The global public policy agenda now resonates with terms such as 'poverty reduction' and 'pro-poor growth'. Poverty, it seems, has been rediscovered by the global community, and the new social agenda differs from the previously dominant 'Washington Consensus' of market and trade liberalization. But – and this is at the heart of the thesis in this volume – poverty reduction and its social agenda, rather than being antagonistic or in opposition to the market, has become an important component of the economic reforms – neo liberalism – promoted by the Post-Washington Consensus (PWC). The new transnational governance of the social welfare agenda differs not only from the Washington Consensus, but also from the Basic Needs model which had recognisable Keynesian and social democratic elements (Higgott 1983).[1] This, above all, provides an institutional framework for debate on a 'social agenda' where the terms of engagement are different from those of the social democratic project that informed the postwar welfare state as well as the earlier welfarist development priorities of international financial institutions. While this new framework arises from within the contours of the neo liberal market model that dominated politics and policy over the last two decades, it does create new alternatives for debating social issues – especially for various nongovernmental organizations – that might challenge some of the assumptions of the prevailing neo liberal model. What we consider in this chapter is not the 'terms of engagement' of the debate, but the institutional framework in which this new governance takes place. It is through this framework for social governance – which we describe as 'contractual governance' – that economic constitutionalism is entrenched within the spaces of social policy making, and thereby privileges the pursuit of economic and market order and the emergence of forms of market citizenship.

This emerging new transnational welfare governance – framed within the PWC – has stimulated the development of new forms of mediation between state and civil society. The agenda of the PWC has clearly been associated with Joseph Stiglitz (Stiglitz 1998a and 1998b), and exemplified in the World Bank's Development Report of 2000/2001 on attacking poverty.[2] The logic of the PWC agenda should be understood not so much as a departure from the policies of structural reform, but as an attempt to evolve an institutional framework to embed the structural adjustment policies of the Washington Consensus era. But the ethos of governance that has emerged is much more than entrenchment of rules and institutions of economic governance; it is equally concerned with enabling 'conforming conduct' within the sphere of civil society. From this perspective, economic constitutionalism seeks to institute processes and structures of governance that activate modes of conduct appropriate to an efficient market economy. Accordingly, civil society becomes an integral element in the management of an efficient economic programme, and, more crucially, in the production of new liberal subjects. It is within the ambit of this economic constitutionalism that transnational welfare governance becomes a significant component of transnational public policy.

Social policy has become central to the governance agenda promoted by international organizations such as the World Bank for two central reasons. First, following the Asian economic crisis, countries such as Thailand (Phananirmai and Hewison 2001) witnessed a rapid expansion in the ranks of the working class as result of two decades of industrialization. As a result, the Asian crisis has magnified the political and social impact of unemployment and prompted agencies such as the World Bank to focus on the politics of managing this unemployment.[3] Political management of unemployment became as much an ideological project as a social policy venture mainly because the objective of many of these social programmes was to shift the burden of unemployment on to communities or individuals. This is a point well made in Weber's (2001) perceptive paper on the global development architecture and micro credit strategies which analyse the role of 'social safety' as mechanisms or instruments of political crisis management. Therefore, social programmes building on notions such as social capital or community empowerment have had the effect of transforming the conventional view of unemployment from a social issue or a social problem into one of social conduct needing regulation and management. The objective of governance reform, now couched in the language of social inclusion, was framed in terms of regulating individual behaviour. Social policy began to take on an entirely different role and is at the forefront of the new governance agenda of multilateral agencies (see Cammack 2001).

In this context, the explanation of poverty developed in the new global social policy is framed not in terms of class inequality, but in the language of social inclusion. Poverty, it is now argued, results either from the lack of social capital – the social networks to which people are connected – or from the inadequacy of individual assets – such as marketable skills or capital to compete in a competitive global economic environment. This market citizenship, built on notions of social capital, is as much a product of global governance as it is of national politics. But what is distinctive about this form of transnational welfare governance is that global policies are directed not so much to specifying policy alternatives, but to constructing or constituting a regulatory environment. This is essentially a political or regulatory space in which actors can engage and deliberate on social policy. It is this regulatory space rather than any specific policy alternatives that define the new transnational welfare governance.

In the light of the foregoing, this chapter will examine not only the substantive policy alternatives proposed by international financial institutions (IFIs) but, more importantly, the modes and mechanisms through which these policies are put into effect. In fact, one of the characteristics that this ethos of poverty reduction has in common with third way thinking is an obsession with governance; not substantive policies, but the nature of governance itself. To underline this zeal on issues of governance one needs only to note that many of the initiatives pursued by institutions such as the World Bank, the OECD, and the EU, are primarily directed at setting up the appropriate mechanisms and modalities of governance, all of which are concerned with constituting a domestic regulatory space in which issues of social policy can be debated and justified.

In itself this is an important feature of this economic constitutionalism. It works indirectly through the specification of the political space for regulation rather than directly through regulation itself. Put differently, the regulatory governance – whether at the transnational or the national level – works through various forms of meta regulation or meta governance – that is, by working on the governance of governance. Governance in this sense becomes the very business of the state as it seeks to constitute new arenas of the fields of governance itself. The crucial shift here is towards the state being organized more on the basis of regulation and supervision of regulation rather than directly engaging in regulating the provision of services. And economic constitutionalism works through these channels of meta regulation rather directly on policy outcomes. In this sense meta regulation becomes the cutting edge of the deeper internal transformations taking place within the state.

In the transnational welfare governance, as with a number of other areas of global public policy, the primary mechanism of meta regulation is through systems of contractual governance. Contractualism here refers to the way in which public policy – in this case transnational policy[4] – and its forms of delivery is organized and secured through contract like frameworks. Importantly, the agents operating these frameworks – be they individuals or local/national government, civil society actors, and even transnational agencies – are required to meet certain standards of performance and conduct as a condition for the receipt of a grant or a benefit. What is more the performance of these standards is monitored and there are specified mechanisms of enforcement. What I suggest here is that this politics of social inclusion is now seen as an important feature of recent welfare strategies (see Chapter 1) which are reliant on the specification of the standards for inclusion. Furthermore, contractual governance turns out to be the major means through which these standards are imposed and assessed. In other words, global contractualism bears more than a passing similarity to various workfare regimes in Australia, the UK, and the US (see Chapter 3) and is seen as the 'hard edge' of social inclusion. But contractualism can be analysed as a framework of meta regulation which is as a strategy of global governance that serves to link global welfare policy more directly to economic imperatives fostering the development of forms of market citizenship.

In these terms the new welfare governance becomes workfare writ large at a transnational level. Clearly, contractualization of global social standards forms a strategy of regulatory governance that seeks to influence the conduct of agents at various levels of governance. But these new social standards are premised on meeting certain obligations. Even at the transnational level, welfarism is transformed from claims that arise out of the political standing of actors (individual or states) to claims that are contingent on the prior and continuing performance of certain obligations. Furthermore, the real significance of these new forms of contractual governance is the emergence of new regulatory structures and arenas in which contestation and debate over social policy making take place.

But it would be erroneous to think of the new contractual regulation as merely a Trojan horse for market imperatives. Elsewhere contractual regulation establishes a framework within which social policy arguments and debates take place. It is the very form of contractual regulation that embodies – to use Schattsneider's (1960) term – a certain 'mobilization of bias' found less in the content of policies than in the broader structural framework of governance that privileges certain policy alternatives over others. But this mobilization of bias is even more encompassing in that the institutional framework tends to favour certain kinds of issues, actors, and even understandings of social disadvantage over others. So, for example, although the principle of participation is an important dimension of the new social policy framework it remains narrowly confined to participation within the economic sphere.

To give another example, the Poverty Reduction Strategy Papers (PRSPs) (discussed below) require that social policies work in tandem with macroeconomic economic policies geared towards sustainable economic growth. Morgan (2003) argues that one of the consequences of meta regulation particularly through the operation of procedural requirements is the 'economization' of regulatory policy making – that is, 'a regulatory politics increasingly shaped by technocratic bargaining in apolitical terms' (Morgan 2003: 490). 'Economization' is a handy term because – if we leave aside the arguments on the pros and cons of this framework – what it does is to implicitly 'economize' social policy making. But – and this is the nub of economic constitutionalism – these imperatives are not imposed through specific policies, but through contract-like arrangements which impose procedural requirements that filter the range of policy alternatives available to domestic policy makers.

Contractual governance, then, is more than just a set of techniques; it has embedded within itself a political bias towards selecting certain policy strategies over others. In this sense, contractualism can be understood as bits and pieces of building blocks of statecraft that reshape the internal architecture of the state as well as the broader relationship between the political community and citizens. Contractualization of global social standards is a strategy of regulatory governance seeking to influence the conduct of agents at various levels of governance. Regulatory governance of these social standards in turn serves to link the global welfare policy more directly to economic imperatives, thereby fostering the development of forms of market citizenship.

However, it is important that we identify two distinctive elements in the contractual regulation of welfare. First, contractual governance provides a set of meta governance procedures which establishes a 'chain of contracts' that link various sites of governance. Contractual governance sets out broad flexible goals and governance arrangements. These goals are then progressively enforced and supervised down the contractual chain to the national and subnational level. Therefore a crucial point that we develop here (see section below) is that these new institutional patterns are linked through what may be termed a *'chain of contract'* to higher levels of supervision and monitoring at both the national and supranational levels. In this way the new transnational social policy is embedded in the organizational and procedural routines of local, national, and transnational political structures and works to exclude certain forms of interests, actors, and issues. Contractualism, far from being a set of technocratic routines, has its own political effects that are echoed in the depoliticization of social governance. Yet the importance of this welfare contractualism rests not on the specifics of a particular policy regime but on the fact that it seeks – not always successfully – to develop a regulatory space for the new social policy. And it is this regulatory space that is organized through a contractual architecture.

Second, contractual regulation works through the enrolment of a range of 'stakeholders' in the process of social policy formulation. These stakeholders, in turn, are expected to engage and participate in the process of social policy formulation and delivery. But this participation is limited to enhancing economic participation within the marketplace. Indeed, the new contractualism is replete with the appeal to the liberal virtues of participation and choice but this participation is one that takes place in the shadow of the marketplace. Hence the most systematic effect of this welfare contractualism is the establishment of a model of access to welfare not as a right – as would be the case with notions of social citizenship – but as a condition of securing greater economic participation.

Contractual welfare governance, in other words, serves to carve out a distinctive terrain of relationship between state and the citizen based on the economic participation rather than on a set of social rights. Indeed, the most important impact of the new contractual governance may lie in fostering new forms of economic citizenship that make access to social goods conditional on participation within the market order. Participation in this form of contractualism marks out a distinctive terrain of relationship between state and the citizen based on economic participation rather than on a set of social rights. These issues are explored in the next section of this chapter.

Chain of contract and the new welfare governance

Ownership, participation and standards are the lexicon of contractualism. At its broadest level, contractual governance sets out a spectrum of goals and objectives that have to be met, such as performance and audit standards, and provides the organizational infrastructure through which governmental and other actors enter into agreements. Nothing better exemplifies this contractual governance of welfare than the joint World Bank/IMF-sponsored Poverty Reduction Strategy Papers (PRSPs) which form the cornerstone of 'pro-poor' policies in low-income developing countries. These documents lay out not just the poverty reduction policies, but a road map of the participatory and audit process that needs to be met in order for the PRSPs to qualify for World Bank/IMF approval. The PRSPs are in turn, linked to the so-called Comprehensive Development Framework (CDF) objectives and are viewed as a way of giving concrete shape to some key objectives of the CDF. But the PRSPs form their own separate chain of contracts because in this process transnational agencies set out broad long-term objectives which are then progressively localized at lower levels of the contractual chain. What is so striking about the PRSPs is that they are not so much policy documents as procedural specifications of contractual architecture that allows various actors drawn from government and NGOs to enter into a series of contracts. Establishing these chains of contracts requires an organization or mechanisms through which these chain of contracts from the transnational level to the local level are managed and organized. The PRSPs therefore play a crucial role in shaping the meta governance that permits significant governance innovations down the PRSP track – such as public and private partnerships and the incorporation of stakeholders into the policy-making process facilitating the enrolment of non-state actors in governance across a broad spectrum of social and economic domains.

Contractual governance referred to in the PRSPs does not specify precise standards but lays out the organizational or the procedural routines that are to be followed if transnational standards are to be met. The PRSPs, as well as the Millennium Account (see below), in one sense reflect a common governance framework through which global social policy is shaped, debated, and delivered. While earlier programmes placed emphasis on policy conditionality, the new contractual global welfare places a high premium on countries meeting various procedural requirements before and during the implementation of aid programs. As Prion and Evans (2004) point out this is based on a gamble that: 'if the

PRSP is taken seriously by both governments and donors, then the relationship between them will change to emphasise domestic (political) accountability to citizens over external (technocratic) accountability to donors' (Prion and Evans 2004: 4). In this sense setting out the procedures for policy formulation rather than actual policy becomes the key governing strategy of the new global policy. But these procedures in turn incorporate economic imperatives in the broader framework of social policy formulation and serve to entrench a system of economic constitutionalism within the domestic policy-making process. Hence the crucial element of the new contractual governance is the way in which transnational agencies set broad flexible goals which are then progressively enforced and supervised down a chain to national and subnational levels. PRSPs have become a crucial element in the new transnational welfare governance. The World Bank and the IMF identify four core principles that underpin the PRSPs (IMF 2004).[5] These are:

1. *Country driven*:   Involves broad-based participation of all the stakeholders.
2. *Results oriented*:   Programs are focused on setting measurable and achievable targets.
3. *Comprehensive*:   Recognises the poverty reduction needs to integrate macroeconomic and economic aspects.
4. *Partnership*:   Requires the participation and enrolment of all stakeholders in a dialogue over poverty reduction policies.
5. *Duration*:   Poverty reduction requires a long-term perspective that requires building institutional capacity.

The PRSPs are prepared by the member countries and this involves a participatory process which includes what are termed domestic stakeholders – governments, local agencies and civil society groups as well as international financial institutions such as the World Bank. PRSPs are a broad agenda-setting document that details the economic and social policies to promote economic growth and facilitate poverty reduction. At its heart, the PRSPs are about a hierarchy of contracts that range from the IFI to national governments and local stakeholders. PRSPs provide a governance framework through which the chain of contractual arrangements are organized, managed and evaluated.

More especially, the PRSPs reflect the hierarchical contractual architecture that is so central to the contractual governance of transnational welfare. This contractual architecture is reflected in four fundamental areas: first, in a sense of country ownership of the economic and social program; the PRSPs are not just owned by the country, but are anchored within its policy-making process; second, within the lower levels of national or subnational policy making a more inclusive and participatory process that involves a range of domestic stakeholders; third, in the imposition of procedural requirements that incorporate the agenda of poverty reduction – so-called 'pro-poor' policies – into stable and sustainable growth policies and in this way it connects economic reform to poverty reduction; and, finally, in the incorporation of a regime of benchmarking and monitoring of programs to ensure that policies and outcomes meet the objectives of the programs (IMF and International Development Association 2002).

The PRSPs, as laid out here, underpin a meta-contractual framework for the governance of social and welfare polices without imposing any particular set substantive policies. This 'meta regulation' is evident in the specification of the procedural requirements that tie pro-poor policies to macroeconomic stability. It is important to note here that both the IMF and World Bank admit that specific causal linkages between the poverty reduction and growth policies are difficult, partly because:

> to understand the linkages between the policies discussed above and growth/poverty reduction requires a good understanding of the macro-micro linkages in particular country context, including the nature of country specific institutional characteristics that determine the efficiency of markets. (IMF 2004: 18)

It is not so much the nature of the specific growth–poverty linkages that are at issue, but the fact that this contractual governance locates welfare within the context of market stability and efficiency. This makes the PRSPs a vital component of economic constitutionalism; social policy is in effect economized.

This meta-contractual governance is about constituting a dynamic framework for governance – not just a one-stop exercise. The IMF (2004) is keen to point to the dynamic nature of this process by noting that it is an 'iterative one, starting with an interim PRSP, leading to full PRSP, followed by annual progress reports, and, a new PRSP, with results from implementation and monitoring feedback back into formulation and implementation of the subsequent strategy papers' (IMF 2004: 14). What this meta governance establishes is not just a hierarchy of contracts but a regulatory framework in which social policy is formulated. In moving towards setting the terms of 'process conditionality' rather than policy conditionality global governance is not imposed from 'outside' but transforms the very structures and institutions of domestic policy making. Perhaps the most important consequence of this process of conditionality is that transnational and core executive agencies within the state effectively take on supervisory rather than a directly allocative role.

The PRSP strategy has been extremely influential in providing a template for a number of international developmental strategies. Possibly most significant of these developmental strategies is the US-funded Millennium Challenge Account (MCA) established by George Bush in March 2002. This was intended to direct US aid to the poorest countries which meet a set of predefined set of standards (Soederberg 2004). Under the MCA the US administration provides aid to very poor countries which are able meet these performance criteria. Some of these performance criteria, influenced by right-wing think tanks like the Heritage Foundation, refer to the control of corruption, promotion of free trade and economic liberalization, investment in education and health care. In terms of reporting, the MCA bypasses official US aid agencies and is accountable to a corporation that reports to an executive composed of representatives from Treasury, State department and other agencies (Dao 2003).

The MCA uses explicitly contractual language. Recipients are expected to sign multi-year contracts that are subject to performance standards. The 'contracts' could be cancelled if the receiving countries fail to make the necessary reforms. Unlike the PRSP, the MCA programme is much more coercive in setting out sanctions for countries that fail to perform, and in comparison with the PRSP appears as more of a neo conservative version of the Post Washington Consensus. In this respect, the cocktail of sanctions that are applied bear a striking resemblance to those adopted by workfare programs in the US. Republicans and right-wing think tanks in the US appear to conceive of the poorest states of the world as the overseas analogue of the 'black single mother'. But the most interesting difference lies in the fact that the MCA proposes a kind of pre-emptive conditionality which means that to be selected for MCA 'contracts' countries must meet criteria which in themselves are biased towards certain forms of development. But these biases are hidden in the often vague generalities of the preconditions required before countries are selected for the MCA contracts. In fact Soederberg (2004: 294) notes that:

> While these conditions reflect the concerns of the official development discourse, i.e. reproducing the imperative of economic growth,

open current and capital accounts, sound macroeconomic fundamentals, good governance and democratic values, the 'empowering
features' seem to be overshadowed by the pre-emptive nature of the
MCA, not to mention the complementary scheme of pre-emptive
conditionality imposed by the IDA.

In this analysis Soederberg rightly notes that this allows the MCA to
exclude certain states on political and strategic grounds. This insistence
on meeting preconditions by both the MCA and the PRSP interestingly
follows a similar template to that imposed by the EU on prospective
candidate members for EU membership. More recently, the EU has proposed Economic Partnership Agreements with African states that govern
aid disbursement through contract-like partnerships that impose obligation on donor countries.[6] These partnership agreements attempt to
incorporate poverty reduction policies with market-oriented economic
policies in a way similar to the PRSP. It is this procedural and contractual
template that both the PRSP and the MCA – despite their obvious and
important differences – as well as the EPA have in common. These tem-
plates establish a contractual form of governance whose various elements are linked together within a chain of contracts that runs all the
way from transnational organization to the individual welfare recipient.

These chains of contract in the new transnational welfare governance
have three central features: first, within the chain of contract there is a
constant tendency for governance to be decentralized such that an obligation of ownership so well described by Cammack (2002) (and also see
Weber 2002), is imposed at ever lower levels so that governance is progressively localized. A chain of contract in these arrangements relies on
what Weiner (2001) calls a 'constant localizing'; and, indeed, a privatiz-
ing of policing. In the case of social policy, the expansion of the social
funds programmes such as the World Bank's Social Investment Fund
(SIF) in Thailand (see below), underscores the extent to which the governance of social policy becomes increasingly localized so that at the
very end of the contractual chain individual beneficiaries are required to
actively engage in the management of their own vulnerabilities and risk.
But this management is defined in terms of responsible economic participation in the market economy.

Second, localization of governance imposes capacities for constant
supervision and monitoring of each level of governance. Within this
new architecture of global social policy *supervision* takes the form of the
development of new forms of audit and transparency through which
performance has to be constantly measured. But, given the insistence on

the importance of 'ownership' in these new social policy programmes, there is a strong tendency to place a great deal of effort in monitoring compliance with broad institutional procedures at all levels of governance. As Pongsapich (2001: 252) points out:

> All operations and project implementation procedures need to have accountability, predictability, transparency, and the participation of all concerned stakeholders. This means that civil society organizations need to become involved in public activities to ensure that all four components of good governance takes place.

In a nutshell, supervision entails the constant policing of each level of governance to ensure fidelity to institutional procedures.

But at the heart of the constant localization of ownership of social policy programmes is a depoliticization that works through constant distancing of the centres of decision making from the actual implementation of the programs. As Cammack (2002: 37) notes in relation to the poverty reduction policies and Comprehensive Development Framework (CDF), it is a:

> ... fundamental goal of the Bank's strategy to impose 'country ownership' of the CDF both because it recognizes that it lacks the means to enforce the strategy itself, and because the legitimation of its project *vis-à-vis* citizens around the world depends on its adoption by national governments, which remain indispensable intermediaries in the project of global governance.

As we have seen in the case of social funds, this distancing extends beyond national governments to more local institutions within civil society. But the overall effect is that claims to legitimacy through ever-proliferating levels of local ownership have the effect of placing political contention of the goals and objectives of social programmes beyond the reach of those who 'own' the programmes.

Finally, we note that the notion of 'chains of contract' carries with it an implicit reordering of the scales of governance. It is this rescaling that Robertson, Bonal and Dale (2002) explore in their sophisticated analysis of the impact of General Agreement on Trade and Services (GATS) on educational services and governance. They point out that:

> through GATS, the conditions are being created for disembedding educational activity from its fixed institutionalized location as a

national regulated redistributional and legitimatory decommodified public good, forcing it into motion and into the global marketplace to be fixed through processes of successive liberalization as part of the built-in GATS Agenda. (Robertson, Bonal and Dale 2002: 488)

In essence, the impact of GATS and what could be called the globalization of education, as they argue, lies in the transformation of 'scales of governance' within the state to include both global and regional dimensions. Hence, as with social policy this new rescaling of educational governance serves to distance the political decision from the actual delivery and implementation of these programmes.

Participation, reflexive regulation and contractualism

One of the important elements of this contractual governance is its reflexive capacity. Procedures constantly require not only that stakeholders be consulted, but that deliberation and participation is seen to be vital in establishing the legitimacy of programs and policies. In fact, along these lines it takes on what Teubner (1983, 1987) has called 'reflexive regulation'. According to Barnard and Deakin (2001: 2), this denotes that the:

> essence of reflexive law is the acknowledgement that regulatory interventions are most likely to be successful when they seek to achieve their ends not by direct prescription, but by inducing 'second-order effects' on the part of social actors. In other words, this approach aims to 'couple external regulation with self-regulatory processes'.

Reflexive governance works not through the direct transformation of policy or structure, as would be the case with policy conditionality, but more indirectly by enhancing the regulatory capacities for participation and external adjustment. These themes are reflected in the critical role accorded to the enrolment of non-state actors for the implementation of social policy. Indeed, many of the new institutional structures which embody principles of participation and deliberation – such as the solidarity programme in Mexico, or Thailand's emphasis on local self-reliance – are geared towards the production and distribution of social goods. More especially, the PRSPs explicitly call for dialogue and participation of a range of both government and nongovernmental stakeholders. The World Bank is keen to emphasize that the PRSP process is not simply about producing a public document, but is in itself a means of furthering a dialogue or deliberation on poverty-related issues. For this reason priority is placed on the enrolment of stakeholders into the policy-making process, but this incorporation of stakeholders is intended to facilitate a deliberation on poverty reduction issues: PRSPs are not only about social inclusion, but also about the politics of social inclusion.

But what kind of participation is this? One of the central dilemmas of the notion of welfare contractualism is that it appeals to the liberal notions of participation whilst at the same time tends to result in illiberal outcomes. In this regard, the observation of Freedland and King (2003: 469–70) in relation to British social policies could easily be applied to the transnational welfare contractualism in that:

> the contractualising of these social, disciplinary or welfare relationships is generally presented as a way of imbuing these relationships with the liberal virtues of consent, freedom of choice and the willing assumption of mutual responsibility. The worry is that arrangements which in principle embody that liberal conception may be implemented by processes which are or become arbitrary, oppressive or one sided character.

But I would argue that the reasons for these illiberal outcomes go beyond the illiberal mechanisms of implementation, and have rather more to do with the fact the claims on the state are contingent on the performance of duties outside of the formal political or representative sphere of the state. Indeed, the language of participation initially strikes a dissonant tone with neo liberal programmes of economic reform.

The question we need to ask is to what extent this deliberative governance creates the basis for a more fundamental transformation in social relations. In fact, the very ideal of deliberation only works so far as it neutralizes the broader context of economic and social power that lies in the background of deliberative institutions. In contrast, deliberative processes in contractual governance promote a particular view of individuals as 'problem solvers' enmeshed in social networks or in communities outside the formal representative structures of the state. More importantly, this marginalizes the political conflict and struggles that are placed within the formal political arena in favour of participation within the managerial civil society. It is not participation per se that counts but, rather, where this participation takes place. Locating this participation outside of political society reinforces the depoliticized management of social governance.

This is where the transnational welfare governance has been especially important in constituting institutional arrangements for participatory governance of the delivery of social services, infrastructure and funds. Exemplar of these new hybrid private/public organization is the experiment with social funds. A distinctive feature of social funds such as Thailand's Social Investment Funds is the emergence of novel institutional forums through which this new social policy is disseminated. Social funds have spread rapidly in developing countries since the Bolivian Emergency Social Fund which was launched in 1987. While the first funds were directed at ameliorating the immediate effects of structural adjustment programmes, they have now been expanded to encompass the more ambitious objectives of new social policy strategies such as poverty reduction and social exclusion as well providing a complex array of participatory mechanisms.

The funds themselves are usually set up as autonomous institutions that provide funding to NGOs, local governments, or community organization for a range of locally based social and economic programmes. To give just one example in East Asia after the Asian crisis the World Bank helped set up the Thai social investment fund. The purpose of this fund was to

> One of the most striking elements of the Thailand Social Investment Fund (SIF) is its emphasis on social capital formation and the way it has catalysed the large voluntary response from Thai society to help those affected by the recent social and economic crisis. Particularly innovative is the social fund's 'Menu 5' window, in which community organization networks – made up entirely of volunteers – distribute social fund financing directly to needy groups in the form of social assistance and cash transfers. (Salim 2001; available at: <http//www1.worldbank.org/publicsector/decenralization/sfupdate.pdf>)

But the real significance of these social funds is that they provide institutional arrangements for participatory governance. In order to underline the role envisaged for participation in social governance, it is worth quoting in full the World Bank observation that

> Participation occurs along a continuum. On one end are 'beneficiaries', who are the recipients of services and resources. More and more successful projects, however, define participants as 'clients' and invest in setting up timely feedback mechanisms to ensure they stay

in touch with what their clients want. In these projects, 'clients' are perceived as those who buy something (for example, financial services) and must agree to pay more than a symbolic fee for it. They also ensure that a clear contract exists with clients, which lets them know what they must do to keep the services coming. The challenge is to devolve the decisionmaking power and control over resources to participants as 'investors' or even 'managers' who make strategic and operational decisions about how services are designed and delivered. But it is important to remember that many people are not willing or able to take on the additional risks and increased responsibilities associated with higher levels of self-management. (World Bank 1996; Available at:<http://www.worldbank.org/wbi/sourcebook/sb0405t.htm>)

The importance of these new institutional fora is that they are located 'in and out of the state', thereby imparting to these institutions a quasi-public character; it amounts to a privatization of public governance. It is the public or the state-like nature of organizations in civil society that has most distinguished the architecture of global social policy. The important dynamic here is not the emergence of some putative alternative to the state in the form of civil society, as some of the more romantically inclined notions of civil society (Keane 1998) would have it, but rather the fragmentation and dispersal of public or state power to organizations and institutions within civil society.

Hence the exercise of some of the functions of public authority by civil society organizations has been one of the distinguishing features of the emerging economic constitutionalism. The 'privatization of public governance' perspective, then, on the one hand, captures the diffusion and dispersal of public power to nongovernmental organizations located outside the formal state apparatus; and, on the other hand, it underlines the way many of these organizations operate *in* and *out* of the state. No doubt, there is tremendous variation in the relative dependency, origin, and purpose of the NGO–state relationship, but the point that needs to be underscored here is the increasing accentuation of the 'state'-like character of these hybrid organizations, which in turn serves to depoliticize this sphere of the civil society.

Following on from this 'privatization of public governance' is an understanding of citizenship as an attribute of market functioning. According to Marshall's (1964, 1981) classic definition of citizenship in terms of the sequential adoption of civil, political, and social rights, the basis of social citizenship rests on our common membership in a broader political community. However, the form of claim making which is associated with the new contractual governance operates with a very different understanding of political community. Here, social claims on the state are understood to flow from the inclusion of citizens in various governance regimes or sites. The social claims that individuals or groups make on the state depend on the procedural rules that regulate the management of these sites of governance. In this sense, contractual regulation forms the primary mode through which these sites of governance are managed and it is through these organizations or sites of governance that social claims are made on the state. The consequence of this theorizing is to 'privatize citizenship'; or, as Somers (2001: 44) puts it, the theory and practice of civil society has:

> been privatized in political argument, now seemingly reduced to a cluster of non-political, anti public, and marketized attributes. Neoliberalism has been able to increasingly hail true citizenship as a form of social activity reflecting the ethically superior private sphere of market priorities.

The global 'workfare' promoted by programmes such as social funds, therefore, differs markedly from the Marshallian model of 'social rights'. Indeed, as Somers' insight suggests, social policy in the regulatory state shifts from the language of social rights to that of customership. Perhaps more strikingly, the new quasi-public governance creates structures of accountability between citizens within privatized governance structures. This, in turn, while attenuating the relationship between state and citizen, has inevitable implications for the practice of citizenship in that it calls for an active model of participation. But this is the new global workfare in participation that takes place not in the public sphere, but in the intermediate hybrid public/private institutional forums such as social funds. It is clearly a form of depoliticized participation or active participation that marginalizes conflicts of power and interests within market societies.

Equally important here is the fact that the purpose of participation and deliberation in these quasi-public organizations is concerned with problem solving or the effective management of policy rather than the achievement of a legitimate political and constitutional consensus. As Steele (2001: 417) notes, a fundamental distinction between deliberative models of democratic legitimacy and problem solving lies in the fact that in the latter:

> the subject matter of deliberation is more likely to be an individual decision for action, rather than the adoption of a formal legal standard or other law. This means that participation of this type is likely to be a requirement of law (if law is involved at all), instead of being a part of the process of legislation.

In other words, participation is not seen as an end in itself; rather, it is seen in an instrumental fashion as a means of achieving better technocratic policy outcomes. More especially, these institutions attempt to develop the strategic capacity of citizens in the implementation of public policies. Interestingly, these developments in global workfare also converge with important trends in European social policy that seek to enhance a problem-solving approach to social policy issues. For example this has taken the form of negotiated bargaining between social partners – labour, capital and other nongovernmental organizations – over social issues (Teague 2001). But this bargaining differs from the older-style corporatist systems in that these deliberative institutions are directed at social inclusion rather than the redistribution of resources.

The crucial point about this depoliticized management is that participation operates in tandem with neo liberal ideas of choice and efficiency. It is useful to place these notions of participation and deliberation as problem solving as it is especially appropriate in a regulatory state which acts like an enterprise rather than a civic organisation (Oakeshott 1975). In a 'civic association', rules do not derive authority from any end outside of the association or from its use for the creation of a desirable set of outcomes. As such, a civic association – though this is no part of the Oakeshott argument – can be identified in terms of the non-instrumental use of public reason. By contrast, in an 'enterprise association' the validity of rules springs not from the association itself but from the ends or purposes of the organization. An enterprise association, therefore, is a purposive and end-oriented organization. From the perspective of an enterprise association, participation is understood in terms of its ability to promote a given set of policy outcomes. In short, it promotes a view of participation as problem solving.

Behind the 'problem-solving' view of participation is an assumption that participation – conceived in local terms – will reveal in fairly short order the real 'needs' of the community: these community interests are somehow seen as being pre-political. But what this account diminishes is the role of representation in articulating and giving expression to various identities and interests in the political community. And the crucial point is that for this representation to take place it has to be mediated through a range of representative organizations, forms, and institutions; this means that there can be no simplistic overlap between the community and interests. Hence,

> representation therefore modifies our understanding of democratic theory, which tells us that people represent their interests in the state through an activity we call politics. It makes visible the mediations as well as the mediators, the practices as well as the practitioners. (Chandhoke 2002: 19)

It is this autonomy of representation – or more precisely the mediation of political practices – that is absent in conceptions of politics that underpin various forms of reflexive governance in the new transnational welfare governance.

Yet it is clear that this participation cannot simply be reduced to neo liberal economics. Certainly the very form of the institutional governance works to provide a framework for a debate on social issues that works to marginalize certain forms of conflict. On the other hand, these new forms of participation do allow various actors to bring issues of social disadvantage to the forefront of the policy debate. More to the point the experience of innovative participatory forums such as the process of participatory budgeting in Porto Alegre promoted by the Left Wing Workers Party does allow considerable latitude for the adoption of at least some elements of a progressive social agenda (Baiocchi 2001). It places the democratization of the state on the agenda and this may be one of the potential progressive pathways from contractual welfare governance. The broader point is this: while the new welfare governance framework emerges out of neo liberalism and therefore constrains the type and form of social policies, it does allow new arguments to be proposed that go beyond neo liberal social policies. To give one example, the recent promotion of basic income models[7] (Van Parijs 2004) reflects a commitment to both individual autonomy and 'effective freedom' within market economies, and is a good example of the way in which social democratic language of welfare may cast for new alternatives and possibilities within the new model of welfare governance.

Nevertheless, within the new framework of global social policy civil society functions not as a spontaneous autonomous sphere – as the neo-Tocquevillians like Putnam (2000) would have it – but, rather, as a managed civil society where core institutions are linked to the delivery of basic social services and welfare. Moreover, new institutions such as social funds are located in the intermediate arena between the public and the private, creating a 'hybrid public organization' that operates through a contractual relationship with central state structures. But, alongside this enrolment of non-state actors in the policy process procedures are established for the deliberation and participation of all stakeholders in the effective management and delivery of welfare policies. In fact, it is these new forms of participation that carve out entirely new arenas of welfare governance within the state.

However, this participation – as we argue – is increasingly about problem solving and inclusion rather than about a contestation and conflict over political representation. This is participation within an enterprise organization that is directed towards 'problem solving' or the management of often pragmatically state-defined vulnerable groups, and, as such, these governance forms are potentially at odds with pluralism and conflict that is essential to the operation of representative political practices not institutions.

In sum, the basic argument then is that these reflexive forms of governance within civil society provide a mode of statecraft or ideological template of institutional innovation that stretches across a broad range of social and economic domains in advanced liberal democracies as well as authoritarian states. The new framework of social policy is not simply about the transformation and reorientation of policies and institutions (although these are important); rather, it reflects a deeper structural transformation of the state.

Contractualism, welfare governance and state transformation

Let me conclude by noting a paradox. On the one hand, the new global social policy places great importance on terms like 'participation' and 'empowerment'. These, of course, have been part of the vocabulary of the left; on the other hand, this emphasis on participation and partnership goes hand in hand – as it has, for example, in US 'Workfare' programs – with a program of market-oriented reform. To understand this paradox we need to locate this enhanced importance of civil society in the context of the emergence of a new form of participation congruent with market reform. Clearly, in relation to various poverty reduction programs, 'the goal is to enable the poor "to engage effectively in markets"; the result is to deliver the poor into greater dependence upon markets' (Cammack 2002: 6). And this is the point: participation within civil society cannot be divorced from the broader programme of economic citizenship of the new regulatory state

From this perspective, the new contractual governance signalled by the regulatory state can be more properly regarded as an attempt to shape new forms of institutional mediation between state and society. Hence, the emergence of reflexive governance represents the growth of a new managerial civil society that meshes in with the rise of the regulatory state. This is what is intriguing about this new contractual governance of global social policy. It seeks to develop a commitment to active 'participation' within a framework of economic and market reform.

What is noteworthy here is the way the new contractual governance provides a set of strategies to regulate the conduct of individual and public agencies. Moreover, contractualism is the basis for new forms of statecraft and as such it is possibly better described as a kind of 'political rule'. Contractual governance furnishes a new mode of statecraft or ideological template of institutional innovation that stretches across a broad range of social and economic domains in advanced liberal democracies as well as authoritarian states. The new framework of transnational welfare governance is not simply about the transformation and reorientation of policies and institutions (although these are important); rather, it provides a pathway for state transformation. It is this transformation of the state towards a new regulatory state that is reflected in the variegated political projects that seek to engage civil society in social and economic governance.

But this emphasis on deliberation and empowerment as policy making marginalizes the relations of power and conflict within which deliberation and participation takes place. Consequently, the defining characteristic of welfare governance is the fact that it provides a way of managing often administratively defined groups and communities – such as the urban poor and children – outside the normal representative spheres of politics. In this context Harriss (2002) provides an excellent account of how the infatuation with the notions of social capital leads to a depoliticized version of development, and points out that:

> ... these ideas are deceptive because they are used to veil the nature and effects of power, and – as I have argued in this book – they hold out the prospects of democracy (in 'civil society') without the inconveniences of contestational politics and of the conflicts of ideas and interests that are an essential part of democracy. (Harriss 2002: 116)

Harriss is correct in making this argument, but the more important point is to recognise how anti-political notions are embedded in the fabric of governance institutions. It is not so much the substantial policy outcomes, but the framework around which the debates on poverty took place. What I mean here is that new forms of governance that characterize the regulatory state carry a particular conception of politics as anti-politics. Let me explain: politics involves a constant conflict as groups seek to gain representation or identity within the polity – indeed, it could be argued that democratic politics is but a by-product of this ongoing struggle for representation. Chandhoke (2002: 18) makes this point about representation neatly by arguing that:

> Politics is a two-way activity ranging from what is experienced into how it is represented in the form of the expressed, and from what is expressed into an interpretation of what is experienced. But politics is also a plural activity inasmuch as it negotiates between different and contested forms of the expressive.

Instead, within the new forms of governance of the regulatory state, politics – even democratic politics – is replaced by a search for technocratic management of various groups and individuals under the broad rubric of social inclusion. But the important political shift here is that the forum for making claims on the state shifts from political society and the language of rights to a managerial civil society where social claims are managed through the language and practices of contractualism. And, in turn, this new managerial civil society presumes the existence of some unified pre-political community lending itself to development of notions of social inclusion, community participation or localism, which underpinned not just the new transnational welfare governance but a far broader array of third way social policies. It is for this reason that the new welfare governance is much more than a reorientation of social policy; it reflects a more profound transformation from social constitutionalism to economic constitutionalism.

5
The New Regulatory State and the Social Market in Korea

Economic crisis and a Korean Third Way

Korean economic governance in the 1980s may well be described as being more Japanese than the Japanese. The Korean state exemplified much better than the Japanese state some of the key defining elements of the developmental state: strong pilot agencies; a coercive set of policy instruments; concentrated and tightly controlled mega enterprises; and a fast and rapid industrialization moving within a short space from labour-intensive industries to more technologically and capital-intensive sectors. Yet, in the aftermath of the Asian economic crisis, Korea has made a remarkable transformation from being the most 'Japanese' of East Asian states to an economy whose governance reforms are modelled on dominant Anglo-American neo liberal programs (Jayasuriya 2000a).

Nevertheless, it would be a mistake to see this Korean venture into economic governance as a simple imitation of neo liberal economic models. Instead, we argue in this chapter that what is most striking about state transformation in Korea is the emergence of a new mode of economic and political governance which, despite commonalities, has a number of important differences from the Anglo-American model. At the heart of this distinctive neo liberalism is the paradoxical combination of market reform with a growing emphasis on social policy and social contracts. This combination forms the cutting edge of a new language or technology of public action that underpins a transformed relationship between the individual and the political community. Hence, what is distinctive about Korea's response to the Asian economic crisis is that alongside the implementation of far-reaching economic reforms, it has also established a new framework – which we call the 'social market model' – of welfare governance. Welfare governance has gone in tandem with the programme of market and economic reform. And here we see a striking difference between the Korean and Anglo-American neo liberal models of economic governance.

In Western Europe and North America the welfare state and its associated programmes are seen as obstacles to the expansion of neo liberal programmes of market reform. By contrast, in Korea, the development of social policy in a range of areas – health and social security – are seen as the pivot around which neo liberal economic reform swings. Social welfare programmes, far from being abandoned or cut back, have proved to be central to the implementation and entrenchment of neo liberal economic reform. Indeed as Peng (2004: 393) perceptively notes about Korea and Japan: 'In the 1990s, however, the exact opposite dynamics were evident in both countries. Japan and Korea both faced economic crises, but these crises were met by extensions in social welfare rather than retrenchment' (Peng 2004: 393). This seemingly paradoxical combination of welfare expansion and neo liberal reform underlines the fact that neo liberal reform is as much a transformation of the internal routines and architecture of the state as a set of economic programmes; in other words, neo liberalism is as much about political and social governance as about market reform. In this context, social contracts become a crucial catalyst in establishing these new forms of statecraft.

Yet these social contracts cannot be readily subsumed under the categories and forms of social citizenship – the grammar of social rights that underpinned the postwar welfare state. The new welfare governance formula introduced in the aftermath of the Asian economic crisis seeks to socially regulate the market in order to produce market or economic order. Unlike the postwar European welfare state, the Korean welfare state did not seek to establish a form of social citizenship in opposition to – or in tension with – the market. Instead, Korean social policies sought to develop forms of 'socialized' citizenship that were compatible with programmes of market reform. Welfare governance was framed within the context of economic rather than social constitutionalism. Kim Dae Jung, of course, did not lead a social democratic party or have a social democratic programme; yet when he came to power in the midst of the Asian economic crisis his programme of economic reform – which included reforming Korean chaebols – required a broad coalition that included organized labour. In fact:

> The strong anti-chaebol sentiment shared by the Kim government and the public resulted in attempts to rein in, rather than nurture, the chaebols. Thus, the breakdown of the traditional alliance between the state and business, and the transition to the new social contract, are features of the post-crisis period. (Hundt 2005: 243)

In this context the political pressures and dilemmas that Kim faced when he took office were similar to those confronted by traditional social democratic parties in Europe, namely: to maintain the support of a labour and progressive constituency while remaining within a globally competitive economy.

Put bluntly, social democracy confronts two apparently irreconcilable imperatives: to maintain legitimacy and support of key political constituencies and at the same time to act within the constraints and requirements of the global economy. New social democracy or the third way so closely associated with the programs and policies of New Labour in the UK was largely an attempt to navigate the choppy waters of legitimacy and economic reform by seeking to establish new forms of statecraft. Kim and the new Korean government on coming to power faced exactly these same dilemmas. Their response was to establish a distinctive 'Korean third way' that bears resemblance not just to New Labour's third way[1] but also to the even earlier experience of social democratic parties in Australia and New Zealand. If anything after Kim's departure and the election of President Roh Moo Huyn elements of this new statecraft have become consolidated ever more deeply within the Korean state. Clearly, the intriguing emergence of a Korean third way is a story that is as much about the reconstitution of the state as it is about economic transformation. Central to this state transformation is the emergence of new forms of economic and social regulation. The nature of this transformation is well expressed by Pirie (2005: 25, 26) who maintains that

> the contemporary Korean state has not simply engaged in a process of policy adjustment and adopted selected neo-liberal policies but rather is consolidating a whole new and unambiguously neo-liberal mode of regulation. ... The development of such a mode of regulation can be best illustrated by focusing on the processes of institutional restructuring, the reconfiguration of the structures of the Korean state itself to meet the dictates of the new global market order.

The Korean case is not simply about reinventing the developmental state (Weiss 1998) or providing a new political foundation for state intervention (Hundt 2005). Rather, it is about the creation of new sets of regulatory practices and routines within the framework of the new regulatory state. But what distinguishes this new Korean regulatory state is not simply the panoply of economic regulatory institutions[2] but the ambitious attempt to establish a new social market model which was not simply about substantive policy changes. These changes in welfare governance have transformed the language of paternalism that had previously underpinned the system of 'enterprise welfare' to one based on a language of public action that was much more legalistic and inclusive. This underlines the fact that statecraft is as much about the changing conception of stateness – the language of public action – as it is about the nuts and bolts of welfare governance. The social market model, in providing the foundations for this language of public action, becomes the crucial cement of the new Korean regulatory state.

A notable and striking feature of the ongoing welfare and economic reforms that Korean policy makers implemented after the Asian crisis is the strong similarity it bears to the ordo liberal conception of the social market economy (previously outlined in Chapter 1). In fact, Kim Dae Jung himself dubbed this model as one of 'productive welfare' to capture the way the emerging model of welfare meshed in with his economic reform programme.

Social policy was seen as a way of forging the social order and stability essential to the economic order. While the model may permit social expansion, these programmes have to be in harmony with, or reinforce market order. It is an idea of welfare that chimes with economic constitutionalism and does not have the marked redistributive component which formed an integral part of the European model of social constitutionalism. At the same time the Korean model differs from what some have called the 'productivist form of the welfare regime' that developed under the umbrella of the developmental state (Holliday 2000). However, while both the social market and productivist welfare model accentuate economic objectives in welfare governance they differ on a crucial point – that the social market model does not make welfare ancillary to the economic imperatives of the developmental state, but rather instantiates market imperatives within the heart of welfare governance. What the Korean third way has in common with the New Labour approach is a political project that seeks to frame the 'idea of welfare' within the context of economic constitutionalism.

This chapter is divided into three sections: the first section explores the creation of a new regulatory state. The shift from the development to the regulatory state in Korea is examined, and it is argued that this shift has led to the establishment of new forms of economic governance as well as new forms of citizenship; the second section considers the role of social inclusion and the tripartite dialogue in the regulatory state. Particular attention is given to the way in which inclusion provides a new technology of public action;[3] the final section analyses the new social contracts and the social market economy. This section explores how the social market model provides a framework for reconciling market reforms with new social initiatives that depart from the previous paternalistic and enterprise-based welfare regime.

Creating a new regulatory state

By and large, scholars of the Korean state – with some notable exceptions, such as Pirie (2005) – have tended to neglect the extent and depth of the transformation of modes of social and economic regulation. One reason for this is probably the prominence of the neo-Weberian model of the strong and weak state among both political analysis and social theorists of the developmental state. Trapped within this unhelpful binary of strong and weak states, the fundamental problem posed by the Asian crisis for statists was to account for the pursuit of financial liberalization, and, through it, the progressive decline of policy capacity in countries that supposedly had 'strong states'. For example, in an otherwise persuasive argument of the link between financial liberalization and the Asian economic crisis, Wade and Veneroso (1998) resort to explaining the origins of this financial liberalization as a policy error. This explanation reduced to its bare bones amounts to the claim that while the state itself was strong, it was weakened only by technocrats buying into the orthodoxy of neo liberalism – be it of the US Treasury or the IMF.

This mode of theorizing is characteristic of a now-commonplace argument gaining popularity within the field of international political economy, which claims that globalization is merely ideational, so that while state or state power itself has not declined in capacity any limitation on state capacity arises through the operation of the ideological dominance of globalization ideas on state elites. But these explanations only serve to underline the fact that the statists confronted with the Asian crisis have found it difficult to account for the propitious decline in the capacities of the developmental state – such as that so well documented by

Wade and Veneroso (1998) and Weiss (1998) – within the terms of its own conceptual framework of state capacity.

The strong state so crucial to the statist research programme[4] turns out to be a chimera that obscures the more important process of state transformation that is taking place under the pressures of global economic and political change. From this vantage point, I argue in this chapter that the crucial transformation that is occurring in East Asia is from the developmental to the regulatory state, rather than the weakening or otherwise of the capacity of the strong state. The central problem with employing neo-Weberian categories like 'embedded autonomy' or 'governed markets' is that it considers state or institutional capacity as a set of institutional attributes that can be readily identified. This in turn depends on a model of state capacity that seeks to identify the key endowments or attributes that a state or public agency may possess and thereby enable to generate transformative powers over policy and structure.[5] In turn, it is these transformative powers that frame the extent and limits of state strength. Even as society is brought 'back in' to the developmental literature through such notions as embedded autonomy, the implicit assumption is that the state itself becomes an actor that intervenes or acts on society to produce certain desired outcomes. But how this state power is produced and the form it takes remains well beyond the horizon of the research programme. State power for the neo-Weberians becomes a kind of *deus ex machina* that is unable to grasp the way in which the state is transformed over time. More problematically, developmental state theorists, because they understand 'policy capacity' as a set of fixed institutional endowments or attributes, are unable to grasp how these capacities change in response to broader changes in the constellation of social and economic interests.

This warrants revisiting Nettl's[6] seminal article which inspired so much of the statist literature on strong and weak states.[7] Admittedly while Nettl's work does provide ample justification for a neo-Weberian reading, it also allows us a glimpse of a constitutive understanding of the state as a set of constituted relationships rather than a fixed entity. In particular, Nettl sought to give conceptual clarity to the various multiple analytical dimensions such as international forces, state–society relations, and conceptions of public authority that serve to constitute what he calls 'stateness' or 'statehood'. Using the conceptual framework of stateness rather than the state as an 'ensemble of institutions' enables us to explore how 'state transformation', or indeed 'state building', is always a socially constituted relationship.[8] By the same token understanding stateness as a dynamic process enables us to conceive of shifts in conceptions of stateness as arising out of modifications of various structures of public authority framework as well as the language and technology through which public authority is exercised and articulated.

The real advantage of this understanding of statehood is that it allows us to see how various statecraft projects are enabled or constrained by the broader structural forces in the global political economy. For example, the developmental state project of the Cold War period in East Asia was enabled by both the Cold War system of security alliances between the US and East Asia and the Bretton Woods system of financial regulation that created the possibility for a regime of national developmentalism. As argued elsewhere (Jayasuriya 2000a, 2001a, 2001b), the transformation of global order in the post-Cold War era made the military alliances less important to the US; but, more crucially, the globalization of finance rendered problematic the very notion of 'national' economic development so central to the evolution of the developmental state.

The developmental state was an artefact of a particular regime of international governance. But at the same time this transformed global political economy provided opportunity for new conceptions of statehood or statecraft to take root. These projects of statecraft sought to develop means and instruments of organizing state power or the frameworks of public authority, particularly those more congruent with (or better able to reproduce) a more globalized political economy. The advantage of this formulation is that it allows us to focus on the process of state transformation and, more importantly, the processes through which new notions of stateness are created. Instead of locating the impact of globalization on some quantum of state power – as the neo-Weberian statist would have it – this approach allows us to explore how globalization changes the internal architecture of the state. What is important is the production and reorganization of state authority and not the diminution of state power and capacity (Jayasuriya 2001b).

Pivotal to these new forms of statehood is the emergence of a form of regulatory state directed towards the production of economic and social order within a globalized economy. In particular, this shifts the function of the state from the direct allocation of social and material goods and resources to a provision of regulatory frameworks (see Jayasuriya 2005). The main features of the regulatory state are: (a) separation of policy from operation through, for example, contracting out of services (b) creation of new and autonomous regulatory institutions such as independent central banks, discussed in more detail below (c) the increasing role of the state as the regulator of regulation; particularly in the determination of the nature and extent of shaping the institutional context of regulatory institutions; and (d) the shift from a discretionary to a rules-based mode of governance in a range of economic and social policy areas. At the same time this new Korean regulatory state is much more than an ensemble of institutions of economic governance. What matters here is that this new regulatory state is able to consolidate a broad range of new social policies framed in terms of a social market model – the 'technology of public action' – that in turn entrenches a new regime of market citizenship. It is this socialization of neo liberalism in the form of a social market that is so distinctive of the Korean social market model. However, before examining this new welfare governance it is important to place these shifts in the context of changes in the regulation of economic order.

Regulating economic order

The transformation towards a new regulatory state in Korea is best illustrated in the independence given to the Bank of Korea (BOK) – the South Korean central bank. The BOK has not had a great deal of legislative or policy autonomy from the executive government, and, in fact, much of the real economic policy-making power in South Korea lay with the Economic Planning Board and the Finance Ministry. According to Maxfield (1994: 561), the 'central bank does little more than implement credit policies in line with overall government spending plans'. However, in the aftermath of the Asian crisis changes in the BOK Act:

> ... at the insistence of the IMF, on December 31 1997, must rank as the single most important piece of legislation enacted since the onset of the economic crisis. Enhancing the authority and autonomy of national monetary authorities always represents a major policy initiative, as, by its very nature, it involves a major shift in macroeconomic policymaking responsibility away from politicians to autonomous technocrats. (Pirie 2005: 31)

In this landmark change in the history of central banking in Korea, there are two key features of central bank independence (see Ministry of Finance and Economy, Republic of Korea 1998). First, the BOK effectively entrenches its autonomy from the Ministry of Finance. While mechanisms of consultation between the ministry and the BOK have been established, the executive is unable to impose a particular course of monetary policy on the Monetary Board. Second, the BOK, regardless of the membership of its Board, will be asked to pursue the objective of monetary stability. In this context, it is of special interest that the IMF intervened to further strengthen the objectives of monetary stability. It did this by adding a clause to make it clear that the BOK will seek to harmonize its objectives with macroeconomic policy, subject to the proviso that this does not conflict with its main objective of monetary policy. This additional clause makes it clear that the prime objective of the BOK is to pursue monetary stability and regulate economic order. In this sense these objectives of economic order and monetary stability strongly parallel some of the key elements of the ordo liberal economic programme.

The BOK is not the only independent economic agency established by the Korean government to oversee the established order; another such institution is the Financial Supervisory Commission (FSC). The FSC was established to oversee, monitor, and regulate the Korean financial sector and it has wide jurisdiction over a range of financial policy issues and circumscribes the discretionary power of politicians. The significance of the FSC lies in the fact that:

> placing such an autonomous and powerful organisation at the heart of the postcrisis process of financial re-regulation, the Korean state sent out a clear signal about its intention to create an 'appropriately' regulated market-based financial system. (Pirie 2005: 36)

This independence is in reality subscribed and limited by political interests. What needs to be understood is that the very creation of these kinds of agencies imposing the disciplines of the global economy exemplifies the nature of the transition from the developmental to the regulatory state. More significantly, the new regulatory infrastructure reflects the overriding importance of a new infrastructure of public action.

This is not all. An equally important change relating to the developing system of jurisprudence has been the introduction of a broad system of administrative review. In this regard Korea has established an administrative court system and expanded the scope and basis on which administrative action could be taken (Ginsburg 2002). Taken together with the growing influence of the Korean constitutional court the 'hard edged' developmentalism of the statists looks simply out of date (Ginsburg 2003).[9] In fact, the growing importance of the new legalism in East Asia, exemplified by Korea's Administrative Law, creates a whole new set of state practices and arenas, which serve to transform even more significantly the prevailing 'developmentalist' notions of public authority and purpose. It provides a new public language and technology around which political claims and contestation find expression. This new language of public action, more than anything else, reflects a deeper underlying shift in conceptions of 'stateness' or 'statehood'.

Furthermore this emergent legalism in turn reflects the importance of a form of 'proceduralism' in economic policy making within the new regulatory state. Proceduralism, in this context, refers to the fact that as these new and relatively autonomous sites of governance take shape, they come to be constituted not by direct application of state law, regulation, or authority, but through more indirect means that enhance or generate the self-regulation capacities of these sites of governance; policy capacity lies in the efficacy with which these indirect techniques enable self-governance. Proceduralism, then, transforms 'stateness' or 'statehood' in two respects: first, governance is seen as establishing the self-regulating capacities of independent agencies; second, and perhaps more importantly, it establishes the meta-level procedures that govern the linkages between various sites of governance.

Social inclusion and tripartite dialogue in the regulatory state

As we have seen with the administrative review system, proceduralism was more than the technical nuts and bolts of governance; it embodied a new language of public action. Legalism was a key dimension of this public language, but equally important was the incorporation of the language of social inclusion and participation into the programme of market reform. The Kim Dae Jung administration initiated a tripartite commission that sought to implement economic reforms through a formalized system of dialogue and partnership. This initiative, envisaged as a 'social pact' although not entirely successful, nevertheless helps to illustrate Kim's ambitious attempt to chart a statecraft that sought to meet the objectives of economic reform and political participation. According to Kong's perceptive analysis:

> the social pact of 1998 was envisioned not as mere crisis-management device but in terms of much more ambitious objectives. These apparently contradictory commitments led to descriptions of Kim Dae-Jung as an impeccable pro US neo liberal or as an reinventor of the

Korean developmental state, both of which contained an element of truth. (Kong 2004: 26)

The problem with these contradictory views of the Kim presidency is that they seek to reduce neo liberalism to a simple economic model. Yet what remains so distinctive of Kim's tripartite strategy is the attempt to develop a form of statecraft that incorporates a new social contract and dialogue articulated within a framework of economic constitutionalism. While participation is important for Kim, it remains within the boundaries of the neo liberal model. Conceived in these terms it becomes in effect the kind of social market envisaged by the ordo liberals who were as keen to create a competitive and inclusive society as they were to establish the institutions of economic order (see Chapter 1). But the crucial point is that at the heart of Kim's political project was the use of social inclusion and dialogue as a new technology of public action, and this is most clearly exemplified in the establishment of the Korean Tripartite Commission.

The Korean Tripartite Commission (KTC) was first established as a consultative body but was later given legal standing and was composed of general meeting and standing committees whose aim was to discuss and deliberate on issues of economic restructuring. Kim evidently intended the KTC to be the lynchpin of a system of social dialogue to entrench the programme of economic and market reform. At one level, the Tripartite Commission reflected the insistence of the World Bank – and, more particularly, the IMF – that governments provide for the participation of civil society – and crucially for the ILO trade unions – in programmes of economic reform. But none of this is to discount the fact the Kim Dae Jung was ideologically predisposed towards these forms of social bargaining. Kim had long tried to reconcile his commitment to a market economy and his commitment to what he called a participatory economy, and tripartism offered one means of reconciling these commitments (Kim 1985).

Furthermore, more than any other factor the domestic political imperatives of sustaining his political coalition provided a strong incentive to put in place deliberative institutions such as the KTC, with a special emphasis on labour market reform. Tripartite consultations on labour-related policies were formulated around the following issues:

- labour policies concerning job security and working conditions and closely related matters which significantly impact upon the national economy as well as society as a whole;

- matters pertaining to principles and directions of restructuring the public sector and others;
- matters related to the improvement of the systems, mindset, and practices, for the development of industrial relations;
- measures regarding the implementation of agreements reached through the KTC;
- matters pertaining to supporting those projects designed to promote cooperation among labour, management and the government. (KTC 2004: 4)

In essence, the Tripartite Commission has three distinctive purposes: first, it set out to achieve labour flexibility, a crucial part of the IMF package in the aftermath of the Asian economic crisis; second, it sought to provide employment stability and social safety that effectively tied welfare reform to economic restructuring; and, finally, it sought to provide a new and cooperative climate for the management of industrial relations in a climate of economic restructuring. In this regard, the KTC was from the outset premised on encouraging dialogue and participation as means of enhancing the legitimacy of economic reform. This participation was seen as a vital cog in the evolving mode of social regulation within the new regulatory state.

The effectiveness of the KTC was significantly shaken by the withdrawal of the Korean Confederation of Trade Unions (KCTU) in 1999. And, in fact, the KTC proved to be marginal to the industrial relations climate at the beginning of the first decade of the twenty-first century. In this respect Kong (2004) points to the absence of links between the party system and organized labour as one reason for the lack of political ballast for the tripartite dialogue. The regional cleavages that underpin the party system seem to work against the consolidation of 'social partnership' institutions. Equally strong intra-labour conflicts, particularly between the KCTU and the Korean Federation of Trade Unions (KFTU), undermined the capacity of labour to deliver a binding bargain with government and business. But perhaps:

> even more detrimental to the development of social partnership was the divergence of expectations about the nature of the new economic pathway. The social pact showed that all parties recognized the unsustainability of the old game of confrontational bargaining within a high growth economy. However there was no consensus over the nature of the new game either. (Kong 2004: 34)

This is certainly a judicious evaluation of the Korean tripartite experiment in which labour groups felt that they had little control over the formulation and implementation of an economic reform agenda. Nevertheless, despite these ebbs and flows the KTC has continued to function, and, in fact, there are signs that Roh's presidential administration expects the tripartite bargaining structures to play a more central role in the management of social and industrial governance.

In some ways the deliberative institution of the Tripartite Commission amounted to a form of societal corporatism,[10] albeit a corporatism very different to that associated with the postwar welfare state in Western Europe. In a way similar to the competitive corporatism analyzed by Rhodes (1998) the tripartite agreement set out to create a consensus over the introduction of more flexible labour market and conditions.[11] Without doubt some of the main features of the KTC seem to approximate to many of the objectives of competitive corporatism – as analysed by Rhodes – especially in the way it sought to introduce a more flexible and competitive labour market and at the same time sought to protect employment security. In this sense, this amounts to a social dialogue about adjustment, not redistribution, of income as was the case with the postwar European corporatism. Put differently, competitive corporatism sought to reconcile the seemingly contradictory elements of labour flexibility and security through a system of negotiated adjustment.

There are a number of important differences between the Korean model and the competitive corporatism of Western Europe. As Kong (2004) notes, Korea lacked the representational monopoly of labour that was a vital element of all forms of European corporatism; it lacked a powerful social democratic party that could secure and implement the cooperative decisions; finally, it lacked the broad-ranging welfare policies that could be negotiated as part of a package of competitive adjustment. Despite these formidable obstacles the KTC formed a significant component in Korea's management of the economic crisis, and, more importantly, it provided a language of social inclusion and deliberation that provided a basis for social regulation within the new regulatory state.

Social dialogue formed part of a political project by Kim Dae Jung to build a coalition that included organized labour to implement substantive neo liberal reforms. This coalition was essential to the simultaneous management of the economic as well as the political crisis; and this is what makes the Korean case so exceptional. Crafting this political coalition required the organization of structures and the public language of dialogue and social inclusion in order to establish legitimacy for the economic reforms that Kim was pursuing. It is here that the KTC differs in important respects from models of competitive corporatism. Competitive corporatism was a defensive strategy that sought to negotiate adjustment to the competitive global economy. On the other hand, the KTC was much more of an offensive adjustment strategy to create new regulatory forms that will consolidate support for economic reform. At least in this important sense the analytical framework of competitive corporatism obscures the key point about the KTC, which was that the dialogue and partnership it sought to establish was in itself – quite apart from substantive outcomes that flowed from the social pacts – a central element in the emergence of the new regulatory state. The dialogue and inclusion mechanisms need to be viewed as the building blocks of the language of public action that formed the backbone of the new form of regulatory statecraft.

In this context, Ost's (2000) analysis of tripartite bargaining in Eastern Europe may be more relevant for the Korean experience. Ost argues that the plethora of tripartite bargaining institutions in Eastern Europe is nothing more than illusory corporatism, very different from the competitive corporatism identified by Rhodes (1998). For Ost this illusory corporatism was a pale imitation of the real social bargaining that obtained in Western Europe. He argues that the tripartite bargaining in Eastern Europe in the post-communist era produced largely nonbinding agreements, excluded the private sector, and was mostly tokenistic. He explains these outcomes in terms of the weak position of labour and class identity after the transition. Tripartism, he suggests, is an elite-driven strategy to manage the political effects of economic transition while making little concession to labour. Ost's analysis has partial relevance for Korea because for one it places importance on tripartism as 'statecraft strategy', and it additionally acknowledges its importance as a legitimization strategy or as a language of public action within the framework of economic constitutionalism. Even so, this East European framework has only limited use in attempting to understand Korean tripartism. For one thing, Korean labour and class identity is strong and if anything has become even stronger during the post-crisis period. More significantly, Korean tripartism played a much more important role in post-crisis economic management than the tokenistic role played by deliberative institutions in Eastern Europe. Moreover, as we explain below, its substantive impact has been felt in the rapid increase in the scope of social policy in the post-crisis period. What is more, tripartism served to reinforce the 'social regulation' of the market; it was the glue that held together the 'social market' model of statecraft pursued by Kim and his successor Roh.

The broader point here is that notions of 'competitive corporatism' (Rhodes 1998) or illusory corporatism (Ost 2000) fail to recognise that what is distinctive about these new forms of social bargaining is that they remain outside the traditional social democratic projects that formed the basis of the Western European corporatism. The new politics of 'inclusion' – which is possibly a better term – takes place within the structures of economic rather than social constitutionalism. Inclusion provides a language and a technology of public action that helped to propel the social policy initiatives pursued by Korean economic reformers. This is not to say that no real concessions were secured by labour; however, these concessions remained well within the boundaries of the new social market economy. These social pacts are not primarily designed to redistribute income or labour conditions; rather, they are intended to provide the public language of social inclusion and the technology of tripartism within the framework of the neo liberal market mode. These regulatory forms illustrate our point that the most significant dimension of state transformation lies in the way it alters – to use Nettl's terminology – conceptions of 'stateness' to offer a new public language that shapes the way citizens relate to public authority. The significance of the new language and practices of inclusion underlines the manner in which the economic reforms undertaken by Kim were related to a more general restructuring of notions of citizenship organized under the rubric of inclusion.

Indeed, this mode of regulation through dialogue was wider than the tripartite experiment. In the area of social policy there has not only been a shift of power towards welfare and health ministries away from economic bureaucracy, but there has also been an equally significant shift towards the constitution of a broader and inclusive policy network (Yang 2004). The significance of this lies in the fact that Kim's administration was able to put together new coalitions or actors that included labour groups, non governmental groups, and social policy bureaucrats, in the Ministry of Health and Welfare (MOHW) who were able to promote a broad and universal social policy agenda (Yang 2004; Kwon 2003b). In fact this:

> new environment elevated the relative power of the social policy apparatus vis a vis the economic apparatus in the area of social policy. The MOHW was further empowered by forming solid social policy network with the democratic KCTU and the progressive People's Solidarity for Participatory Democracy. (Yang 2004: 203)

The new participatory governance and its associated public language was vital to cementing new political coalitions as well as creating new arenas on which there emerged, as Yang clearly illustrates, a new politics of social policy.

New social policies and the social market economy

It will be clear from the foregoing that in the aftermath of the Asian economic crisis and the collapse of the developmental state project the possibility of a new statecraft project opened up. Importantly, this was facilitated by a new coalition around the Kim Dae Jung administration. Of course, as we have seen with the case of the Tripartite Commission, this coalition was highly fragile and vulnerable. But what welded this coalition together was a common project of statecraft anchored around a notion of a social market economy. This statecraft was not simply about the implementation of economic reform but also about changing the institutional architecture – the routines and institutions of governance – of the state through forms of regulatory governance. But in itself this regulatory governance was simply not enough to keep the coalition together; rather, what was required was the formulation and implementation of new social policies that could put some ballast into the politics of social inclusion and dialogue. In fact, this is what occurred, but this social policy, in contrast to that of the classical welfare state model, was directed not towards securing equality against the market but towards including citizens within the market economy. Indeed, Kim's use of the term 'productive welfare' during the 2000 campaign neatly sums up the driving idea behind the adoption of new social policies after the Asian economic crisis.

This rapid growth of a range of new welfare programmes and policies in the midst of neo liberal economic reform remains the most intriguing dimension of the new Korean regulatory state. Certainly prior to the Asian economic crisis some important steps were taken in developing comprehensive welfare programmes – especially significant was the introduction of the National Health Insurance scheme in 1995. This was a universal programme which was partially funded by the government. But labour market, employment and other social assistance programmes were rudimentary and depended on the kind of 'enterprise welfare' that was such an identifying feature of the developmental state (Kwon 2003a). In the wake of the economic crisis there were significant increases in both new programmes as well as the broadening of the scope of the eligibility for existing programmes.

To give an indication of this political commitment, the social expenditure as a proportion of GDP increased from 5.2 per cent in 1997 before the Asian economic crisis to 11.4 per cent in 1998 (Gough 2003). Even at its present level these figures still make Korea an effective welfare state laggard, but this still remains a significant increase in the state commitment to social expenditure. Moreover, reflecting the importance of labour market programmes in this 'social market' statecraft was the increase of labour market programmes from almost nothing before the crisis to about 4 per cent of GDP in 1998 (OECD 2000). In part, these new employment and labour market programmes were an outcome of the deliberation of the Tripartite Commission. The commission, in agreeing to labour market reforms, explicitly endorsed a series of programmes to deal with employment. The master plan of the commission included expansion of the Employment, Labour Market Issues and Insurance Program as well as a reinforcement of new employment services. But, critically for our argument, these new labour market programmes were designed to improve the capability of workers in the market rather than merely providing job security (Yi and Lee 2003). Labour market programmes play a decisive role in the new social market economy because they link labour market training to the welfare and work system rather than to the provision of employment security. It is these 'welfare to work' linkages that allow us to make the crucial distinction between the social market economy and the postwar European welfare state.

One important component of this new labour market programme directed at the unemployed was the Employment Insurance Scheme. The Ministry of Labour outlines the main functions of the unemployed insurance system in the following terms:

The Employment Insurance System is both a social security system and a comprehensive labor market policy including employment security programs to promote corporate restructuring, prevent unemployment and boost employment, and vocational ability development programs as well as unemployment insurance programs which are a traditional function of providing unemployment benefits to the unemployed. (Ministry of Labour, Korea 2005)

The Employment Insurance Scheme is of limited duration, and, in comparison with other programmes in OECD countries, is not generous, but the point as suggested in this chapter is that these insurance programmes are linked to workforce participation to create new forms of market citizenship.

Insurance for the unemployed remains one aspect of the broad gamut of labour market policies introduced. A similarly important part of labour market policy is the role that Korean policy makers have given to employment policy which, in its most recent formulation, focuses on alleviating labour shortages for small and medium-sized enterprises. This is achieved by linking schools to the labour market, and denotes a heavy emphasis on the development of vocational skills and building life-long skill development. There is also an emphasis on the provision of specialized employment services to target groups such as women and the disabled (Ministry of Labour 2005). The central policy thrust of these employment policies is directed at enhancing the capabilities of the individual to participate in the economy. Enhancing the capacities of individuals to work in the economic sphere is one of the hallmarks of welfare within the structures of a social market economy or economic constitutionalism.

One of the most important social policy initiatives occurred in 1999 when the Korean government introduced the Minimum Living Standards Guarantee Law, a measure which established the minimum threshold of public assistance for the poor. The programme recognised the right to benefit, but also acknowledged the importance of relative poverty which was an important departure from the earlier rationale for welfare. But this was not its only point of departure from the earlier paternalistic welfare regime. The new law effectively 'legalized' access to benefits in a way that was not prevalent in the previous system of welfare paternalism. This itself is a good illustration of our argument that the regulatory state is as much about the changing forms of 'stateness' about the purpose and form of public authority – the language of public action – as it is about substantive policy outcomes. Hence the real significance of the Minimum Living Standard Guarantee lies in the fact that it shifted 'welfare' from the ideology of paternalism to a more legalistic understanding of access to welfare, although this is not a rights based approach.

Indeed, this new-found legalism can be identified across the spectrum within various areas of social and economic governance. Nothing more clearly illustrates the transformation of the developmental state than the way its panoply of 'administrative guidance' and executive discretionary power has given way to the flowering of a growing and assertive legalism and constitutionalism in economic and political decision making. New forms of welfare are a broader subset of these new forms of stateness – the creation of a new technology of public action. Welfare legalism became a vital element in the constitution of new forms of market citizenship.

Underpinned by the new legalism, citizenship and the related growth of a new welfare regime remain at the sharp edge of the new regulatory state.

The strength of the social market and the economic constitutionalism framework approach used in this volume allows us to engage with the broader debate over the differences between recent developments in welfare and earlier patterns of welfare state development. Korea has been characterized as a 'productive welfare state' by Kwon (1997, 1999), and more recently as a 'productivist' regime by Holliday (2000) (see also Deyo 1992). In fact, for Holliday (2000) Korea formed a fourth world of productivist welfare that stood independently alongside Esping-Andersen's (1990) three worlds of welfare: Liberal, Conservative, and Social Democratic. The essence of the productivist regime was that social policy was strongly tied to the economic concerns or imperatives; non-state-based welfare was prominent and welfare was tied to ideas of paternalism and developmentalism. The question that this poses for us is: to what extent have recent changes in welfare policy and programs in Korea signalled a shift towards a different kind of welfare state.

For some, like Ramesh (2003), changes in welfare orientation in the wake of the crisis reflect a more profound transition from productivist welfare regimes to the more familiar systems of welfare found in Western Europe. In their recent work Peng (2004) and Wong (2005) have put forward a similar argument, suggesting that the increased attention to welfare in Korea and Taiwan reflects a more substantial transformation from the developmental state. Put bluntly, these authors tend to argue that welfare is being normalized and East Asia is no longer the exception. Peng (2004) argues that this normalization comes from two interrelated pressures. First, there are what he calls post-industrial pressures which, according to him, refer to economic globalization as well as shifts in demographic and family relations. The more interesting of these pressures of post-industrial forces – since it is rather difficult to think of globalization as a post-industrial pressure – is the changing dynamics of gender and family relationships. Peng points here to the growth of more egalitarian family relationships and changing attitudes towards state involvement in welfare. Relatedly, he notes the extent to which policy discourse has been feminized. The second set of pressures which, in effect, translate these structural factors into the policy and political process has been the political opening provided by key regime shifts that enabled 'progressive agents to carry through with their social policy goals' (Peng 2004: 408). The upshot of these changes is that the:

> ... shifts in economic and political conditions in the 1990s are forcing politicians and policy makers to take social policy more seriously, and as a result, there has been a decoupling of social policy from economic policy. In Korea and Japan there is evidence that new social policies are playing a more facilitative role rather than subjugative role to economic development. (Peng 2004: 416–17)

His argument here is that it is the interaction of both the post-industrial pressures and internal political dynamics that facilitated the emergence of key actors that sought to develop a more autonomous and less economically subordinate role for social policy. In other words, the Korean welfare became less exceptional and productivist.

However, Holliday (2005) has doubts about this and has argued that recent welfare changes – though substantive – still remain broadly productivist in character, and that Korea is still a bad fit with any of Esping-Andersen's worlds of welfare. Summing up these changes he notes that

> there were obviously productivist elements, notably the pre eminent status of education, the routine privileging of industrial workers, and the limited attention paid to social security. In the matrix of possible state forms, South Korea was clearly developmental, but with a much less individualistic approach than Singapore. It was clearly moving from elitism towards pluralism. (Holliday 2005: 156)

In a similar vein, Kwon argues that, despite significant changes, Korean welfare policy remains a broadly productivist welfare developmentalist state. Korea still remains exceptional. There is something to be said for the productivist argument. As we suggested, the predominant aspect of the recent welfare argument is the pursuit of – to use Kim Dae Jung's words – 'productive welfare'. But is 'productive welfare' the same thing as productivism? The notion of social market economy advanced here better captures the significant changes in welfare in the post-Asian crisis period. The social market economy model differs from productivism in two important respects.

First, much of the discussion on welfare takes place outside the broader changes in the state structure and organization and notions of stateness. Productivism as a model of welfare was a good fit with the developmental state, but the shift towards a regulatory state created new forms of productive welfare outside the paternalistic approaches of enterprise welfare. One of the key changes in the welfare model in Korea is to be found in the fact that it has a legalistic basis quite separate from the developmental goals and objectives of the 'developmental' or productivist welfare state. The real significance of this is that the new welfare thrust in Korea helps to constitute new forms of social citizenship that are different from the paternalism and enterprise welfare of the developmental state. The Korean welfare regime is now enmeshed in new structures of economic constitutionalism that differ from both the social constitutionalism of the European welfare state and also the welfare regime of the developmentalist state.

Second, at the core of this shift from productivism to the social market is the gradual movement towards a more liberalized and flexible labour market. In one sense productivism and the model of enterprise welfare remain premised on tightly controlled labour markets. In moving towards a more flexible labour market the new welfare programmes served not only to trade off lost benefits with some – albeit limited – social spending. This trade-off remained the main rationale for the Tripartite Commission. But it was more than a simple trade-off. The new welfare orientation also served to facilitate the opening of the labour market through the provision of welfare and employment services that were non-enterprise-based. Indeed, the Asian economic crisis, and in the Korean case the prospect of imminent bankruptcy, forced many large domestic corporations to reduce their enterprise welfare systems which included many meagre paternalistic welfare and education benefits that had been such a hallmark of the productivist model. This, in turn, forced the state to assume some welfare responsibilities. But, more importantly, shifting these welfare benefits into the public sphere enabled the movement of political issues of labour market flexibility. In this sense, at least, welfare underpinned Korea's movement towards more flexible labour markets.

It is this relationship between labour markets and the welfare system that underscores one of the defining elements of the social market economy: the location of welfare within the imperatives of the market economy. To the extent that these programmes establish new social contracts they remain contracts in which a market citizenship is defined in terms of the imperatives of economic order, and recall that this was one of the central motifs of social market that emerged from ordo liberalism (see Chapter 1). In fact, Korean economic and social governance through social market forms strikingly parallel ordo liberal conceptions of the social market, albeit one with 'Korean characteristics'.

This economic constitutionalism represents a form of 'socialization of neo liberalism' rather than the development of the classical welfare citizenship around what we have called a 'social democratic' grammar of politics. The problem with critics of the 'productivist welfare model' such as Peng is that they make the assumption that the transition out of productivism must necessarily be towards a welfare state along the lines of social citizenship. If the argument advanced in this chapter is valid the policy movement is out of 'enterprise welfare' but into an economic constitutionalism whose dominant 'idea of welfare' – to use Pinker's phrase – is built around a politics of social inclusion.

Social market, regulation and statecraft

Korea stands out as an intriguig test case for the politics of the new welfare governance. Struck hard by the Asian economic crisis of 1997–98, Korea responded by placing a higher priority on social policies and expenditure. In part, the explanation for the growing weight of the social welfare priorities is to be found in the dual transition that Korea went through in 1997–98. The first transition is the acceleration of Korea's transition from activist economic policies to a more neo liberal set of economic policies that required the dismantling of the developmental state apparatus; the second transition is the broader process of democratization that culminated in the election as president of the opposition leader Kim Dae Jung. This dual transition allowed Kim Dae Jung to simultaneously pursue a policy of both economic and welfare reform. More to the point, these policies came together in a new regulatory state that not only established new procedures and institutions of economic governance, but also established different forms of social regulation. It is this state transformation that lies at the heart of Korean policy in the aftermath of the Asian crisis.

Social regulation of this kind is best understood in terms of the development of a new social market model. The essence of this social market model was to establish market imperatives with the welfare state, creating a form of market citizenship. As such, the social market model was distinct from the traditional welfare state which establishes social citizenship in opposition or in terms of ameliorating market forces through various redistributive mechanisms, and also from the various forms of East Asian productivism that made social policy an ancillary to the developmental state. The social market model entrenches a welfare regime suited to the economic constitutionalism that defines the Korean state. But we need to be clear that this social market model was an exercise in statecraft which sought to change both the practices and the language of public action. For example, in the Korean case one of the especially important developments has been to grant a new legal basis to welfare state programs that are different from the paternalistic orientation of what Holliday (2000) terms 'productivist welfare'. Statecraft is not simply about creating new structures of public authority; it is also concerned with giving new meaning to the purposes under which that public authority is exercised.

To sum up, as a statecraft project the social market model has three elements. First, there is an inclusive element that promotes the active participation of social actors in the formulation of social policy. This is more than mere symbolism as, in itself, it assists in giving legitimacy to the broad tenor of economic and social programmes implemented in the post-Asian economic crisis period. Second, there is a concerted expansion of welfare programmes which give effect to a broad range of new social contracts. These welfare programmes, at least in the Korean case, led to the paradox of both welfare expansion and neo liberal economic reform. Finally, and most importantly, these new social contracts serve to create new forms of market citizenship within the new social market model. This social market model is distinct from the welfare productivism of the old developmental state as well as the European-style welfare state. In this sense, the new Korean welfare governance is very much a part of the third way in seeking to develop 'ideas' of welfare within structures of economic constitutionalism.

6
Statecraft and Social Contracts: A Populist Market Citizenship in Thailand

Neo liberal populism as statecraft: Thailand's new social contracts

In Thailand the election of the Thai Rak Thai (TRT) in 2001 led by Thaksin Shinawatra and its subsequent consolidation of electoral power in the 2005 election with a stunning landslide victory signalled a significant transformation of Thai politics.[1] As a political party, the TRT represents an intriguing combination of conflicting political and economic elements. This involved: the pursuit of nationalist policies while being committed to a broad range of neo liberal policies; and a strong authoritarian streak combined with mastery of the electoral process and led by one of Thailand's richest businessmen yet who has appealed to poor farmers and urban voters with an attractive range of social policies (Hewison 2005).[2] These factors have served to change the fundamental character of Thai politics. But the question of how and why this amalgam of political elements came together remains problematic.

However, a quick and ready answer to this combination of seemingly antagonistic political elements is populism.[3] This is altogether too easy an answer. The Thai situation presents a populist politics of a peculiar kind – one that links populist politics with a commitment to neo liberal economics. It is a curious populism because these movements have traditionally been associated with the presence of dirigiste economic and social policies. On the face of it, pursuing neo liberal policies seems antithetical to the way populist politics has traditionally played out, especially on its home turf of

Latin America. In fact, in Latin American politics the emergence of politicians such as Menem in Argentina and Fujimori in Peru with a sustainable political project led to the coining of the term 'neo liberal populism' by scholars to identify the special character of this hybrid of neo liberalism and populism. The TRT, with Thaksin at the helm, embodies a distinctive language, style, and politics of populism that slots neatly into this category of 'neo liberal populism'. Thaksin, in particular, has shown a remarkable ability to weave this new populist politics alongside a broad acceptance of the market model in a manner that enables Thaksin to carve out new forms of market citizenship under the rubric of a populist political project. In this chapter we will explore the nature and form of this project of populist market citizenship.

We need to preface this analysis of the concept of neo liberal populism by first considering Thaksin's political programme as a distinctive statecraft project. This programme is at once a statecraft project that seeks to reshape both the internal governance of the state as well as creating new forms of market citizenship by constituting new relationships between the individual and the political and civil community. Looked at from this angle the neo liberal populism is a statecraft project, one that not only seeks to transform the framework of public authority but also the nature and purpose of public policy. These elements, in turn, facilitate the emergence of new forms of 'stateness', that is, a transformation in the language, technology and institutions of public action[4] that draws pointed attention to a neglected dimension of statecraft in the literature on neo liberal populism. An important aspect of this populist statecraft in Thailand is that it works through – this again differs from the standard accounts of neo liberal populism – the implementation of a range of innovative social contracts and policies. Social policy stands at the heart of this statecraft of neo liberal populism.

As in the case of Korea, social policy remains essential to this statecraft because it allows for the creation of new forms of citizenship. In order to properly analyse the nature of neo liberal populism in Thailand we need to analyse this populism not simply as a means of implementing shock market therapy – a description which certainly would not apply to the TRT government – but also as a broader project that aims to regulate social and economic governance. And it is for this reason that questions of welfare governance go far beyond the implementation of the social policies: it fundamentally reconstitutes the nature of the state. As we shall argue, these new social contracts introduced by the TRT are at the cutting edge of a new project of statecraft that reorganizes the state institutions, routines and practices as well as creating new relationships between citizens and the political authority. In the Thai case this new populist project lends itself to a form of anti politics which finds expression in an increasingly authoritarian governance.

Neo liberal populism: from market reform to statecraft

Populism, then, is pivotal to understanding this new form of statecraft, but this populism – as we have seen in the case of TRT economic nationalism – is a very different beast to that of the classical inward-oriented protectionist form of Latin American populism which depended on an active and interventionist state. In contrast, the Thai case represents an unexpected and surprising populism that meshes, albeit not always smoothly, with the neo liberal programmes of economic reform promoted by the TRT. Surprisingly, due to the constraints of policy placed on the capacity of political leaders to deliver on populist policies and programmes, it was assumed that neo liberalism would be inhospitable to populism. But far from being vanquished, populism appears to have sought a new lease of life in both newly industrialising and advanced industrial economies.

Indeed, in Latin America, Roberts (1995) has argued that a breed of populist leaders, such as Menem in Argentina and Fujimori in Peru, were able to turn populist politics into support for neo liberal policies. Populism, Roberts argues, is multidimensional and is characterized by the following features: personalistic and paternalistic rule, a multi-class coalition, a rather ambiguous ideology, and an economic project that uses redistributive methods to consolidate political support. On this definition populist programs go hand in hand with the pursuit of programs of economic reform – a paradoxical combination of neo liberalism and populism which Roberts was the first to identify as a neo liberal populism[5] which was a political and ideological form:

> associated with the breakdown of institutionalized forms of political representation that often occurs during periods of social and economic upheaval. Its emergence demonstrates that populism can adapt to the neoliberal era and that it is not defined by fiscal profligacy; indeed, even when constrained by fiscal austerity and market reforms, personalist leaders have discovered diverse political and economic instruments to mobilize popular sector support when intermediary institutions are in crisis. (Roberts 1995: 82)

This formulation moves us beyond simplistic definitions of populism as a particular kind of interventionist and dirigiste economic programme, seeing it instead as a political project that takes on various forms in different phases of the global political economy.

In the understanding of populism as a constantly transforming political programme it is useful to be aware that there is a striking convergence to similar mutations within social democracy, particularly when it seeks to adapt to neo liberalism through the third way or the new social democracy. There is a strong similarity here to the problems of social democracy. Whilst the new social democracy or third way politics is an attempt to construct a social democratic project of statecraft within neo liberalism, neo liberal populism also strives to mobilize populist notions of the nation and citizenship within neo liberal economic forms. Just as the new social democracy is a social democratic moment within neo liberalism, then neo liberal populism is a populist moment within a highly globalized economy. In fact, given that populism is often seen as analogous to social democracy in Latin America the parallels between new social democracy – the third way – and the neo liberal populism are striking. Furthermore, what is remarkably similar is both the new social democracy and neo liberal populism attempt to craft a political programme that seeks to 'socialize' neo liberalism while being bound by the structural constraints imposed by the global economy.

In this sense, the real significance of neo liberal populism lies not so much with the first generation leaders such as Menem or Fujimori but with the second wave of neo liberal populism exemplified in the later election of those such as Mexico's Fox, Columbia's Uribe, Peru's Toledo and even Argentina's Kirchner. These leaders, while they adopt a populist political style, have not embarked on the drastic and radical neo liberal reforms undertaken by those such as Menem and Fujimori. More to the point, these leaders now find that the pursuit of neo liberal market models in the late 1990s will lead to neither political nor economic success. Assessing these trends Weyland (2004), a leading proponent of the framework of neo liberal populism, suggests that, while the ties between neo liberalism and populism may have been weakened, the new second-generation leaders remain committed to neo liberal economic models and are still within the precincts of neo liberal populism. He suggests two reasons for this: first that economic reform has weakened intermediary political organizations such as trade unions and has paved the way for the emergence of strong populist leaders who bypass formal political institutions, often through the use of plebiscitary instruments; second, that as the market model has matured populism turns towards administrative and governance reform that:

> promote the unity of the people by calling for an end to factional conflict and ideological rifts. Since the market system has defeated its ideological rivals and since even most sectors of the left have accepted its basic principles, severe political polarization has diminished in Latin America. Contemporary neoliberal populists seek to reinforce this 'end of ideology'; by depicting as the main task of politics the pragmatic 'administration of things.' (Weyland 2004: 1110)

Weyland is perceptive here in noting a shift towards governance and administration rather than towards the shock therapy of neo liberal market reforms. But this shift is not so much a weakening of the market model; rather, it reflects a further deepening of neo liberalism which has the intention of developing more regulative forms of statecraft. Whereas the first wave of neo liberalism was really about rolling back the state – what Peck and Tickell call rollback neo liberalism – the concerns of the second generation of neo liberal populists are more with the issues of statecraft and governance. The latter seek to construct new forms of social and economic governance to provide a political platform and develop new forms of statecraft that are compatible with a globalized economy. It is in this sense that the second generation of neo liberal populists converge with the third way social democratic strategies in developing forms of market citizenship around various strategies of welfare governance. In other words, neo liberal populism has become a political project of statecraft that reshapes the institutions, structures, and practices of state power.

Neo liberal populism as statecraft then has three central characteristics. First, it is primarily concerned not so much with expanding the market model but with the reregulation of economic and social governance in order to provide market order along the lines of economic constitutionalism (see Chapter 1). What distinguishes neo liberal populism from other regulatory projects is that this re-regulation occurs outside formal representative institutions and reinforces populist styles of leadership and rule. But what is equally significant in the second generation of neo liberal populism is that these populist styles of leadership are accompanied by concerted efforts to establish new structures of accountability that emphasize often locally based policy formulations to the political debate in national legislature or assemblies. The substantive effect of these emerging patterns of populist representation is to erode the mediating structures of democratic politics (Chandhoke 2002: 18).

Second, an essential dimension of this new re-regulation is what we may call the 'socialization' of neo liberalism – that is, programmes and policies aimed at the regulation of social governance. In turn, these forms of social regulation help to produce new regimes of social citizenship which, unlike postwar social democratic regimes of social citizenship, place social governance within, rather than in opposition to, the market. Paradoxically, these new regimes of market citizenship mean that social policy or the new social contracts take on renewed importance within neo liberal populism. Of course, all populist politics, as Roberts (1995) notes, depend on the use of distributive benefits to reinforce and build populist constituencies, but what characterizes this second wave of neo liberalism is not these 'distributive policies' per se, but the fact that these policies are a component of a wider project to produce new forms of citizenship or political community. These new social contracts or forms of populist market citizenship attempt to regulate civil society by producing more competitive and enterprising subjects. In this way, strategies of neo liberal populist statecraft – in part through its new social contracts and social policies – creates a new relationship between citizens and political authority.

Finally, these new social contracts are ideologically justified and legitimized as instruments that will move politics beyond contestation and pluralism. What makes the market citizenship of this neo liberal populism so ideologically distinctive is its rhetoric to portray its policies as benefiting the 'people' in an immediate way while moving beyond the pluralism and political conflict of the past. It is a populism that finds its appeal on moving towards a new politics based on a 'new consensus'. Significantly, 'overcoming such "factionalism" is a common populist theme, and founding this new consensus on generalized acceptance of basic market principles is of interest to neo liberals' (Weyland 2004: 1111). But this new anti-politics is played out not in doleful terms of technocratic governance but with the harsh brass of populism; it is this anti-politics that make the new social policies so crucial to the statecraft of neo liberal populism.

At first glance, Thailand does not seem to fit in with the neo liberal populism. Nor is it possible to slot Thaksin into the mould of the first wave of neo liberal populist leaders. The programme on which he won the first election was notable because it blamed the previous government for adhering too closely to IMF/World Bank programs. If anything, then, it implied a rejection of certain elements of the IMF economic model. But this becomes problematic because Thailand, over the last three decades, has assiduously followed World Bank prescriptions on economic policy and, indeed, was cited in the famous Miracle Report of the World Bank as a notable exponent of the effectiveness of the Washington Consensus policies.[6] Ironically, it is these kinds of East Asian success stories that initially spurred Latin American neo liberal populism. Thaksin, indeed, was intent on rejecting those elements of the IMF model that hurt domestic capitalists like himself and this is a fact that distinguishes him from the first wave of neo liberal populism.

This was, however, not a rejection of the market model as such, but only of those very specific elements of the IMF package and the austerity programme of the previous Chuan government that had dampened economic growth. In fact, as the economy recovered, and, more importantly, once domestic capital was secured Thaksin seemed ready to pursue a sharper neo liberal agenda. Yet, this was not the main aim of his political project. As argued previously, the TRT programme was a project of statecraft that aims to regulate the market model through the reshaping of social and economic governance. This was primarily achieved by appealing to groups such as the urban and rural poor by promising new benefits in return for political support, as well as creating new forms of entrepreneurial conduct (Hewison 2003a, 2003b, 2005; Jayasuriya and Hewison 2004).

In these terms the policies and programmes pursued by the TRT had the intention of creating a new form of citizenship and political community. It was, above all, these new social policies that, more than anything else, allowed the TRT to consolidate its grip on political power and, more significantly, enabled it to win a resounding victory in the election of February 2005. Thus, liberal populism in the Thai context was directed towards the reshaping of the institutions, routines and practices of the state. What needs to be emphasized is that neo liberal populism is not simply a programme of economic reform but a more deep-seated programme of political reform. For this reason alone, the TRT and its programme needs to be located within the domain of neo liberal populist statecraft.

Indeed, this project of neo liberal populism statecraft arose in response to what Jayasuriya and Hewison (2004) have termed 'a governance project' promoted by both the World Bank and the previous Chuan government,[7] and exemplified by a range of governance programmes. These pertain mainly to bureaucratic and administrative reforms aimed at improving the technocratic management of economic reform. But it was much more. Unlike earlier structural adjustment programmes, this governance project envisaged a more active and regulatory role for government. After identifying the relationship between financial instability and perceived weakness in transparency and corporate governance, Robert Rubin, the US Secretary of the Treasury, argued that these problems: 'require the help of the international community and a reorientation to the role of the government and the political will to implement that reorientation' (Robert Rubin, quoted in Hewison 2003b).

Going even beyond this reform of economic governance, this governance statecraft project sought to regulate civil society through the implementation of a number of programs such as the Social Investment Fund (SIF) (see Chapter 3). Nurtured by ideas of social capital, the SIF sought to develop participatory programs for local policy making. In fact a key component of the World Bank response to the Asian economic crisis was the attention and emphasis given to the social dimensions of the crisis by sponsoring the Bank's rubric of poverty reduction.

However, this governance project of the Bank and the Chuan government soon gave way to the more populist statecraft of Thaksin and the TRT. To be sure these two statecraft projects have much in common. Both employ a distinctly anti-political language and rhetoric that marginalizes political contestation and conflict. Yet the populist statecraft of Thaksin and the TRT proved to be a much more successful scheme. An immediate and obvious reason for this is that the fiscal austerity imposed by the IMF and the sluggish economic performance allowed them to appeal to populist language and to frame the political debate in nationalist terms. The more substantive reasons for the success of the TRT were that its programmes, as Hewison and Jayasuriya (2004) argue, were more closely aligned with domestic capital. In addition to being less dependent on rigid neo liberalism, they also contained a harder, more ideologically resonant notion of nationalism, which used social contracts to construct a broad-based coalition. It is these new social policies that have become the sharp edge through which this new neo liberal populist statecraft creates new institutions and forms of social regulation which, in turn, reinforce the neo liberal market model. This new welfare governance forms a new 'technology of public action'[8] that works to produce new relationships between the political authorities and the citizenry.

Thailand: the strategies of populist governance

Before analysing the nature of this new infrastructure of public action, we need to consider briefly how the electoral and political success of the

TRT has reshaped Thai politics: first, the TRT was a different kind of political party – as much a media creation by its leader as a programmatic political party. Thaksin – of course, being Thailand's richest businessman and most prominent figure in the corporate sector – saw his party very much as a vehicle by which he could, with the support of other key elements of domestic capital, capture the electoral market. Indeed, the tactics and strategies that he used to set up the party bore a striking similarity to the way in which he captured a market for his own business. But, more importantly, the party itself had no social roots or even a clear ideological programme. It was simply a structure, an electoral organization, created mainly for the purpose of securing governmental power. Above all, his party organisation and campaigning style reflected an understanding and use of American forms of political marketing (Nelson 2001), such that:

> the TRT election campaign was also emphatically new in several ways. The party spent two years setting up a local network, and used the principles of pyramid selling in an attempt to sign up enough party members in each constituency for electoral victory (Pasuk & Baker 2004: 83).

Second, one of the ramifications of this way of selling the party to the Thai electorate was to eliminate the local political bosses who wielded so much influence in the old system of money politics. In itself, this was in part a consequence of the fact that the party was highly effective in using marketing techniques to sell both the party and its leader in the 'soft nationalism' that became its trademark brand. None of this is to say that old 'money politics' that has been so central to Thai politics was replaced by new US-style political marketing, but what the TRT effectively did, as Pasuk and Baker (2004) suggest, was combine money politics with the strategic use of US political marketing. However, what was so unique about the TRT's approach to electoral politics was its ability to create a more centralized system of 'money politics' that to some extent bypassed or subordinated local systems of political patronage and money politics. In other words, the election of TRT highlights the emergence of a new form of centralized money politics rather than the decentralized patronage politics that was such a characteristic of Thai electoral politics.

Third, the TRT has been adroit in managing the constitution, something which was once thought to be its Achilles' heel. The constitution itself was a product of what might be called a 'governance' project strongly associated with the previous regime of Chuan Leekpai. The governance statecraft and the constitution were composed of two potentially antagonistic elements. One was that the constitution established a range of bodies that were designed to produce horizontal accountability for the executive. These bodies included the Constitutional Court, the Election Commission and the National Counter Corruption Commission, as well as procedures and regulations which governed the appointment of members to regulatory bodies in sectors such as telecommunication. The other element was that alongside these instruments of horizontal accountability the constitution facilitated the continuity and stability of executive government. To this end, it limited the capacity of Parliament to move motions of 'No confidence' in the government and limited the MPs' right to resign from parties. All of this solidified the extent of executive power.

The common thread that runs through these two antagonistic elements is a form of anti politics that seeks to smooth the exercise of executive power towards technocratic ends. Thaksin has cleverly managed the constitution by effectively taming – though not replacing – the new institutions of horizontal accountability. This was most notably apparent when the Constitutional Court backed down over his own eligibility to stand for Parliament; at the same time Thaksin was able to use those parts of the constitution that facilitated the exercise of executive control over Parliament in order to smooth the way for the TRT to marginalize and dominate the political opposition.

Equally important was the fact that the TRT as a political party based its appeal on Thai nationalism. This was noticeable in its very name, 'TRT', which translates as 'Thai loves Thai'. But this was very much a 'soft' nationalism that was not inconsistent with the commitment to globalization. As Pasuk and Baker (2004: 79) note, this nationalism was not:

> ... anti globalist in the long term. Less advanced countries needed to integrate with the world at their own pace so they could participate on 'fair and equal terms' and retain their cultural identity. The priority was to restore the national government's duty to manage the economy.

Clearly, this form of 'culturalist nationalism' with its appeal to history, and to past glories, differs from what we may call 'developmentalist nationalism' which characterized much of the colonial politics leading to decolonization in Asia. Identity politics of nationalism, as practiced here, is hostile to those aspects of political globalization, such as respect for international human rights obligations, but is quite consistent with economic globalization. In fact Thaksin has argued that: 'having debates and so many different opinions is just selfishness. And it is on the increase. These things slow the society down. Everyone has to unite for the country to progress' (Thaksin quoted in Pasuk and Baker 2004: 139). Here, Thaksin seems to argue that this kind of cultural nationalism is a necessary concomitant of globalization.

Similarly, this new cultural nationalism has not prevented Thailand from forging strong links with the US and its war on terror, and as a reward for these efforts it has been granted Non NATO ally status (Macargo 2005). Thailand, along with Singapore and Australia, has become key components of US strategic policy in Asia. In fact, Macargo (2005) even argues that Thaksin has been the most pro-American Thai prime minister in the post Vietnam period. Given the traditionally close links between the US and Thailand this is a striking confirmation of the fact that Thaksin's nationalism plays well with the neo conservative ideology that characterizes the Bush administration. Quite apart from these considerations the war on terror has served to re-legitimize those national security doctrines and practices that were such a pervasive element of Thai state practices during the cold war (Glassman 2004; Rodan and Hewison 2004). Hewison (2003a, 2005) has persuasively argued that the TRT victory and its nationalist rhetoric reflect the interests of those domestic capitalists whose enterprises were badly hurt by the IMF-sponsored austerity programme.

> [In the] post-crisis setting, domestic capital's economic survival and growth required a political vehicle that allowed it to seize the state. In Thailand's political environment, with a new and reformist constitution, this could only be achieved through the electoral process. (Hewison 2005: 312)

In this argument, the TRT was a vehicle through which domestic capital was able to blunt the edge of those reforms that hurt its strategic economic interests. But this was an electoral victory that was made all the more significant by the fact that the policies of the new government were justified under the rubric of a soft 'identity politics'. Hence the policies of the new government cannot be easily dismissed merely as instrumental actions of vested economic interests. This was certainly the case, but these policies were also framed within an overarching economic nationalist programme that appealed to a broad coalition. But to the extent that this was a form of economic nationalism it was not inconsistent with the broad thrust of neo liberal programmes.

Much of Thaksin's economic programme relied on reversing the IMF's fiscal austerity policies to provide what became a substantial fiscal stimulus to the economy. However, as the business and financial press (Lian 2003) was to quickly make the point, Thaksin's economic policies in no way – nor could it – undo the programmes of economic liberalisation to which successive Thai governments over nearly two decades have been committed. In fact, as the economy has consolidated, Thaksin has moved to implement an ambitious agenda of utility and infrastructure privatization. For example, the TRT government sought to privatize the Electricity Generating Authority of Thailand (EGAT) but this was – in part due to labour pressures – put off in March 2004. But in October 2004 new plans were announced and it is expected that after his resounding win in the general election of 2005 there will be another concerted effort to privatize EGAT (Thomas, Hall and Corral 2005). In essence, this economic nationalism of the TRT government was a far cry from the mercantilist programmes with which it is customarily associated; this nationalism was essentially a political and ideological programme designed to secure benefits for domestic capital within a global economy.

This is a significant point because the sort of economic nationalism pursued by the TRT does not depend on the construction of the kind of nationalist developmental strategy such as that pursued by Korea at the height of the Cold War. To the extent that Thaksin's economic policies are nationalist they are geared towards creating a more competitive edge for domestic capital in international markets. While neo liberals:

> may chafe at such policies, they scarcely provide more support for Thai capitalists than what is on offer for most capitalists from states elsewhere in the world, nor do they necessarily outstrip the statist forms of support offered to international capitalists by organizations like the IMF and the World Bank. (Glassman 2004: 59)

More specifically, this domestic capitalist class has transnational links and alliances which precluded the emergence of a national developmentalist agenda that might have formed the ideological backbone of dirigiste policies (Glassman 2004).

The more general point here is that as we move from an international to a global economy it becomes impossible to counterpoise the interests of domestic capital to foreign capital. Domestic capital itself is fractured and connected to the global economy and global capital. From this perspective, it is impossible to draw a simplistic typology of protectionist and internationalist interest within the capitalist class, because capital (both foreign and domestic) has contradictory and mixed interests in the pursuit of various strategies of foreign economic policies. The point then is that global economy means that the 'concept of the domestic bourgeoisie is related to the process of internationalization, and does not refer to a bourgeoisie "enclosed" within a "national" space' (Poulantzas 1978: 74). The point is simply that while the TRT may have pursued policies bearing some elements of economic nationalism these policies only reflected competing interests within a globalized economy rather than an effort to carve out nationalist developmental strategy – something in any case impossible in a globalized economy.

Statecraft, social contracts and new entrepreneurial capacities

But the kernel of this new populism is to be found in the way in which it seeks to establish a distinctive social contract between the citizens and the state. This is one that seeks to promote new kinds of entrepreneurial subjects rather than the social citizenship associated with the post-Second World War welfare state. These new social contracts, as Hewison (2003b, 2005) points out, differ markedly from the old developmental contract which sought to deliver trickle-down social benefits through economic prosperity. Instead, the new social contract 'involves the promotion of domestic capital by the government of the remaining rich, while delivering increased social protection to the poor' (Hewison 2003b: 19). This presents a substantial commitment that goes beyond the developmental contract which prevailed during the 'boom years' of the Asian miracle. The new populist market citizenship means that Thailand is committed to developing – however falteringly – a much more extensive social infrastructure. However, unlike the European welfare state, most of these policies are directed at the creation of a more competitive and entrepreneurial society. In this sense at least Thaksin represents a Thai version of the third way as ideologically important as New Labour in Britain.

The new populist politics of Thailand, like many of the third way programmes, explicitly articulates a new social contract. In fact, Thaksin himself, as Pasuk and Baker (2004) point out, has been explicit in calling for a new social contract. But this social contract is about enabling or creating those forms of market-conforming conduct rather than participating in the broader political community. As such, the terminology of the social contract differs sharply from the way this has been understood in the formulation of the postwar European social settlement in terms of social protection. Social contract is defined here in terms of economic rather than social constitutionalism. In other words, Thaksin's use of the term social contract is instructive because it does not necessarily signify the introduction of an insurance society and its various associated forms of social solidarity. Rather, it points to the way in which the state enters into a contract with its citizens to enable them to participate more actively within the market. And here is the nub: social governance is seen in terms of the activation of various forms of entrepreneurial abilities and capacities.

Some of these key entrepreneurial policies outlined below include: the Village Fund, the People's Bank, the Obe Tambon Project, the Asset Conversion Program, the Health Scheme (see Looney 2003, Hewison 2003a for more details on these programmes).

The Village Fund

This was a key campaign promise of the TRT government and was designed to provide one million bahts to Thai villages. It works through the provision of targeted projects designed to renovate the rural economy, with the aid of community and village leaders identifying projects, by providing loans for projects at subsidized interest rates. The Village Fund was aimed not just at supporting agriculture, but also at facilitating entrepreneurial rural farmers through subsidized credit. In many respects, the Village Fund stands out as the flagship programme of the new social contract in Thailand.

According to a senior government official:

> The objective of this fund is to act as a revolving loan facility, available for individuals and households within the community, to borrow for local investment. The fund will be used to support the process of self-sufficient development at the community level, hence stimulating the economy, and strengthening the peoples' capacity to meet their subsistence requirements. (Boonyaratpalin 2005)

The People's Bank

One of the major functions of the bank is to provide credit to various micro enterprises to allow groups and individuals with no formal access to credit the ability to develop their businesses through access to credit institutions. Similar credit-related schemes have been created for the urban poor (see Looney 2003).

One Tambon project

This programme is designed to get Thai Tambon (subdistricts) to specialize in the production of one product in which it has a comparative advantage. The key assumption is that:

each community has a comparative advantage in one or more of these traditional products. The project's role is to assist the communities in modernizing the production and distribution process of these products so that they can be competitive at the national and international levels. The government's role is to identify candidate products and then to assist their development through providing necessary support for their eventual success. (Looney 2003: 6)

Perhaps the most significant aspect of the One Tambon Project was its localism – that is, the emphasis it places on local communities. Localism, of course, was an important element of the Thai NGO response to the Asian economic crisis (Hewison 2000) and the TRT was able to use aspects of this ideological language of localism. More especially, the One Tambon Project served to underline the importance of 'community' to the new social contracts. Implicit in this notion of community was its conceptualization spatially as 'neighbourhood communities'. This marginalizes the communities as a 'class' in favour of communities that are spatially specific. It is the management of these localized communities that becomes a central objective of the welfare governance. Various forms of localism are seen as being crucial in activating these new inclusive forms of participation. This is mainly because it 'might be a way of reorganizing social exchange in a more individualistic way, activating reciprocity on a territorial basis against the abstraction of universal rights' (Procacci 2001: 63). Localism, in this view, becomes the basis for a conception of citizenship that is at odds with the insurance or entitlement understanding of social citizenship.

The asset conversion programmes

This is a programme that seeks to give individuals and groups, such as the urban poor and rural farmers, secure property rights so that they can use these rights to access credit and other services in the formal economic sector. Hence their description as an 'asset conversion programme' based on the assumption that the causes of poverty are due to the inability of individuals to convert their assets into credit. On this account, groups such as the urban poor who have no formal title to the property they own and are unable to mortgage these assets into credit in the formal market. These asset conversion schemes are an instrument of social policy, but endowed with a particular technology of public action directed at creating and broadening property ownership within the community. A key driving assumption of these asset conversion programmes is that economic independence is not just the key to greater social well-being, but is also essential to the production of new liberal subjects who see themselves as owners of assets rather than active members of the political community. Asset ownership in the new populist programmes is seen not merely as an economic instrument, but as essential to the membership of civil society rather than membership of the political community. On this score asset conversion has many similarities with the New Liberal understanding of property examined in Chapter 1.

The asset conversion programme involves two key initiatives: first, it aims to create assets for farmers, small businessmen and the urban and rural poor. Under the land distribution scheme that has existed for a few decades in Thailand, small farmers are given land but are not allowed to mortgage these assets. Similarly, in urban areas there are street hawkers who own stalls but are unable to realize the economic gains from these assets. In this case the Thaksin government has adopted administrative measures to allow farmers or the urban poor to convert or realize their implicit assets for economic gain (Lian 2003). Secondly, the assumption is that the asset conversion programme, by moving people into the formal market, will substantially reduce the rates of interest charged within the informal market. Moving individuals from the informal to the formal market system will therefore increase the saving and credit of underprivileged groups. As Lian (2003: 2) points out:

> Given that the large part of the Thai informal economy involves economic activities that are either illegal or not facilitated by the formal market mechanism, the capital creation initiative could cyclically create and structurally boost the formal economy.

Regardless of the debate over the economic benefits or otherwise of the asset conversion programme, what is important to emphasize here is the manner in which the new populist policies are directed towards creating 'enterprising' subjects – an enterprise culture for a market economy.

Health scheme

Besides these entrepreneurial programmes, one of the most important social programmes is the national health scheme that, in effect, amounts to a programme of a universal health coverage. The so-called

30 Baht Scheme, while not perhaps intended to provide a universal national health scheme, has in effect provided the foundation for a system of universal health care. Although the programme has run into a number of financial problems, it is clear that it is electorally popular and the Thaksin government remains committed to its main features. Disregarding the circumstances and the specifics of how this health scheme came about, it is clear that it has many of the attributes of social citizenship identified with the classical welfare state. At least on this score the 30 Baht Health Scheme runs counter to the entrepreneurial thrust of the TRT social policies.

Apart from the universal health insurance programme overall, the broad tenor of the social policies introduced by the Thaksin regime is geared towards the creation of entrepreneurial forms of conduct. Approaching it in this manner highlights the innovative way in which these various governance projects seek to impose market discipline through the constitution of new forms of social policy. But it is here that we see the real importance of these new third way policies which give a new meaning to the notion of market citizenship seeking to include individuals within the economic sphere. This is a very different form of claim making couched in terms of inclusion and participation within the market rather than in the form of social solidarity in opposition to the market as was the case with social citizenship. The common structural logic between otherwise very different third way strategies lies in the attempts to constitute a mode of sociability different from that which informed the social democratic grammar of the social question.

Towards authoritarian statism?

The election of the Thaksin government has transformed the Thai political system in significant ways. Much of this transformation is towards a form of populism. And there is little doubt that Thaksin fits the populist bill on several counts. He embodies a highly personalized style of leadership that continually invokes the idea of the Thai people, appeals to a notion of albeit 'soft' Thai nationalism, and depends on a broad cross-class constituency; he also endeavours to keep his coalition together with the introduction of a broad range of social policies. Given that Thailand had both a constitution with well-developed checks and balances as well as a steady commitment to neo liberal economics, the rapid consolidation of this populist politics is indeed surprising. However, as we have seen, the constitution presented few obstacles to Thaksin, who succeeded in marginalizing those elements of the constitution such as the Constitutional Court that may have restrained the consolidation of executive power. At the same time he neatly used those provisions of the constitution that enabled him to effectively sideline the parliamentary opposition such as through its restriction on the right to launch motions of no confidence.

Thaksin's relation to neo liberalism is far more complex. He clearly does not fit in with what we have called the first wave of neo-liberal populism; indeed, his programme was explicitly designed to protect domestic capital from the effects of the post-Asian economic crisis IMF package. But clearly this does not mean a wholesale retreat from the market model. In fact what is evident is that as Thaksin consolidates his power he is intent on pursuing economic reforms, such as the privatization of utilities. But the real significance of his populist programmes lies in the way that these governance programmes have attempted to 'socialize neo liberalism' through the introduction of a range of new social contracts. 'Thaksinomics', as it has now been dubbed, is more appropriately seen as a way of constituting a new form of market citizenship and welfare governance that is very different from the model of social citizenship that informed the postwar welfare state.

Thailand provides a good illustration of this new form of market citizenship. The organization and delivery of new social contracts, as Hewison (2003a, 2003b, 2005) has argued, have been central to the policy agenda of the government of Thaksin Shinawatra. In short, what is significant about the Thaksin government is that even though it is led by one of Thailand's leading capitalists and counts among its number some of Thailand's richest individuals, it has been defined largely in terms of its social policy agenda.

Social policy has been a pivotal component of the new statecraft that has enabled Thaksin to mobilize around a political project that creates a new relationship between state and the – imagined – political community around what we call the enhancement of entrepreneurial capacities. To the extent that this is a social contract it involves a new form of contract that is based not on social rights – claims against the market – but in the mutual obligation of individuals to participate in the market economy. Participation and inclusion suggest an understanding of citizenship that differs sharply from a view of social claims based on rights or entitlements within political society. In the new populist social contracts, social claims are based on performance and conduct within the formal economic system. These contracts put into place by the TRT are directed at creating new modes of sociability and conduct that promote entrepreneurial responsibilities by individuals and groups who, through these efforts, manage to achieve greater economic independence and participation.

It is in this sense that the particular market model that Thaksin is seeking to establish is properly described as the statecraft of neo-liberal populism. Weyland (2004) makes the valid point that the second wave of neo-liberal populism – that is, the marriage of neo liberalism and populism – is much more concerned with social rather than economic issues. Thaksin clearly falls into this second wave. However, we need to view this neo-liberal populism not simply as the tilt back towards the social away from narrowly economic issues, but as a broad-based effort to reshape the internal architecture of the state. What this chapter argues is that the 'socialization' of neo liberalism that we see in various third way governance projects frames issues of poverty and inequality in a way that is entirely different from that which governed the social democratic logic of the old social question. In other words, neo-liberal populism is a project of statecraft that is directed towards changing both the purpose, infrastructure and institutional practices of public authority.

Neo liberal populists like Thaksin seek to constitute new modes of sociability that operate within market forms through quite innovative social policy projects. These, in effect, form new technologies of public action that create new forms of social regulation. But the clear consequence of these new modes of social association and the related notions of inclusion on which they depend is the mobilization of conceptions of community that marginalize material and class relations of conflict. To the extent that these social policies appeal to targeted groups they remain policy-defined categories such as the 'urban poor' who are not political actors, but those whose status is defined by the access to – and inclusion within – the market.

Alongside these changes is a drift towards a new form of authoritarian politics. Political opposition is made illegitimate or a part of the discredited structure of old politics. In Thaksin's words:

> Upon coming to office, many ruling parties try to do all they can to hang on to power, while those in the opposition try their utmost to topple the government and assume power themselves. Virtually anything initiated by the government is resisted by such opposition without considering whether the government's actions are in the best interests of the people. *Such adversary politics may not be for the best interest of the people. On the contrary, it may be a betrayal of our*

social contract to the people. (Thaksin quoted in Pasuk 2004; emphasis in original)

But this is authoritarian politics that does not go back to the blunt notion of coercion and intimidation of the military era. Rather, this new politics is more akin to what Poulantzas over three decades ago called 'authoritarian statism'. He defines authoritarian statism as that which:

> differs considerably from that of the national-popular body composed of free citizens – individuals who are equal before the law – or, to put it another way, from that of the institutionalised dissociation between public and private which is the cornerstone of traditional representative democracy. (Poulantzas, 1978: 238)

Running through this new authoritarian statist mode of political regulation is an attempt to shape and discipline social conduct in civil society in a way that is inimical to the development of the pluralism and antagonism so vital to democratic politics. But the most significant consequence of this new populist market citizenship is to shift social claims away from the representative structures of political society towards a managerial and technocratic governance of civil society. Depoliticization and neo-liberal populism converge with various forms of third way politics in seeking to shift social claims from political society to a new managerial civil society. It is these new forms of social and political regulation that form the cutting edge of neo liberal populist statecraft.

7
The New Politics of Inclusion

Statecraft and ideas of welfare

This volume started off with the puzzle that the recent emphasis on social policy or social development went alongside the dominance of the neo liberal market model. There is, in both advanced industrial and newly industrial countries, an anxiety linked to two main factors: the effects of privatization and deregulation on inequality, and the legitimacy of market reforms. In response to these anxieties there has been a concerted effort to place issues of social disadvantage and poverty at the centre of a new social agenda. Not surprisingly, international development agencies have turned their attention to a determined effort at promoting what has now entered the development lexicon as 'pro-poor policies' which are now considered to be vital to both good economic and political governance. Indeed, the very fact that developmental agencies now assess even their most cherished economic policies in terms of their impact on poverty is a striking departure from the era of the earlier 'Washington Consensus'. In a similar fashion, the European Union has made the fight against social exclusion one of its objectives. At the European Council meeting in Lisbon in March 2000, member countries were asked to take decisive action to eradicate poverty by 2010 (Atkinson 2002), and members were also required to come up with national plans for social inclusion within the framework of the EU's open method of coordination. To the extent that this is an emerging politics of welfare, it is one framed in terms of inclusion or participation within the market or economic life.

It is this new politics of inclusion that is most distinctive of recent initiatives in social and welfare governance and has been described as a 'new pluralism' by Midgley (2003). He suggests that it: 'has halted the apparently inexorable expansion of state welfare and, at the same time, found an equilibrium that rejects the totalising intentions of institutionalism as well as the insensitivity of residualist thinking' (Midgley 2003: 4). Identifying similar trends in the transformation of the welfare state in advanced industrial states Gilbert (2002) brands this as an 'enabling state'. Whatever the label given to these new initiatives, what links these inclusive strategies, ranging from the UK's New Labour third way to the World Bank's pro-poor policies, is a concern with the exclusion of those inflicted by 'diswelfare' – that is, groups and individuals who have lost out in the headlong rush towards programmes of market reform, deregulation, and privatization. What is noteworthy about these social policies is that they are framed in terms of linking the worlds of welfare and work. At the same time these new strategies for social inclusion create a political space for 'new opportunities for differentially situated poor groups to challenge their economic and political exclusion' (Houtzager 2003: 1). Inclusion and its associated welfare governance are directed at enhancing individual capacities and endowments for participation within the economic mainstream. It is also equally concerned with delimiting a new terrain for engagement and deliberation on issues of poverty and social exclusion.

Without much doubt this preoccupation with issues of poverty and exclusion is more than just warmed-up neo liberalism. Even if the policies that define these new inclusionary programs are tepid, its most decisive effects may lie in providing for a new space for engagement on issues of poverty. But, then, what of the answer to our puzzle? It is to be found in unravelling the complexities of neo liberalism not merely as a set of market-oriented programmes and policies, but as a series of variegated statecraft projects that seek to reconstitute the state. In a nutshell, we need to understand the emergence of these new strategies of inclusion within the context of the steady erosion of both the developmental state in newly industrializing countries such as Korea and the welfare state in advanced industrialized countries of Western Europe. What is most distinctive about the new welfare is that it establishes modes of social regulation and arenas for debating social policy that remain within the precincts of the market model. While conceding that the deliberation and engagement over social issues is more salient in the first decade of the twenty-first century the terms of this engagement of the politics of inclusion are different from that which distinguished the social democratic experiment of the postwar era. This above all indicates 'clear rejection of the principles of social democracy: a commitment to equality and redistributive justice, principles of co-operation, sharing of risks and solidarity' (L. Jayasuriya 1996). It is the terms of this social engagement and its articulation within the state that provides the rudiments of the answer to our initial puzzle. 'Inclusion' is an expression of an underlying political or statecraft project which establishes forms of social regulation that are congruent with the dominance of neo liberalism.

The social policies explored in this volume – be they in the form of workfare policies in the UK, Australia or the USA, transnational social policies and the social market in South Korea or populist market citizenship in Thailand – are a component of statecraft projects. Statecraft, then, can be seen in terms of the initiation and implementation of policies by political agents that 'elaborate and regularize fundamental relationships between state and society' (Malloy 1991: 4). Put differently, it focuses not so much on the state as on the processes of state transformation. Social policies here are the blunt edge through which new projects of statecraft are implemented and serve to establish new forms of social regulation within the state. But, more importantly, these statecraft projects help to reconstitute the relationship between citizens and the broader political community or simply put, it alters regimes of citizenship.

It is this emphasis on social policy as statecraft that distinguishes this volume compared with other contemporary approaches to social policy. In analysing these new initiatives Gough (2000: 19) makes the valid point that 'in an increasingly competitive world of welfare states can provide a competitive advantage to capitalism with different moral underpinning and welfare outcomes'. Although Gough is persuasive on this point, and in fact may well provide one answer to our initial puzzle, these taxonomies of welfare (e.g. Gough 2000, and Esping-Andersen 1990) overlook the fact that the postwar strategies of welfare were not just fused with capitalism, but underpinned a 'social democratic grammar' of politics. Instead what we find is that this social democratic experiment has been severely eroded. In this regard the most problematic aspect of classificatory approaches lies in the tendency to regard 'welfare' as a given; but, as Pinker has reminded us, 'ideas of welfare' have always remained complex and highly variable. No doubt classificatory systems have value in comparative social policy analysis, but these classificatory regimes obscure the broader context of state transformation which gives rise to – and is in turn reinforced by – certain structures and ideas of welfare. Welfare is statecraft.

Therefore the argument is that we need to understand neo liberalism not merely as an economic programme, but rather as a set of often diverse political or statecraft projects intended to reshape the bound-aries of the state and also the nature of the relationship between state and civil society. It is within the interstices of this developing statecraft that we need to identify and locate political projects such as British Labour's third way or Kim Dae Jung's social market project. Third way welfare governance is couched in terms of inclusion and participation within the market and this clearly differentiates it from the social citi-zenship model of welfare as compensation or redistribution to redress the vagaries and inequalities produced by the working of market forces. One of the consistent themes running across the analysis depicted here is this shift in ideas of welfare from social to economic constitutionalism and the ramifications of these changes on what Nettl (1968) called 'stateness' or conceptions of statehood.

In this regard, the burden of the argument advanced in this volume is to understand the evolving 'inclusive' welfare governance as a statecraft project. This approach is exemplified in the analysis of social gover-nance in newly industrializing countries. To cite an example, this is well illustrated in the analysis of East Asian social policy, particularly that of Korea. In this instance, we have endeavoured to go beyond the limita-tions imposed by the classificatory approach to understanding Korean social policies. For many years, East Asian social policies have been seen as welfare laggards and have been variously described as Confucian wel-farism, productivism, societal welfare or enterprise welfare. But these welfare laggards have made significant strides in matters of welfare pro-vision and cognate social programmes (Ramesh 2004). Yet the analysis of these emerging welfare regimes in East Asia has been strangely trapped in a futile debate over whether these welfare initiatives signal a move towards one of Esping-Andersen's 'worlds of welfare'; or, alterna-tively, if these welfare regimes are, as Holliday (2005) argues, still essen-tially productivist in the sense that they are subordinate to the developmental state. On both sides of this argument there is a hidden teleological trajectory implying that any social policy change has to be conceived of in terms of whether or not it meets the standards and requirements of the European welfare state.

But this orientation to social policy misses the point that what has changed in both the advanced industrializing and newly industrial state is the very terms of engagement over social questions – that is, the analysis, understanding and response to the social inequalities created by the capitalist market. The strength of this statecraft perspective approach to social governance is that it allows us move beyond this unhelpful debate and identify the new politics of inclusion as a political response that manages both domestic pressures for legitimacy and the international imperatives of competitive global economy. The collapse of both the social democratic model and the developmental state has altered the context of welfare governance in both advanced industrial and newly industrializing countries.

In the case of Korean social policies, we argue (see above, Chapter 5) that they are best understood in terms of the development of a new social market statecraft model. But the crucial point here is that this social market model was distinct from the traditional welfare state which entrenches social citizenship through various redistributive mechanisms. At the same time it needs to be distinguished from the various forms of East Asian productivism which made social policy an ancillary to the developmental state. Therefore the identification of recent Korean developments in social policy within the ambit of the European welfare models or a mutation of the productivist approach fails to recognise that the social market model is in fact a distinctive social policy within the constraints of a neo liberalism context. The social market model was a political exercise in statecraft which sought to change both the practices and language of public action that articulated welfare governance. Furthermore, the South Korean example also serves to underline the fact these projects of statecraft are not simply about creating new frameworks of public authority, but provide new meaning to the purposes under which that public authority is exercised. In this sense welfare or the social market model is as much about constituting forms of stateness (Nettl 1968) – that is, boundaries between state and society – as it is about welfare. In brief, welfarism in South Korea needs to be seen as part and parcel of a much broader state transition from the developmental to the regulatory state.

But we need to be careful here and underline the fact that these projects are not simply the product of one template. There are considerable differences between the coercive populist social policies of Thaksin and the much more participatory social market model of South Korea. Gilbert (2002: 47) notes that the enabling state:

> ... will not take one distinct form. Just as there have been different types of welfare states, variation within the basic pattern of the enabling state are likely to emerge in response to historic and cultural differences among the advanced industrial nations.

However, both advanced and newly industrializing countries exhibit a reframing of social policy within the framework of the market.

And, despite their many differences, all these statecraft projects are, in one way or another, variants of the 'third way'. Here, the notion of the 'third way' is used as a generic term to depict how welfare and social policy is reframed within the structures of 'economic constitutionalism' (see Chapter 1).

What is distinctive about this volume is that it suggests that social policy analysis is not about social policies per se, but rather about the organization of the regulatory spaces in which these policies are formed – the terms of engagement of the social policy debate. For instance, the extent to which the third way can be recognised as an ideology lies not in terms of programmatic ideas, but in its central concern with governance itself. At the same time, inclusion, as we suggest in Chapter 5 on Korea, is something like a technology of public action that shapes the organization of these emerging forms of welfare governance. This was evident in the analysis of recent initiatives of transnational welfare governance which led us to the conclusion that the substantive effect of this governance was that it was directed not so much to specifying policy alternatives as to shaping an institutional framework around which social policy alternatives are debated (see Chapter 4).

Germane to our argument is that these institutional frameworks themselves embody their own political bias. Frameworks of welfare governance are distinguished by, to use Schattschneider's (1960) telling phrase, 'mobilization of bias'. This bias is evident less in the content of policies than in the broader framework of governance that privileges certain policy alternatives over others, favours certain kinds of issues, advantages certain actors, and legitimates specific forms of understandings of social disadvantage over others. In this respect, our approach differs from those such as Houtzager (2003) who seek to discover 'a polity in which societal actors and state agents compete for, and reach out to, excluded groups, while such groups will coalesce into political actors and negotiation coalitions from below and across the public–private divide' (Houtzager 2003: 22). While this approach to the politics of inclusion has the admirable benefit of incorporating the state into the analysis, it fails to answer the more fundamental question of how these welfare strategies articulate the basic relationship of individual citizens to political authority.

For example, the widespread use of contractual forms of governance in workfare-type policies tends to privilege an understanding of individual autonomy as economic independence rather than a notion of democratic citizenship (Chapter 3). Along similar lines, in the analysis of Thailand it was shown that the mechanism through which populist social policies such as asset conversion helped to shape new forms of entrepreneurial conduct and subjects (Chapter 6). And, furthermore, our analysis of the transnational global social policy of the World Bank revealed how the procedural requirements of the PRSP privilege those policy alternatives that work in tandem with macroeconomic economic policies geared towards sustainable economic growth. These market disciplines are not imposed through specific policies, but through a system of contractual governance that imposes procedural requirements which act as a sieve to filter the range of policy alternatives available to domestic policy makers. And this is the point about the 'mobilization of bias'; it acts like a sieve that favours certain actors, issues and understanding above others and this is an inherently political process.

But there is one final twist to this 'mobilization of bias': these new institutional frameworks function in a way that depoliticizes social governance. Much of the proposed policy solutions as well as the broader governance structure in which these policy alternatives take shape posits a particular conception of politics as management and consensus where this: 'focus on legitimation is ultimately depoliticizing. As it posits in advance a unified community, it withdraws the revolutionary energy long associated with claims to universality' (Dean 2002: 171).

It is in this sense that the emerging governance of welfare provides for a form of politics as anti-politics. This is clearly seen in the ways in which transnational social policy works to move the forum for making claims on the state from the political society couched in the language of rights to a managerial 'civil sphere' where social claims are organized through the language and practices of contractualism (see Chapters 3 and 4). This, in turn, implies the identification of prior pre-political community whether it is framed in terms of community participation or localism. But the broader point is that these new regulatory spaces of social policy are pushed outside of the formal political arena; and this is an aspect that is missing in the approach taken by Houtzager (2003) to the politics of inclusion.

In short, the statecraft approach allows us to examine more clearly how the terms of engagement over the social issues in the new welfare pluralism reflects a distancing from the 'grammar of politics' that constituted the social question in the postwar social democratic experiment. The growth of the so-called third way politics from Lula in Brazil, New Labour in Britain to South Korea identifies a political imperative to reconstitute the social question within the logic of the market: a search for a 'social democracy without social democracy, that is to say a search for ways of responding to the "social question" outside of the terms of engagement of the social democratic model'. This is not to say these attempts have been a mere façade for market policies; far from it, it has meant a real departure from hard-edged programmes of market reform and, as we have seen in the Korean case, led to the introduction of substantial social initiatives. But these initiatives differ from postwar social constitutionalism in that it 'subordinates social welfare policies to economic considerations, such as the need for labour force flexibility, international competition, and the imposition of limits on deficit spending' (Gilbert 2002: 43). The 'social' is situated not in opposition to the logic of the market but within the imperatives of the economic order.

But the most important point is that the transformation of terms of engagement on issues of social policy and governance is related to the serious erosion of the salience of class or labour as social forces that drove the postwar social democratic experiment and the associated framework of welfare governance. It was not just the force of economic circumstances that made class marginal as a political force but also an imaginative underpinning of those:

> 'communities of interest' that provided the backdrop for democratic politics in the twentieth century. The working class was never only a homogeneous category of wage earners. Whatever the stage of capitalism, the working class was always in the process of being formed. It had to be made into an operative unity – one with recognized public meanings and an active political presence. (Eley 2002: 397)

These underpinnings of the political vocabulary of pluralism formed the bedrock of those institutions and practices of representation that were at the heart of the welfare state (Jayasuriya 2005).

As the 'idea of welfare' – to use Pinker's useful phrase – mutates from social constitutionalism to economic constitutionalism, there is a more profound change in the organization of social relations and associations. It is in this sense that neo liberalism brings with it a new form of liberal sociability which transforms in a basic way the understanding of social association. It does this by framing social policy along lines of economic participation and seeking to create new subjects whose identities and interests are not determined on the basis of membership of interest or class communities, but by the degree to which these individuals possess those capacities to participate and compete within the productive mainstream of the economy. Indeed, it creates a normative framework that is more congruent with the traditions of the ordo liberalism and the New Liberalism of during the early twentieth century (see Chapter 1).

In fact, a striking aspect here is a move away from an insurance or redistribution framework – social policy as income management – to an understanding of social policy, and, more broadly, the social sphere, as the furthering or reinforcing of an inclusive and participatory market economy. This, above all, constitutes a significant reconstitution of the language of liberalism.

The next sections of this chapter examine how this 'mobilization of bias' is exemplified in the way in which the 'idea of welfare' has changed from the social constitutionalism of the postwar period to the emerging structure of economic constitutionalism. But this mobilization of bias is evident not simply in the privileging of certain policy alternatives – important as this is – but in a more significant transformation of the nature of social association.

The 'social question' and the social democratic grammar of politics

The 'social question' which animated postwar social democracy in Western Europe was driven by an underlying set of social and political relations that made possible a social democratic grammar of politics through which the social question could be framed. It is this social democratic order that has now been fundamentally challenged by neo liberalism, posing problems for social democrats and others who wish to pursue the social question in this new phase of neo liberal economics. In this context, 'third way' politics has become highly visible and salient for those committed to neo liberal economic ideology – be they in the advanced industrial or in newly industrializing countries.

'Third way' political projects represent not so much an integrated set of programmes, or, even less, a third way between social democracy and neo liberalism, but rather a concerted effort to incorporate the 'social' within the frame of the emerging economic constitutionalism. What it allows is a pathway towards a mode of neo liberal sociability or a 'social democracy without social democracy'. And, even more significantly, this liberal sociability carries with it a particular model of social association. In fact, it could be said to constitute a new form of the 'social question'.

To help situate this understanding of the new 'social question', we contrast two models of social association: one based on the centrality of class and its struggles for recognition and representation within the social democratic grammar of politics; and the other, on those communities that are defined not in terms of material relations of conflict but in terms of access to market participation. The emergence of the latter model of social association represents a shift between the insurance and compensatory models that underpinned the postwar welfare state and the participatory society model that characterizes social regulation in various political projects.

A more generic understanding of the various third way formulations in Western Europe as well as the NICs reflects the emergence of a particular form of neo liberal politics. This is one which departs decisively from the core issues and concerns of the postwar social democratic political project. Social democracy in Western Europe – we will return to the newly industrialized democracies shortly – was never static; it was a constantly evolving set of programmes and policies (Eley 2002). However, what was common to all these manifestations or variations of social democratic policies was that they were driven by an attempt to respond to what is revealingly called the 'social question'. The essence of these policies was that they were defined in terms of working towards redistribution through forms of income management. This was largely a matter of reducing the insecurities, inequalities, and vulnerabilities created by capitalist industrialization, and was to be achieved, at least in the postwar period, without any major dislocations or instability within the market order (see, for example, Moene and Wallerstein 1995; Judt 1997, Moschonas 2000).

By formulating the social question in this way the social democratic project, despite all its concessions to the market, opened up a range of political possibilities. This was mainly through the contestation and competition between the ideological logic and social forces of the 'market' and social solidarity. While postwar social democracy in its Keynesian version radically altered the terrain particularly through the contestation between the market and social solidarity, the essential components of the 'social question' – the terms of engagement if you will – remained constant. However, the social question so framed is much more than a particular set of programs and policies.[1] It is structured within a grammar of politics[2] and specific ideological and organizational traditions that defined postwar social democracy.

Indeed, as Moschonas (2000) argues convincingly, social democracy and the social question that underpinned it 'specified a *"way of seeing" the social and the economic, a model of problems and solutions*, which furnished the outline and prototype of "normal politics", particularly during the trente glorieuses' (Moschonas 2000: 6) (author's emphasis). In a highly original piece of analysis, social democracy, for Moschonas, constitutes something like a relatively distinct 'system of action' (p. 313), which incorporates electoral, organizational, and ideological elements, among others. These elements in turn serve to carve out a distinctive space within postwar Western European politics. It is beyond the confines of this chapter to explore these elements in detail, but for our purposes what is important is that it was only within this broad system of social democratic action or grammar of politics that the 'social question' was given shape, organization, coherence, and meaning.

Pivotal to the social question is the fact that in advanced capitalist democracies the constitutional as well as the growing societal recognition has given shape to a larger politics of 'interest' and representation. In short, the essence of 'social constitutionalism' was the mediation and negotiation of social interests. And integral to this social settlement was the central role of labour in the social constitutional framework of postwar social democracy.[3] Despite the institutional compromises of the post war social settlements

> class kept its centrality. It was necessary for making sense of the society under capitalism – from the organizing of social life and the mapping of human differences to the charting of inequalities in the social distribution of value produced in the economy. (Eley 2002: 394)

In this context, the impact of neo liberalism has been to critically undermine this accepted grammar of politics in the social democratic state. However, under neo liberalism all of the elements of the social democracy – electoral, organizational, and ideological – have undergone changes. In each of these elements there has been significant – albeit modest – modifications that ultimately add up to far-reaching changes in the underlying grammar of politics. It is not possible to examine in this volume the detailed specifics of these changes, such as electoral dealignment. Nevertheless, it needs to be mentioned that these changes have the ability to influence the capacity of social democratic parties to sustain the social democratic experiment of the postwar period. Taken as a whole, these changes tend to clog the arteries of social democracies and the chances of fending off a fatal attack will depend to a considerable extent sharpening various adroit survival strategies within the context of neo liberal dominance.

Admittedly the prognosis then is far from terminal and, without doubt, social democratic parties continue to thrive within a variety of neo liberal conditions. But the real thrust of this analysis is that the core of social democracy – its underlying social and political order – confronts real and substantial challenges. Indeed, the analysis of Thatcherism by

Hall (1988) and Hall and Jacques (1989) – although sometimes seen unfairly as a precursor to New Labour's third way – was intended to alter dramatically the thinking of the political left about the evisceration of both the material and the ideological foundation of the postwar social democratic compromise. These theorists maintained that Thatcherism remained unique in seeking to create a new political project – a neo liberal programme – that would fill the political void created by the collapse of the social democratic compromise. Differing from Giddens (1998), whose understanding of these changes had an air of sociological inevitability, Hall's analysis placed more weight on the profound changes that were occurring within the underlying grammar of social democratic politics.

It is clear, then, that the advent of neo liberalism has posed fundamental challenges for social democratic politics. Social democratic politics had either to adjust to the new realities of neo liberal politics or be excluded from political power. It is this political void that new policies of social democratic programmes sought to fill. But the clear ramification of this process was the abandonment of the social experiment and the social question that formed the backdrop of social democratic politics for much of the twentieth century. This, however, does not mean – as we have consistently argued – that social democracy – either as a political force or even as political rhetoric – disappears. But what it does mean is that it leads to a longer-term unravelling of the ideological and organizational foundation of the postwar social democratic compromise. Despite the extent to which postwar social democracy reflected a drastic revision of the classical socialist programmes and policies, it still pitted the logic of the market beside that of social solidarity. Welfare was at the heart of this often conflictual and contradictory logic of the market and social solidarity. And it is above all this politics of social conflict that is absent in the new economic constitutionalism. So that 'social democracy' is on the verge of a change in identity because it is no longer capable of embodying that 'social experiment of enormous promotions and because it is no longer capable of definitively turning its back on the logic and politics solidarity either. It thus finds itself in strategic "intermediate" because its identity its intermediate' (Moschonas 2000: 295).

But how relevant is this argument for those newly industrializing countries (NICS) whose organizational and ideological traditions of social democracy have been marginal? In the case of Brazil with Cardoso's PMDB, and Lula's Workers Party, some argument can be made for the claim that these social democratic parties confront the same challenges and problems encountered by their counterparts in Western

Europe.[4] Nevertheless, this is hard to sell in relation to countries such as Korea or even Thailand where an attempt has been made to develop a new form of social policies and contracts. Rather, the relevance of this argument possibly lies in Western Europe and other countries such as the NICs seeking to socialize neo liberalism, and in Western Europe, there has been a convergence towards a form of third way politics.

This convergence has followed different paths in Western Europe and the NICs. In Western Europe there has been a defensive adjustment to the impact of the process of market reform in dissolving the material and ideological foundations of the social democratic compromise. But, in many of the NICs the third way programmes examined in this volume represent an effort to formulate a new social question in a context where previously a social democratic response to these questions appears to have been foreclosed. Importantly, in both instances – the West European and the NICs – this convergence has sought to reshape the 'social question'. For many Western European states there has been a steady retreat from the postwar social democratic compromise. In either case the significance of third way politics lies in the fact that it represents an effort to develop a model of socialized neo liberalism or market citizenship in the absence of what may be termed a 'social democratic grammar of politics'. It is within the framework that we need to understand 'third way' politics as strategies of statecraft that seek to reshape the relationship between citizens and the political community.

A new social question?

Sociability conceived of in neo liberal terms implies a model of social association whose core social categories are determined by the degree of accessibility to market participation. For example, a group such as the urban poor is identified and targeted for intervention on the basis of its exclusion from the economic mainstream rather than being identified as a political group seeking recognition and representation through political contestation. To take another example, in the transnational social policy of the World Bank, groups are defined in terms of their various endowments of social capital. Whatever be the case, forms of sociability depend on building social ties that are independent of the material relations of conflict within the economic sphere. This model of social association stands out sharply against the centrality of class and class conflict that defined the social democratic experiment of the postwar period. As a result, the new welfare governance can be interpreted as a mode of social regulation through the implementation of new forms of contract between citizens and the state. These initiatives are directed not at enhancing social citizenship but at regulating various forms of entrepreneurial conduct within society.

These forms of social regulation are to be found not merely in the substantive content of social policies, but in the very governance of these welfare programmes. Through systems of contractualism these programmes facilitate a new framing of the 'social' that diminishes the political conflicts between social collectivities, which was such a distinctive component of the politics of the social citizenship of the welfare state. In much of 'third way' thinking this convergence is clearly not about any specific set of programmes or policies, but, rather, about seeking to foster certain forms of governance arrangements that aim to overcome the conventional binaries – public vs private, state vs market, and national vs international. These arrangements have served to define the left and right ideological spectrums of advanced industrial democracies in such a manner that the third way is

> less a concrete programme of government with specific proposals in the manner of, say, neo-liberalism or Keynesianism, than a framework deliberately designed to overcome certain dualisms and realign values and policies in hitherto unthinkable ways. To a great extent this is an ongoing project whose precise boundaries and implications have yet to be settled. (Bastow, Martin and Pels 2002: 2)

Indeed, in this way the pivotal dualism that the third way and associated welfare strategies attempt to transcend is that between the 'social' and the 'market' so that the social is now cast within the broader frame of economic participation and independence.

One notable consequence of this erosion of the material and ideological foundations of the social democratic project has been a growing depoliticization of social conflict. Perhaps the most glaring example of this shift is the new language of public discourse embodied in notions of values and ethics that permeate the new social democracy. In fact, this constitutes a common thread running through the various diverse third way programs to the extent that they all suggest that the content of social democracy is to be found in a broad set of values. These values are identified as fairness and justice rather than in terms of the confrontation over a set of economic and social relations. In this respect, 'a key aspect of all third way ideologies is the emphasis on ethics and morality – often though not always – tending towards an anti materialism' (Bastow, Martin and Pels 2002: 276). This is most evident in various forms of workfare programmes introduced in the US, Britain, and Australia, emphasizing duties and responsibilities – not rights – of communities. Society, Mrs Thatcher famously said does not exist, but in contrast, Pels (2002: 195), in a perceptive analysis, notes that for third way ideas, society: 'does not merely exist, but immediately also exists as the *good* society, as a form of solidarity which implies a social duty for individuals to build 'a genuine community of citizens'.

The third way, therefore, remains a hybrid combination of communitarianism and market freedom which may take on an illiberal authoritarian form. Not surprisingly, third way ideologies end up moralizing the economy in terms such as 'community' and 'responsibility'. But to the extent that this is a form of anti-materialism it works to occlude the material relations of conflict and power embedded within capitalism. The social is defined within – rather than against – the economic order. And this is the real importance of these various formulations of neo liberal sociability. It works to neutralize social conflicts by making the market the site of ethical rather than social contestation. Accordingly, the notion of social capital, which will be examined in the next section, has been used to constitute an arena of managed welfare governance that lies outside of political society.

Before turning to social capital it would be useful at this point to distinguish between political and civil society. Political society reflects the conflicts and plurality of interests that are so essential to the functioning of representative politics. In this conception of politics the allocation of rights is central to the emergence of the welfare state. Civil society, in the way used here, is not understood in terms of Oakeshott's 'civic association' which can be defined in terms of an association in which individuals and groups willingly pursue their own autonomous 'ends'. But rather what we find in the new welfare governance is a civil sphere that is managed and administered by the state for broadly economic objectives – an enterprise association in Oakeshott's (1975) terms. In this instance, a managerial civil society is one in which the state governs indirectly in a situation where groups and/or communities are often administratively defined. What matters here is that claims against the state are not founded on rights but on meeting various standards or criteria of social inclusion.

In essence, the new politics of social inclusion calls not just for a new model of social association – based on market inclusion – but constitutes a set of governance arrangements that lies outside of political society. It is within these governance arrangements that social claims are made on the state. Further, this managerial civil society enables the state to manage groups and individuals by differentiating between them in terms of criteria such as economic participation; managerial civil society allows the state to distinguish and constitute different arenas of governance for various communities and groups – be they single mothers, or the unemployed or migrants. Governance is directed at the indirect regulation – through techniques such as contractual governance – of individual control and values. Hence the most important consequence of the new welfare governance lies in shifting the language and practice of liberalism from the pluralism of social interests to a new anti-pluralist liberalism of values.

Social capital and neo liberal sociability

But there is within this new politics of social inclusion an intensive effort to enhance the capacities of individuals to participate within the market economy. One of the driving assumptions of various projects of social inclusion is that the failure to enter the economic mainstream, whether through lack of employment or income, reflects a lack of those attributes or endowments which are seen as an essential component in enhancing effective participation in the economy. Inclusion demands that public policy be directed at developing those capacities that individuals require to participate in the market economy.

But what this implies is a very different understanding of social association grounded not in terms of class, but on the degree to which individuals and groups possess those attributes necessary for functioning within the market economy. Nothing better illustrates these new models of social association than the way the concept of social capital has been used within the World Bank and other international agencies to develop new social policy strategies. In other words, the argument is that poverty and inequality are often considered to develop, or are sustained, because of a lack of social capital.

Social capital in this context denotes the contractual relations that denote a web of networks and social relationships that individuals can draw on in times of social and economic emergency (World Bank 1998).

The World Bank (2001: 47) defines social capital as:

> The role of social and political exclusion is particularly important. Some groups are excluded from political participation because they are too few in numbers to attract government attention, too weak to lobby effectively for their rights and interests, or too unimportant as voters or taxpayers in the eyes of the government. The poor may also

face social exclusion, both in the form of social discrimination (e.g., discrimination against women, ethnic or religious minorities, orphans, and single mothers) and in the form of not having adequate social capital – the networks of influential norms and established relationships that enable people to act in concert for mutual benefit.

Social capital is, in essence, the stock of capacities and skills that individuals possess and through which they compete in the economic mainstream. As such, this concept of social capital underlines a new framework for understanding social disadvantage and broader social relations embedded in various social processes. Public policy, in turn, is directed at modifying or enhancing those relationships. Social policy in particular is geared towards promoting forms of social conduct which are able to withstand the risks and vulnerabilities of the global economy.

These ideas were well illustrated by the World Bank's response to the Asian economic crisis in Thailand during 1997–98. On the one hand, World Bank policies and programmes during and after the crisis were driven by the recognition that the economic crisis required not merely a narrowly economic response, but also policies that dealt with the social fallout from the economic crisis. The Bank, by framing the social impact of the crisis in terms of social capital and community capacity, tended to deny, or at least to marginalise, the class inequalities of the social crisis. But what is noteworthy in the Bank's approach: 'is a desire to deny aspects of social relations that might be considered to operate within groups arranged horizontally in society. Specifically, the Bank appears to want to deny any class element in the social impact of the crisis' (Hewison 2002: 6).

This focus on social capital leads to an understanding of the 'social' that occludes underlying relationships of power that shape markets. Inequality is now defined in terms of participation in the economic sphere, rather than in terms of the redistribution of resources. Moreover, insofar as the capacity of individuals to weather the economic crisis is determined by endowments of social capital, it becomes a crisis of social capital. Framed in these terms the notion of social capital conveys a model of social organization and association very different from that which underpinned traditional postwar welfare state programs. Society,[5] as conceived by proponents of the social capital viewpoint, is composed of 'norms' and 'relationships' that can be mobilized for economic development (Fine 1999).

Social capital, at least in the formulations of the World Bank and other agencies, forms a new framework for justifying social expenditure in the terms of privileging economic inclusion within the market model rather than compensation or redistribution of material resources; and it is clearly based on a market rather than a social citizenship. From this perspective, social capital as an organizing framework tends to select those factors such as social norms, networks, relationships, and, more generally, a 'culture' that tends to exclude the structural and power inequalities embedded in economic institutions. In a sharp critique of social capital Harriss (2002: 119) points out that:

> civil society exists in a field of power – or that there are differences of power within the civil society – hardly seems to cross the minds of those who wish to see the space of civil society expanded, and that of the state (and perhaps of the market) reduced. The discourse is in fact deliberately apolitical, in way that is ultimately supportive of neoliberal orthodoxy.

In the formulations of the Post-Washington Consensus (PWC) of the World Bank and other multilateral agencies, civil society is used in the specific sense of paying due heed to the management and mobilization of social capital entrenched in civil society. And it is this social capital which is mobilized for the successful management of economic reform. From this perspective, multilateral agencies have inevitably sought to place a greater emphasis on the management and incorporation of nongovernmental organizations in the development of participatory decision-making processes. This is clearly evident in the meaning attached to social capital framed in terms of – and designed to enhance – the more effective participation and capabilities of individuals within the economic life of the community (see Chapter 2). This rationale is reflected in the emphasis placed on norms, values, and conduct that enable individuals to manage the vulnerabilities and risks of the global economy.

Whereas the earlier governance programmes of international agencies concentrated on developing the hard institutional infrastructure – such as credible legal institutions and strong property rights – needed for a market economy, the social capital perspective on governance complements this macroinstitutional framework with a sharper focus on the development of an appropriate set of values and norms. In fact, this thinking transcends the earlier debate about the relative efficacy of states and markets that drove both the Washington Consensus agenda and the debate over the East Asian 'economic miracle'. The clear highwater mark of the latter agenda as documented in the World Bank's

Miracle Report (World Bank 1993) stands in stark contrast to the subsequent bank's *Road to Recovery Report* (World Bank 1998) which was framed more in the language of norms, networks, and civil society, embodied in social capital. The critical point that underpins the 1998 Bank Report is that social capital embodies an understanding of individual independence as being one that is able to withstand the risks and vulnerabilities of the global economy. Within this conceptualization, programmes that embody ideas of social capital are seen as conducive to producing liberal subjects who possess the attributes of economic independence rather than political subjects participating within the public sphere. This provides another example of the manner in which the emergent neo liberal sociability reconstitutes liberalism not in pluralist terms, but in the degree to which an individual is able to meet certain standards of conduct and in this it converges with the ordo liberal ideas of an entrepreneurial society.

All of these new governance programmes highlight the consistent attempt made to socialize neo liberalism. It encompasses not just the 'social' but a new understanding of the state as one of enabling and regulating the forms of social conduct necessary to regulate economic order. Here social governance becomes a vital element in the regulation and management of the economic order, and aimed at creating a competitive and inclusive society. To this end it seeks to foster and regulate new forms of social conduct capable of withstanding the risks and future vulnerabilities of the ebbs and flow of the global economy. But these new forms of agency or capacities are directed not at the structures of economic and political power but at *managing* the spatial and individual deficiencies of social capital which are deemed to prevent the full economic participation of individuals.

The underlying objective of this policy strategy of new social programmes and policies – in a manner similar to workfare programmes in the US – is to link social citizenship not to membership in the political community but to the degree to which individuals are able to participate in the sphere of work. It calls on a model of social association that is defined on the basis of the extent to which groups are endowed with stocks of social capital. Consequently, the new welfare governance is directed towards managing often administratively defined groups – on the basis of social inclusion – rather than on the pluralism or the politics of 'interests' that drove the postwar model of social citizenship. It is at this point that concepts like social capital become more than mere technocratic labels, becoming seen as integral to demarcating an arena of welfare governance that lies outside the representative structures of political society.[6]

Inclusion and social democratic politics: new pathways

Returning to the initial puzzle of this volume our argument, then, is that various challenges to the neo liberal market model in newly industrial-izing countries such as Brazil and South Korea or Thailand indicate not the end of neo liberalism, but the transformation of the state that is tak-ing place in these countries. In this volume we have sought to concep-tualize and analyse these emerging forms of social policies as part of a broader statecraft project. Statecraft transforms statehood by transform-ing the rules, institutions and practices that determine the internal char-acter of the state as well as the broader political grammar that shapes the relationship of citizens to the broader political authority. Analysing social policy within this framework of state transformation presents a more meaningful and theoretical defensible way of understanding the political dynamics of social policies as against others such as those which focus on the various 'worlds of welfare' (e.g., Esping-Andersen). Welfare is statecraft. And this why the diverse programmes that we have examined in this study constitute multiple third ways that develop new regulatory spaces of social regulation that reshape the boundaries of state and society within the dominant model of neo liberalism.

One of the central characteristics of this socialized neo liberalism, especially in the NICs, as argued in the foregoing sections, has been the promotion of a new form of sociability, one that reconstitutes the social within the context of market virtues and values. These new social con-tracts that have been instituted by transnational agencies such as the World Bank or those adopted by countries such as Thailand need to be distinguished from the social democratic framing of the 'social ques-tion'. The clear dividing line here between the 'old' and the 'new' social question is to be found in the fact that these new social contracts are designed to further the promotion of economic independence and par-ticipation within the market as against an earlier preference for com-pensating or insuring against the effects of the market. It is this shift from income management to an inclusive society and the associated fos-tering of the entrepreneurial capacities of individuals that distinguishes this neo liberal sociability.

According to this argument, what is often understood as a challenge to the neo liberal market model turns out to be a way of entrenching a form of market citizenship. But this is not as simple as it sounds. It can-not be understood as a way of bringing back the 'social' into what has been conceived primarily as an economic agenda. Instead, the argument in this chapter has been to demonstrate that what is seen as the third way – and this goes beyond British New Labour – is an attempt to develop new modes of sociability that are congruent with the process of economic reform. Importantly, these new forms of sociability, then, stand in contrast to what we have described here as the 'social democratic logic' of the 'social question' that defined politics for much of the twentieth century. Instead of the social question being defined in terms of the collectivist social project that sought, however weakly, to seek compensation from the vagaries of the market, the new social question tries to locate 'social' governance within the economic sphere. It entails a radical shift that leads to the creation of a very different model of social association geared towards inclusion and participation within the market.

More significantly, this accentuation of inclusion also implies a different model of social association that appeals to forms of community and identity that are not based on class. It is at this point that these new third way projects represent an ideological hybrid of communitarianism and free markets, and also one that often combines with various forms of populist politics. This kind of politics leans heavily on notions of community that seek to manage various *'gemeinschaft'* communities such as families, ethnic groups, and/or territorial-based communities. Similarly, it seeks to target groups such as the 'urban poor', or 'working poor', whose defining feature is the exclusion from market participation rather than in terms of political struggles for recognition and representation. Invariably, these new neo liberal forms of sociability differ markedly from the politics of interest that sustained the postwar social democratic experiment in advanced capitalist states.

But our overriding conclusion is that the new politics of social inclusion provide the rudiments of statecraft that work to reorganize and restructure state power and modes of political representation. The more crucial issue this poses is whether the socialization of neo liberalism is only symbolic and merely reflects the dominant concerns of the neo liberal orthodoxy. There is much here – as we have argued – that reflects the dominant assumptions of neo liberalism. But neither is it a chimera. What the prevailing focus on social disadvantage and exclusion in varying social policy contexts does is to create a new framework in which issues of poverty and social disadvantage are deliberated. In this sense the new poverty debate contributes not so much in the articulation of specific and substantive policy recommendations, but in providing a context in which the deliberation over policy alternatives takes place. The core of the argument advanced here is that these new frameworks have created a space as well as new interests and identities around which policy deliberation now takes place. However, within this framework a number of innovative governance approaches seem possible and it does provide at least some space for progressive solutions to problems of poverty and social disadvantage.

The new welfare governance, then, provides a window into a fundamental transition from a liberal language of pluralism and interests to an 'anti-pluralist' language of values and legitimacy. My argument is that the transformation of the postwar welfare order reflects a deeper change from the constitutionalization of social interests – especially that of labour – that remained at the heart of the social state in the postwar period. In essence, this social state was underpinned by a set of embedded democratic relations defined by 'communities of interest', and the imaginative underpinning that enabled these interests to operate politically (Jayasuriya 2005). In contrast, the emerging politics of inclusion and welfare marginalizes the conflicts of interests and leads to the emergence of a politics of anti-politics. And it is this transformation, utilizing the language of liberalism, that stands out as the most salient and visible feature of the politics of inclusion.

It is clear that the terms of engagement over the social question have been irrevocably altered in recent years and we need to search for a progressive solution by extending the boundaries of the framework of the social market. I agree with Gough (2000: 216) that after 1989 capitalism is 'the only game in town'. But the game can be played according to different rules and here once again institutional precision is required'. In essence, we need to engage with the new framework and tease out its possible radical implications of economic constitutionalism – there is no going back to the postwar social democratic experiment. And the urgent task is to seek to articulate the new welfare governance in a way that recognises and acknowledges politics, and, through this approach, to develop a rights-based understanding of social inclusion. As pointed out earlier (see Chapters 2 and 3), a potential pathway for progressive change is to democratize emerging practices of social governance within the state. For example, we need to consider more carefully the prospects and possibilities of developing new forms of democratic proceduralism that develop robust forms of procedural rights within these new institutional practices. At the same time these practices need to be subject to public overview and scrutiny. In short, one possible avenue for developing or furthering aspects of the social market framework is to constitutionalize the new welfare governance, that is, by building in 'procedural rights' – such as the right of review for all citizens (Allars 2001).[7]

At the same time the new economic constitutionalism enables a more critical approach to property ownership than is implied in various third way formulations. Pierson (2005: 145) makes the valid point that:

> it is the very changes that are said by advocates of a Third Way to make a 'classical' social democratic strategy less easy to prosecute (above all, the supposed impact of globalisation) that mandate a renewed emphasis upon questions of property.

In other words, if the Keynesian income management is politically and economically unfeasible then there is a case for a return to an even earlier social democratic and socialist emphasis on the distribution and democratization of property and economic power. In fact, as we argued in Chapter 1, New Liberals like Green and Hobhouse and Hobson[8] were centrally preoccupied with the distribution of property and its implications for both the democratic functioning or capacities of individuals – reminiscent of Sen's idea of capability – and also as economic efficiency. These New Liberal precursors to economic constitutionalism may well lead us to exploring avenues for broadening and democratizing property ownership through such mechanisms as collective pension funds. But this would mean exploring not so much the idea of social market as what Elson (1988) has termed a 'socialization' of the market. Reframing the property and property rights as a complex social product – along the lines initiated by New Liberalism – would be an essential starting point. In this way, it might be possible to explore the strengths, limitations and possibilities of a more robust social democratic version of economic constitutionalism. But that remains a project for the future.

Notes

1 Economic Constitutionalism and Social Inclusion: Transforming Liberalism

1 For an excellent overview of some of the key features of the neo liberal revolution see Robison (2006). Robison's introduction is especially useful in highlighting the politics behind many of the neo liberal policies pursued over the course of the last two decades.

2 For an analysis of these ideas in the context of the development of a new Post-Washington Consensus, see Jayasuriya and Rosser (2001).

3 See Hartog (1983) for the notion of the 'technology of public action'. (See also Chapter 5 for a further elaboration of this concept.)

4 Cardoso is a sociologist by training who was leader of the school of dependent development. While some have suggested that he has broken with the dependency tradition it should be noted that he likes to situate his project in terms of a broader modernization strategy. At least on this score he has some continuities with his earlier dependency work (see Powers 2001).

5 Surprisingly he leaves out the tradition of New Liberalism in shaping the integrationist welfare tradition.

6 This was noted by Foucault in his famous College de France lectures in 1979 (Lemke 2001; Burchell et al. 1991).

7 Joerges and Rödl (2004) point out that he was not in the inner circles of the Freiburg School.

8 As Lemke (2001: 194) points out, 'the *historical* significance of this hypothesis is that it rejects a concept of history that attempts to derive socio-political changes from the economic transformation processes of capitalism'.

9 See Hobhouse (1922), and also White (2004), on Hobhouse and asset-based social policy.

10 See Green (1906). Green's writing on property and rights have been the subject of much recent scholarly analysis. Indeed, he seems to anticipate a number of more recent debates between communitarians and liberals over the nature of rights.

11 See Hobson (1974). Freedan (2004) provides a particularly illuminating analysis of Hobson's views on welfare and poverty.

12 Prabhaka (2003) provides a very good analysis of stakeholding in the programs and policies of New Labour.

13 For a recent overview of some of these arguments about property see Pierson (2005).

2 Capability, Freedom and the Third Way

1 See Giddens (1998) and Jayasuriya (1999b) for an overview of some of the key elements of the new social democracy. For a flavour of some British third way thinking, see Hargreves and Christie (1998).

2   For an overview of recent developments in European Social Democracy see Kitschelt (1994). For an analysis of the structural constraints imposed on traditional social democracy by globalization see Scharpf (1996) and Jayasuriya (2001b).

3   See also Mullender (2000) who argues that the third way represents a form of qualified moral consequentialism that is similar to the pragmatism that Finlayson identifies.

4   See, for example, World Bank (1997) for an illustration of the new emphasis on state capacities.

5   For one influential attempt to locate the new social democracy in relation to both classical social democracy and neo liberalism see Giddens (1998).

6   One of the problems with Giddens's notion of the traditional welfare state is that it tends to gloss over some of the significant differences in European and North American welfare structures and institutions. For a detailed survey of these differences see Esping-Andersen (1990). Moreover, his notion of the social investment state has some affinity with Scandinavian welfare states that have sought to integrate welfare and labour market policies.

7   See, for example, Rhodes (1992) for a discussion of the problems and prospects for European social policy.

8   See Walters (1997) for an excellent account of how this language serves to marginalize the traditional notion of unemployment.

9   This is exactly the point made by Huber and Stephens (1998) in their excellent account of the 'Swedish Model'.

10   Giddens's work, for example, largely skirts around the key issues of equality and freedom in the new social democracy.

11   In short this argument would suggest that postwar social democracy was only possible under conditions where capital mobility was restricted and the Bretton Woods system provided exchange rate stability. It is this postwar world that Ruggie aptly characterized as a form of 'embedded liberalism'. See, for example, Scharpf (1996), J Ruggie (1983).

12   Although assets need to be thought of in broader terms than just skills, this does point to the potentially radical implications of the new social democracy.

13   Unlike our argument, Giddens prefers to analyse the new social democracy in terms of a shift in modernity rather than in terms of the evolution of the new forms of market economies.

14   Much of this approach draws heavily on Beck *et al.*'s (1994) work on risk society. See also Franklin (1998) for a flavour of some recent work.

15   Sen is best known for using the capability approach to understand issues of poverty and development. See Sen (1981, 1985). He has developed the more general normative implications of his views in these writings but a particularly useful articulation of his philosophical views of equality and freedom can be found in Sen (1980, 1992). The latter is a very useful overview of the key concept of capability. Useful reviews of his work can be found in Cohen (1994) and Crocker (1992).

16   Sen also argues that equality is an important imperative in all social and political theories because it reflects a deep concern with equal concern and regard for individuals.

17 Capability 'represents the various combination of functionings (beings and doings) that a person can achieve' (Sen 1992: 40).
18 We need to bear in mind that that functionings are personal features where capability to function relates to what it is possible for a person to do. And this is important.
19 Sen (1985: 318) points out, in this regard, that 'we do not drown the information about a person's disadvantages in the loud noise of utilities, as welfarists would do. A person, as we argued before, is more than the location of utilities, and it does matter what kind of deal he is getting'.
20 Anderson (1999: 313).
21 Anderson (1999) provides a superb critique of what she calls luck egalitarianism contrasting it with a conception of democratic equality. While she does not draw on the republican notion of liberty used in this volume the argument strongly parallels ours.

3 The Illiberal Politics of Neo Liberal Welfare Contractualism

1 For the key features of illiberalism see Holmes (1993, 1995).
2 See Dyzenhaus (1996a) for an intriguing analysis of the way Schmitt's critique of liberalism as apolitical can be utilized to analyse aspects of Rawls's notion of political liberalism.
3 Indeed even in the area of disability, dependency is increasingly viewed in a pejorative and negative manner.
4 Tax credits have been a major component of the social policy reforms of both the Blair and the Clinton administrations.
5 In fact the virtue of King's (1999) analysis is to draw the connection between workfare and a range of other illiberal and coercive programmes, including eugenics.
6 This is not new. See, for example, the Moynihan Report. See also Jencks (1992).
7 And one might as well also add in recent World Bank thinking on social policy which gives a prominent place to civil society. See Chapter 4.
8 Friendly Societies, of course, had a major impact on the development of Australian welfare policy.
9 For an analysis of these notions of procedural autonomy which have played an important role in feminist ideas of individual autonomy see Mackenzie and Stoljar (1999).
10 See also Yeatman and Owler (2001).
11 On this notion of connectedness see O'neil (1996).
12 For the initial discussion of relational autonomy see Nedelsky (1989).
13 For a discussion of the strategies of recontexualization as a critical resource see Lacey (1998) who develops a particularly persuasive argument.
14 For a parallel view of rights as instrumental in securing and upholding collective goods that are essential to the public culture of specific political communities, see Bellamy (2000).
15 As Plant (1985: 23) eloquently argues: 'I believe that those who defend the welfare state as a means to freedom do have to be careful that the

institutional arrangements which they endorse do actually secure the maximal range of choice and maximal amount of responsibility for such choices by citizens'.

4 Contractualism and Transnational Welfare Governance

1 Higgott (1983) provides the best introduction to the impact of modernization theory and basic needs approaches to global development. What is interesting about this basic needs approach and indeed some of the modernization perspectives are some of the implicit social democratic notions that underpinned its developmentalism. In this sense modernization theory remained a precarious balance between discipline and some emancipatory notion of development. In one sense, modernization theory has returned in the guise of global governance, but with a strongly disciplinary focus.

2 For an overview of these debates see Jayasuriya and Rosser (2001).

3 On the Asian crisis and its aftermath see World Bank (1998, 2000, 2001). Jayasuriya and Rosser (2001) trace the intellectual convergence of these new governance programs with ordo liberal ideas.

4 Although in this chapter I examine transnational welfare governance, it needs to be understood that the influence of contractualism on global public policy is broader. For example, the accession process of candidate member states to the European Union has all the hallmarks of the contractual governance being discussed in this chapter. Accession depends on establishing partnership or contractual agreements involving the fulfilment of an often onerous set of domestic governance 'preconditions' – including not just economic governance but areas such as border control – before membership of the EU (Grabbe 1999).

5 For an incisive analysis of these institutional features see Cammack (2002).

6 The objectives of the EPA are the eradication of poverty, the liberalization of economies and sustainable economic development.

7 See the entire issue of *Politics and Society*, volume 32 (1) for a survey of the basic income argument. There are similar proposals for stakeholding or initial capital grants.

5 The New Regulatory State and the Social Market in Korea

1 In fact, it might be said that the Australian and New Zealand experiments have much in common with the South Korean reform programme in that it had to actively pursue market reform, not simply to adjust to a new neo liberal environment as was the case with New Labour.

2 For an initial assessment of the emergence of a new Korean model see Mathews (1998).

3 Here, the ideas of 'technology of public action' are borrowed from Hartog (1983) and Novak (2004).

4 For the notion of a research program see Lakatos (1970).

5 For attribute notion of policy capacity see Evans and Rauch (1999) and Weiss (1998).

6 See Nettl (1968). This was a seminal article that inspired much of the statist literature of the 1980s, including Evans, Rueschemeyer, and Skocpol (1985).

7 See Evans (1997) for an analysis of the impact of Nettl's article on statist paradigm.

8 For an elaboration of a similar relation see Jessop's (2002) notion of strategic relational capacity.

9 Ginsburg provides an excellent overview of the developing systems of judicial review in East Asia. In fact, given the authoritarian traditions of these states these new systems of judicial review are more remarkable than the transformation in the system of economic governance.

10 See Pekkarinen *et al.* (1992) for a discussion of societal corporatism. L. Jayasuriya (2000) has a good discussion of corporatism in the context of third world welfare.

11 For a good survey of European social pacts see Fajertag and Pochet (1997).

6 Statecraft and Social Contracts: A Populist Market Citizenship in Thailand

1 This chapter draws on some of the ideas examined in Jayasuriya and Hewison (2004).

2 Hewison (2004) provides the best understanding of the political and economic context within which the TRT came to power.

3 Not so simple in Southeast Asia where, in contrast to Latin America, populist politics has not been a defining feature of the region. Certainly, in Thailand populist politics has not been very prominent.

4 See the work of Nettl (1968) for a concise definition of stateness.

5 The work of Roberts (1995) and Weyland (1996, 2004) have been among the most important contributions to the literature on neo liberalism.

6 Of all the countries in Southeast Asia, Thailand has historically been the most accommodating of the policies of the World Bank (see Hewison 1989)

7 See also Shivakumar *et al.* (2000).

8 For this concept see Chapter 5.

7 The New Politics of Inclusion

1 This failure to locate the political context of the social question mars an otherwise illuminating piece on the social question in Judt (1997).

2 This is a term taken from Laski (1925).

3 See Jayasuriya (2005) for an analysis of social constitutionalism in terms of the broader framework of the postwar global liberal order.

4 Indeed, an argument could be made that the recent metamorphosis of populism to neo liberal populism reflects a common set of dilemmas to the extent that populism was a substitute for social democracy See Roberts (2002).

5 The point here is not a definitional one, but rather the way the concept of social capital and civil society is used to become a broader element in new

forms of symbolic politics. Consider, for example, how the term 'community' has replaced 'society' in the rhetoric and justification of social welfare pro- grammes. It is important here to note how this usage reflects the application of the notion of social capital to articulate a particular anti-political notion of citizenship.

6   See Ehrenberg (1999) for analysis of the how the term 'civil society' has been used in a way that can marginalize the role of political associations and con- testation in favour of a conception of associational organizations independent of formal representative structures of the polity.

7   Allars (2001) provides the kind of analysis of review rights that is essential if the new welfare governance is going to be made much more political.

8   In fact, Pierson (2005) makes this point in his analysis of property and the third way.

References

Abrams, M. and R. Richard (1960) *Must Labour Lose?* London: Penguin.

Adorno, T.W. and M. Horkheimer (1979) (translated from German by John Cummings), *Dialectic of Enlightenment*. London: Verso.

Allars, M. (2001) 'Citizenship rights, review rights, and contractualism'. *Law in Context* 18 (2): 79–111.

Amsden, A. (1989) *Asia's Next Giant: South Korea and Late Industrialization*. Oxford: Oxford University Press.

Anderson, E.S. (1999) 'What is the point of equality?'. *Ethics* (109): 287–337.

Atkinson, T. (2002) 'Social inclusion and the European Union'. *Journal of Common Market Studies* 40 (4): 625–43.

Baiocchi, G. (2001) 'Participation, activism and politics: the Porto Alegre experiment and deliberative democratic theory'. *Politics and Society* 29 (1): 43–72.

Baker, C. (2004) 'Pluto-populism: Thaksin, business and popular politics in post-crisis Thailand', in E. Hedman and J. T. Sidel (eds), *Populism and Reformism in Southeast Asia: The Threat and Promise of New Politics*. New Haven: Yale University Southeast Asia Studies Monograph Series.

Barnard, C. and S. Deakin (2001) 'Market access and regulatory competition'. *Jean Monnet Working Paper* 9/01. Available at http://www.jeanmonnetprogram.org/papers/01/012701.html.

Bastow, S., J. Martin and D. Pels (2002) 'Third ways in political ideology'. *Journal of Political Ideology* 7 (3): 269–80.

Beck, U., A. Giddens and S. Lash (1994) *Reflexive Modernization*. Cambridge: Polity Press.

Beeson, M. (2002) 'Japan's reluctant reformers and the legacy of the developmental state', in A. Cheung and I. Scott (eds), *Governance and Public Sector Reform in Post Crisis Asia: Paradigm Shift or Business as Usual?* London: Curzon Press.

Bellamy, R. (1999) *Liberalism and Pluralism: Towards a Politics of Compromise*. London: Routledge.

Bellamy, R. (2000) *Rethinking Liberalism*. London: Pinter.

Berlin, I. (1958) *Two Concepts of Liberty*. Oxford: Oxford University Press.

Bessant, J. (1999) 'From entitlement to obligation in the Australian welfare state'. *Australian Journal of Social Issues* 34 (2): 103–18.

Beveridge, W. (1942) *Social Insurance and Allied Services*. London: His Majesty's Stationery Office.

Bevir, M. (2003) 'Narrating the British State: an interpretive critique of the New Labour's institutionalism'. *Review of International Political Economy* 10 (3): 455–80.

Bobbio, N. (1996) *Left and Right: The Significance of a Political Distinction*. Cambridge: Polity Press.

Boonyaratpalin, S. (2005) 'Statement to the IFAD Governing Council'. Available at http://www.ifad.org/events/gc/25/speech/thailand.htm (accessed 2 February 2005).

Bourdieu, P. (1977) *Outline of a Theory of Practice*. Cambridge: Cambridge University Press.

Brison, S.J. (2000) 'Relational autonomy and freedom of expression', in C. Mackenzie and N. Stoljar (eds), *Relational Autonomy: Feminist Perspectives on Autonomy, Agency and the Social Self*. New York and Oxford: Oxford University Press.

Buckler, S. and D. Dolowitz (2004) and 'Can fair be efficient? New Labour, social liberalism and British economic policy'. *New Political Economy* 9 (1): 23–38.

Burchell, G., C. Gordon and P. Miller (eds) (1991) *The Foucault Effect*. Chicago: Chicago University Press.

Business Week (2003) 'Under suspicion in Thailand', *Business Week Online*, 15 April. Available at http://www.businessweek.com/magazine/content/02_15/b3778129.htm (accessed 13 December 2003).

Cammack, P. (2001) 'Making the poor work for globalisation?'. *New Political Economy* 6 (3): 397–408.

Cammack, P. (2002) 'The mother of all governments: the World Bank's matrix for global governance', in R. Wilkinson and S. Hughes (eds), *Global Governance: Critical Perspectives*. London: Routledge.

Cammack, P. (2004) 'Giddens' way with words', in S. Hale, W. Leggett and L. Martell (eds), *The Third Way and Beyond: Criticisms, Futures and Alternatives*. Manchester: Manchester University Press.

Carney, T. and G. Ramia (1999) 'From citizenship to contractualism: the transition from unemployment benefits to employment services in Australia'. *Australian Journal of Administrative Law* 6 (3): 117–39.

Cerney, P. (2004) 'Mapping varieties of neo liberalism'. *IPEG Papers in Global Political Economy*, No. 12, May.

Chandhoke, N. (2002) 'Governance and pluralisation of the state: implications for democratic practices in Asia'. Paper presented at International Conference on: Governance in Asia: Culture, Ethnic, Institutional Reform, and Policy Change, City University of Hong Kong, 5–7 December.

Cohen, G.A. (1994) 'Amartya Sen's unequal world'. *New Left Review* 203: 117–29.

Cohen, G.A (1995) 'Incentives, inequality and community', in S. Darwall (ed.), *Equal Freedom*. Ann Arbor: University of Michigan Press.

Cohen, J. (1999) 'Trust, voluntary association and workable democracy: the contemporary American discourse of civil society', in M.E. Warren (ed.), *Democracy and Trust*. Cambridge: Cambridge University Press.

Considine, M. (2001) *Enterprising States: The Public Management of Welfare to Work*. Cambridge: Cambridge University Press.

Crocker, D.A. (1992) 'Functioning and capability: the foundation of Sen's and Nussbaum's development ethic'. *Political Theory* 20 (4): 584–612.

Dao, J. (2003) 'With rise in foreign aid, plans for a new way to give it'. *New York Times*, 3 February, p. A 5.

Deacon, A. and K. Mann (1999) 'Agency, modernity and social policy'. *Journal of Social Policy* 28 (3): 413–35.

Deacon, B. (with M. Hulse and P. Stubbs) (1997) *Global Social Policy: International Organisations and the Future of Welfare*. London: Sage.

Dean, J. (2002) *Publicity's Secret*. Ithaca, NY: Cornell University Press.

Department for Education and Employment, United Kingdom Government (1998) *The Learning Age: A Renaissance for a New Britain*. London: The Stationery Office.

Department of Family and Community Services, Australian Government (2000) *Participation Support for a More Equitable Society*. The Interim Report of the Reference Group on Welfare Reform. Canberra: Department of Family and Community Services.

Deyo, F.C. (1992) 'The political economy of social policy formation: East Asia's newly industrialized countries', in R.P. Appelbaum and J. Henderson (eds), *States and Development in the Asian Pacific Rim*. Newbury Park, CA: Sage Publications.

Donnison, D. (1976) 'An approach to social policy'. *Australian Journal of Social Issues* 11 (1): 4–31.

DSS (Department of Social Security), United Kingdom (1998) *New Ambitions for Our Country* (The Field Report). London: Stationery Office.

Dworkin, R. (1981) 'What is equality? Part 2: Equality of resources'. *Philosophy and Public Affairs* 10 (1): 283–345. Reprinted in: R. Dworkin, *Sovereign Virtue: The Theory and Practice of Equality*. Cambridge, MA: Harvard University Press, 2000.

Dyzenhaus, D. (1996a) 'Liberalism after the fall: Schmitt, Rawls and the problem of Justification'. *Philosophy and Social Criticism* 22 (3): 9–37.

Dyzenhaus, D. (1996b) 'The Legitimacy of Legality'. *University of Toronto Law Journal* 46: 129–80.

Ehrenberg, J. (1999) *Civil Society: The Critical History on an Idea*. New York: New York University Press.

Eley, G. (2002) *Forging Democracy: The History of the Left in Europe, 1850–2000*. Oxford: Oxford University Press.

Elson, D. (1988) 'Market socialism or socialisation of the market'. *New Left Review* 1/172: 3–44.

Esping-Andersen, G. (1990) *The Three Worlds of Welfare Capitalism*. Cambridge: Cambridge University Press.

Eucken, W. (1950) *The Foundations of Economics: History and Theory in the Analysis of Economic Reality*. London: Hodge.

Evans, P. (1995) *Embedded Autonomy: States and Industrial Transformation*. Princeton, NJ: Princeton University Press.

Evans, P. (1997) 'The eclipse of the state? Reflections on stateness in an era of globalization'. *World Politics* 50 (1): 62–87.

Evans, P. and J. Rauch (1999) 'Bureaucracy and growth: a cross-national analysis of the effects of "Weberian" state structures on economic growth'. *American Sociological Review* 64 (4): 748–65.

Evans, P., D. Rueschemeyer and T. Skocpol (eds) (1985) *Bringing the State Back In*. Cambridge, MA: Cambridge University Press.

Ewald, F. (2000) 'The return of the crafty genius: an outline of a philosophy of precaution'. *Connecticut Insurance Law Journal* 6: 47–61.

Fajertag, G. and P.P. Pochet (eds) (1997) *Social Pacts in Europe*. Brussels: European Trade Union Institute.

Ferguson, J. (1990) *The Anti-Politics Machine: 'Development', Depoliticization and Bureaucratic Power in Lesotho*. Cambridge: Cambridge University Press.

Ferris, J. (1985) 'Citizenship and the crisis of the welfare state', in P. Bean, J. Ferris and D. Whynes (eds), *Independence of Welfare*. London and New York: Tavistock.

Fine, B. (1999) 'The developmental state is dead – long live social capital?'. *Development and Change* 30 (1): 1–19.

Finlayson, A. (1999) 'Third way theory'. *Political Quarterly* (3): 271–9.

Francis, C.B. (2001) 'Quasi-public, quasi-private trends in emerging market economies'. *Comparative Politics* 33 (3): 275–94.

Franklin, J. (ed.) (1998) *The Politics of Risk Society*. Cambridge: Polity Press.

Fraser, N. (1997) *Justice Interrupts*. New York and London: Routledge.

Freedan, M. (2004) *Liberal Languages: Ideological Imaginations and Twentieth Century Progressive Thought*. Princeton, NJ: Princeton University Press.

Freeden, M. (1978) *The New Liberalism: An Ideology of Social Reform*. Oxford: Oxford University Press.

Freedland, M. and D. King (2003) 'Contractual governance and illiberal contracts: some problems of contractualism as an instrument of behaviour management by agencies of government'. *Cambridge Journal of Economics* 27 (3): 465–77.

Freeman, J. (2000) 'The private role in public governance'. *New York University Law Review* 75: 543–675.

Friedman, D. (1988) *The Misunderstood Miracle: Industrial Development and Political Change in Japan*. Ithaca, NY: Cornell University Press.

Fukuyama, F. (2000) *The Great Disruption: Human Nature and the Reconstruction of Social Order*. New York: Simon & Schuster.

Gamble, A. and G. Kelly (1996) 'The politics of ownership'. *New Left Review* 220: 62–97.

Gerber, D.J. (1994) 'Constitutionalizing the economy: German neo-liberalism, competition law and the "New" Europe'. *The American Journal of Comparative Law* 42: 25–84.

Germain, R. (1997) *The International Organisation of Credit: States and Global Finance in the World Economy*. London: Cambridge University Press.

Giddens, A. (1994) *Beyond Left and Right: The Future of Radical Politics*. Cambridge: Polity Press.

Giddens, A. (1998) *The Third Way: The Renewal of Social Democracy*. Cambridge: Polity Press.

Giddens, A. (2000) *The Third Way and Its Critics*. Oxford: Polity Press.

Gilbert, N. (2002) *Transformation of the Welfare State: The Silent Surrender of Public Responsibility*. New York: Oxford University Press.

Gilbert, N. and H. Specht (1974) *Dimensions of Social Welfare Policy*. Eaglewood Cliffs NJ: Prentice Hall.

Ginsburg, T. (2002) 'Comparative administrative procedure: evidence from Northeast Asia, *Constitutional Political Economy* 13 (3): 247–64.

Ginsburg, T. (2003) *Judicial Review in New Democracies: Constitutional Courts in Asian Cases*. Cambridge: Cambridge University Press.

Glassman, J. (2004) 'Economic "nationalism" in a post nationalist era: the political economy of economic policy in post crisis Thailand'. *Critical Asian Studies* 36 (1): 37–64.

Gough, I. (2000) *Global Capital, Human Needs And Social Policies*. Basingstoke: Palgrave Macmillan.

Gough, I. (2003) 'East Asia: The limits of productivist regimes'. Paper Presented at the International Sociology Conference Research Committee 10 on: *Poverty, Social Welfare and Social Policy*, University of Toronto. Available at http://individual.utoronto.ca/RC19_2003/papers.html.

Grabbe, H. (1999) 'A partnership for accession? The implication of EU conditionality for the Central and East European applicants.' *RSC Working Paper 99/12*. Florence: European University Institute.

Green, T.H. (1906) *Prolegomena to Ethics*. Oxford: Clarendon Press.

Habermas, J. (1996a) *Between Facts and Norms*. Cambridge, MA: The MIT Press.

Habermas, J. (1996b) 'Three Normative Models of Democracy', in Seyla Benhabib (ed.), *Democracy and Difference. Contesting the Boundaries of the Political*. Princeton, NJ: Princeton University Press.

Hacking, I. (1996) 'In pursuit of fairness'. *The New York Review* (September): 40–3.

Hale, S., W. Leggett and L. Martell (2004) *The Third Way and Beyond: Criticisms, Futures and Alternatives*. Manchester: Manchester University Press.

Hall, S. (1988) *The Hard Road to Renewal: Thatcherism and the Crisis of the Left*. London: Verso.

Hall, S. and M. Jacques (eds) (1989) *New Times: The Changing Face of Politics in the 1990s*. London: Lawrence & Wishart.

Hargreaves, I. and I. Christie (1998) *Tomorrow's Politics: The Third Way and Beyond*. London: Demos.

Harriss, J. (2002) *Depoliticising Development: The World Bank and Social Capital*. Delhi: Leftword.

Hartog, H. (1983) *Public Property and Private Power: The Corporation of the City of New York in American Law, 1730–1870*. Chapel Hill: University of North Carolina Press.

Hay, C. (1999) *The Political Economy of New Labour*. Manchester: Manchester University Press.

Held, D. (1998) 'The timid tendency', in M. Jacques (ed.), *Marxism Today: Special Edition*, Nov./Dec. 8.

Hewison, K. (1989) *Bankers and Bureaucrats: Capital and State in Thailand*. Yale University Southeast Asian Monographs, No. 34. New Haven: Yale Center for International and Area Studies.

Hewison, K. (2000) 'Resisting globalization: a study of localism in Thailand'. *The Pacific Review* 13 (2): 279–96.

Hewison, K. (2001) 'Thailand's capitalism: development through boom and bust', in G. Rodan, K. Hewison and R. Robison (eds), *The Political Economy of South-East Asia: Conflicts, Crises, and Change*. Melbourne: Oxford University Press.

Hewison, K. (2002) 'The World Bank and Thailand: crisis and social safety nets'. *Public Administration and Policy* 11 (1): 1–22.

Hewison, K. (2003a) 'Crafting a new social contract: domestic capitalist responses to the challenge of neo liberalism,' in G. Ungpakorn (ed.), *Radicalising Thailand: New Political Perspectives*. Bangkok: Chulalongkorn University Institute of Asia Studies.

Hewison, K. (2003b) 'The politics of neo liberalism: class and capitalism in contemporary Thailand'. SEARC Working Paper 43, available at: http://www.cityu.edu.hk/searc/WP.html.

Hewison, K. (2005) Neo-liberalism and domestic capital: the political outcomes of the economic crisis in Thailand'. *Journal of Development Studies* 41 (2): 310–30.

Higgott, R. (1983) *Political Development Theory*. New York: St Martins Press.

Hobhouse, L.T. (1922) *The Elements of Social Justice*. London: Allen and Unwin.

Hobson, J.A. (1974) *The Crisis of Liberalism: New Issues of Democracy*. London: Harvester.

Hodgson, G. (1999) *Economics and Utopia: Why the Learning Economy is Not the End of History*. London: Routledge.

Hohfield, W. (1946) *Fundamental Legal Conceptions as Applied in Judicial Reasoning*. New Haven: Yale University Press.

Holliday, I. (2000) 'Productivist welfare capitalism: social policy in East Asia'. *Political Studies* 48: 706–23.

Holliday, I. (2005) 'East Asian social policy in the wake of the financial crisis: farewell to productivism?'. *Policy and Politics* 33 (1): 145–62.

Holmes, S. (1993) *The Anatomy of Antiliberalism*. Cambridge, MA: Harvard University Press.

Holmes, S. (1995) *Passions and Constraints: On the Theory of Liberal Democracy*. Chicago: University of Chicago Press.

Honig, B. (1993) *Political Theory and Displacement of Politics*. Ithaca, NY: Cornell University Press.

Houtzager, P. (2003) 'Introduction: from polycentrism to the polity', in P. Houtzager and M. Moore (eds), *Changing Paths: International Development and the New Politics of Inclusion*. Ann Arbor, MI: Michigan University Press.

Huber, E. and J.D. Stephens (1998) 'Internationalization and the social democratic model: crisis and future prospects'. *Comparative Political Studies* 31 (3): 353–97.

Hundt, D. (2005) 'A legitimate paradox: neo liberal reform and the return of the state in Korea'. *Journal of Development Studies* 41 (2): 242–60.

IMF (International Monetary Fund) and IDA (International Development Association) (2002) *Review of the Poverty Reduction Strategy Paper (PRSP) Approach*. Washington: IMF. Available at http://www.imf.org/External/NP/prspgen/review/2002/032602a.htm.

IMF (2004) *Report on the Evaluation of Poverty Reduction Strategy Papers (PRSPs) and The Poverty Reduction and Growth Facility (PRGF)*. Washington: IMF. Available at http://www.imf.org/External/NP/ieo/2004/prspprgf/eng/index.htm.

Jackson, B. (2004) 'The uses of utilitarianism: social justice, welfare economics and British socialism 1931–48'. *History of Political Thought* 25 (3) 508–35.

Jayasuriya, K. (1999a) 'Globalization, law, and the transformation of sovereignty: the emergence of global regulatory governance'. *Indiana Journal of Global Legal Studies* 6 (2) (Spring): 425–55.

Jayasuriya, K. (1999b) Review essay: 'Revisionist social democracy'. *Australian Quarterly* 71 (3): 25–39.

Jayasuriya, K. (2000a) 'Authoritarian liberalism, governance and the emergence of the regulatory state in post-crisis East Asia', in R. Robison, M. Beeson, K. Jayasuriya and Hyuk-Rae Kim (eds), *Politics and Markets in the Wake of the Asian Crisis*. London: Routledge.

Jayasuriya, K. (2000b) 'Capability, freedom and the new social democracy'. *Political Quarterly* 71 (3): 282–99.

Jayasuriya, K. (2001a) 'Globalisation, sovereignty, and the rule of law: from political to economic constitutionalism?' Special Issue, *Constellations* 8 (4): 442–60.

Jayasuriya, K. (2001b) Globalisation and the changing architecture of the state: regulatory state and the politics of negative coordination'. *Journal of European Public Policy* 8 (1): 101–23.

Jayasuriya, K. (2002) 'The new contractualism: neo liberal or democratic?'. *Political Quarterly* 73 (3): 309–20.

Jayasuriya, K. (2003) 'Workfare for the global poor: anti politics and the new governance'. Working Paper No 98 Asia Research Centre, Murdoch University. Available at http://wwwarc.murdoch.edu.au/wp/wp98.rtf.

Jayasuriya, K. (2005) *Reconstituting the Global Liberal Order: Legitimacy and Regulation.* Oxford: Routledge.

Jayasuriya, K. and K. Hewison (2004) 'The anti politics of good governance: from global social policy to a global populism?' *Critical Asian Studies* 36 (4): 571–90.

Jayasuriya, K. and A. Rosser (1999) 'Economic orthodoxy and the Asian crisis'. Working Paper, No. 93, Asia Research Centre, Murdoch University.

Jayasuriya, K. and A. Rosser (2001) 'Economic orthodoxy and the East Asian crisis'. *Third World Quarterly* 22 (3): 381–96.

Jayasuriya, L. (1996) The Challenge of the Welfare State in Reclaiming Social Democracy in Sri Lanka. Sixth J.E. Jayasuriya Memorial Lecture. Colombo: J.E. Jayasuriya Memorial Foundation.

Jayasuriya, L. (2000) *Welfarism and Politics in Sri Lanka: Experience of a Third World State.* Perth: University of Western Australia.

Jencks, C. (1992) *Rethinking Social Policy: Race, Poverty and the Underclass.* Cambridge, MA: Harvard University Press.

Jessop, B. (1993) 'Towards a Schumpeterian workfare state?' Preliminary remarks on post-fordist political economy'. *Studies in Political Economy* 40: 7–39.

Jessop, B. (2002) *The Future of the Capitalist State.* Oxford: Polity Press.

Joerges, C. and F. Rödl (2004) ' "Social Market Economy" ' as Europe's social model?' EUI Working Paper Law No 2004/8 European University Institute. Available at http://www.iue.it/PUB/law04–8.pdf.

Johnson, C. (1982) *MITI and the Japanese Miracle: The Growth of Industrial Policy.* Stanford, CA: Stanford University Press.

Joppke, C. (1999) *Immigration and the Nation-State.* Oxford: Oxford University Press.

Judt, T. (1997) 'The social question *redivivus*'. *Foreign Affairs* Sept./Oct.: 95–117.

Katznelson, I. (1996) *Liberalism's Crooked Circle.* Princeton, NJ: Princeton University Press.

Keane, J. (1998) *Civil Society: Old Images, New Visions.* Cambridge: Polity Press.

Kim, D.J. (1985) *Mass Participatory Economy: A Democratic Alternative for Korea.* Cambridge, MA: Harvard University Press.

King, D. (1999) *In the Name of Liberalism: Illiberal Social Policy in the USA and Britain.* Oxford: Oxford University Press.

Kitschelt, H. (1994) *The Transformation of European Social Democracy.* New York: Cambridge University Press.

Kong, T.Y. (2004) 'Neo liberalisation and incorporation in advanced newly industrialising countries: a view from South Korea'. *Political Studies* 52 (2): 19–42.

Korea Tripartite Commission (KTC) (2004) *Introduction to the Korea Tripartite Commission.* Seoul: Korea Tripartite Commission.

Krieger, J. (1999) *British Politics in the Global Age: Can Social Democracy Survive?* Oxford: Polity Press.

Kwon, H.J. (1997) 'Beyond European welfare regimes: comparative perspectives on East Asian welfare systems'. *Journal of Social Policy* 26: 467–84.

Kwon, H.J. (1999) *The Welfare State in Korea: The Politics of Legitimation.* London: Macmillan.

Kwon, H.J. (2002) 'Welfare reform and future challenges in the Republic of Korea: Beyond the developmental welfare state?' *International Social Security Review* 55: 23–38.

Kwon, H.J. (2003a) 'Transforming the developmental welfare states in East Asia policies', UNRISD Workshop on Social Policy in a Developmental Context, Bangkok. Unpublished paper. Available at http://www.unrisd.org.

Kwon, H.J. (2003b) 'Advocacy coalitions and the politics of welfare in Korea after the economic crisis'. *Policy & Politics* 31: 69–83.

Lacey, N. (1998) *Unspeakable Subjects: Feminist Essays in Legal and Social Theory.* Oxford: Hart Publishing.

Lakatos, I. (1970) 'Falsification and the methodology of scientific research programmes', in I. Lakatos and A. Musgrave (eds), *Criticism and the Growth of Knowledge.* Cambridge: Cambridge University Press.

Laski, H. (1925) *A Grammar of Politics.* London: Allen & Unwin.

Latham, M. (1998) *Civilising Global Capital.* Sydney: Allen & Unwin.

Le Grand, J. (1998) 'The Third Way begins with Cora'. *New Statesman* (March): 26–7.

Lemke, T. (2001) 'The birth of "bio politics": Michael Foucault's lectures at the College de France on neo liberal governmentality'. *Economy and Society* 30 (2): 190–207.

Levitas, R. (1996) 'The concept of social exclusion and the new Durkheimian hegemony'. *Critical Social Policy* 46: 5–20.

Levitas, R. (1998) *The Inclusive Society? Social Exclusion and New Labour.* London: Macmillan.

Lian, D. (2003) 'Thailand: capital creation – the next step' Morgan Stanley. Available at http://www.morganstanley.com/GEFdata/dig ests/20030116-thu. html (accessed 18 May 2005).

Lister, R. (1997) *Citizenship: Feminist Perspectives.* New York: New York University Press.

Lister, R. (1998) 'From equality to social inclusion: New Labour and the welfare state'. *Critical Social Policy* 18 (2): 215–26.

Looney, R. (2003) 'Thailand's Thaksinomics: a new Asian paradigm'. Centre for Contemporary Conflict, Naval Postgraduate School, Monterey California. Available at http://www.ccc.nps.navy.mil/rsepResources/si/dec03/eastAsia.asp.

Low, L. and A.T. Choon (2004) *Social Insecurity in the New Millennium: The Central Provident Fund of Singapore.* Singapore: Marshall Cavendish.

Macargo, D. (2005) 'Can Thaksin lead Southeast Asia Time Asia'. Available at:<http://www.time.com/time/asia/2005/thai_thaksin/viewpoint.html> (accessed 10 February 2005).

Mackenzie, C. and N. Stoljar (eds) (2000) *Relational Autonomy: Feminist Perspectives on Autonomy, Agency and the Social Self.* New York and Oxford: Oxford University Press.

Malloy, J. (1991) '*Statecraft, Social Policy and Governance in Latin America*'. Working Paper 151 Kellogg Institute for International Studies at the University of Notre Dame. Available at: http://www.nd.edu/~kellogg/WPS/151.pdf.

Marshall, T.H. (1964) *Class, Citizenship and Social Development.* New York: Doubleday & Company.

Marshall, T.H. (1981) *Rights to Welfare and Other Essays.* London: Heinemann.

Mathews, J.A. (1998) 'Fashioning a new Korean model out of the crisis: the rebuilding of institutional capabilities'. *Cambridge Journal of Economics* 22 (6): 747–59.

Maxfield, S. (1994) 'Financial incentives and central bank authority in industrialising nations'. *World Politics* 46 (4): 556–88.

Mead, L. (ed.) (1997a) *The New Paternalism*. Washington: Brookings Institution.

Mead, L. (1997b) 'The rise of paternalism', in L. Mead (ed.), *The New Paternalism*. Washington: Brookings Institution.

Mead, L. (1997c) 'Welfare employment', in L. Mead (ed.), *The New Paternalism*. Washington: Brookings Institution.

Midgley, J. (2003) *Assets in the Context of Welfare Theory: A Developmentalist Interpretation*. Working Paper No. 03–10. St Louis: Centre for Social Development Washington University.

Migdal, J., A. Kohli and V. Shue (eds) (1994) *State Power and Social Forces: Domination and Transformation in the Third World*. Cambridge: Cambridge University Press.

Miller, D. (1989) *Market, State and Community: Theoretical Foundations of Market Socialism*. Oxford: Clarendon Press.

Miliband, D. (1994) *Reinventing the Left*. Cambridge: Polity Press.

Ministry of Finance and Economy, Republic of Korea (1998) Press statement on 'Outline of new legislation to reform the central banking and financial supervisory systems'. Available at http://kiep.go.kr/imf/hot-2-2l.htm.

Ministry of Labour, Republic of Korea (2005) *Working Conditions*. Available at http://www.molab.go.kr:8787/English/ladm/ind_rel_lab.jsp (accessed 1 March 2005).

Moene, K. and M. Wallerstein (1995) 'How social democracy worked: labour market institutions'. *Politics and Society* 23 (2): 185–211.

Morgan, B. (2003) 'The economization of politics: meta-regulation as a form of nonjudicial legality'. *Social and Legal Studies* 12 (4): 489–523.

Morrow, J. (2001) 'Private property, liberal subjects and the state', in A. Simhony and D. Weinstein (eds), *The New Liberalism: Reconciling Liberty and Community*. Cambridge: Cambridge University Press.

Moschonas, G. (2000) *In the Name of Social Democracy. the Great Transformation: 1945 to the Present*. London: Verso.

Moynihan, D. (1969) *Maximum Feasible Misunderstanding*. New York: Free Press.

Muller, A. (1966) *Wirtschaftsordnung and Wirtschaftspolitick*. Frankfurt: Verlag Rombach.

Mullender, R. (2000) 'Theorising the third way: qualified consequentialism the proportionality principle and the new social democracy'. *Journal of Law and Society* 27 (4): 493–516.

Nabi, I. and J. Shivakumar (2001) *Back from the Brink: Thailand's Response to the 1997 Economic Crisis*. Washington, DC: World Bank.

Nedelsky, J. (1989) 'Reconceiving autonomy: sources, thoughts and possibilities'. *Yale Journal of Law and Feminism* 1: 7–36.

Nelson, M. (2001) 'Thailand's House election of 6 January 2001: Thaksin landslide victory and subsequent narrow escape', in M. Nelson (ed.), *Thailand's New Politics*. KPI Yearbook 2000. Bangkok: White Lotus Press.

Nettl, J.P. (1968) 'The state as a conceptual variable'. *World Politics* 20 (4): 559–92.

Neumann, F. (1944) *Behemoth: The Structure and Practice of National Socialism*. New York: Oxford University Press.

Neumann, F. (1986) *The Rule of Law: Political Theory and the Legal System in Modern Society*. Leamington Spa, England: Berg.

Norrie, A. (ed.) (1993) *Closure or Critique: New Directions in Legal Theory*. Edinburgh Law and Society Series. Edinburgh: Edinburgh University Press.

North, R. (1981) *Structure and Change in Economic History*. New York: Norton.

Novak, W. (2004) 'Law and the State Control of American Capitalism 1877–1932' NYU School of Law, New York University. Available at http://www.law.nyu.edu/tlhc/novak_20sept04.pdf.

Nussbaum, M. (2000) *Women and Human Development: the Capabilities Approach*. New York: Cambridge University Press.

O'Malley, P. (1992) 'Risk, power and crime prevention'. *Economy and Society* 21 (3): 252–75.

Oakeshott, M. (1975) *On Human Conduct*. Oxford: Clarendon Press.

OECD (1989) *Employment Outlook*. Paris: OECD.

OECD (1994) *New Orientations for Social Policy*. Paris: OECD.

OECD (1999a) *A Caring World: The New Social Policy Agenda*. Paris: OECD.

OECD (1999b) *Development Co-operation Report*. Paris: OECD.

OECD (2000) *Policy Brief: Labour Market Reform and Social Safety Net Policies in Korea*. Paris: OECD.

O'neil, O. (1996) *Towards Justice and Virtue: A Constructive Account of Practical Reasoning*. Cambridge: Cambridge University Press.

Ost, D. (2000) 'Illusory corporatism in Eastern Europe: neo liberal tripartism and post communist class identities'. *Politics and Society* 28 (4): 503–30.

Pasuk, P. (2004) *Thailand Under Thaksin: Another Malyasia?* Asia Research Centre Working Paper No. 109. Available at http://wwwarc.murdoch.edu.au/wp/wp109.pdf.

Pasuk, P. and C. Baker (2004) *Thaksin: The Business of Politics in Thailand*. Bangkok: Silkworm Books.

Peacock, A. and H. Willgerodt (1989) *German Neoliberals and the Social Market Economy*. London: Macmillan.

Peck, J. and A. Tickell (2002) 'Neo liberalizing space'. *Antipode* 34 (3): 380–404.

Pekkarinen, J. *et al.* (1992) *Social Corporatism: A Superior Economic System*. Oxford: Clarendon Press.

Pels, D. (2002) 'Socialism between fact and value: from Tony Blair to Hendrik de Man and back'. *Journal of Political Ideologies* 7 (3): 281–99.

Peng, I. (2004) 'Post industrial pressures, political regime shifts and social policy reform in Japan and South Korea'. *Journal of East Asian Studies* 4 (3): 389–425.

Petersmann, E. (1991) *Constitutional Functions and Constitutional Problems in International Economic Law*. Boulder, CO: Westview Press.

Petras, J. and H. Veltmeyer (2003) 'Whither Lula's Brazil? Neoliberalism and the "third way" ideology'. *Journal of Peasant Studies* 31 (1): 1–44.

Pettit, P. (1993) 'Negative liberty, liberal and republican'. *European Journal of Philosophy* 1: 15.

Pettit, P. (1997) *Republicanism: A Theory of Freedom and Government*. Oxford: Clarendon Press.

Phananirmai, M. and K. Hewison (2001) 'Governance and social policy in Thailand', in OECD, *Towards Asia's Sustainable Development: the Role of Social Protection*. Paris: OECD.

Pierson, C. (2005) 'Lost property: what the third way lacks'. *Journal of Political Ideologies* 10 (2): 145–63.

Pinker, R. (1979) *The Idea of Welfare*. London: Heinemann.

Pirie, I. (2005) 'The new Korean state'. *New Political Economy* 10 (1): and 25–42.

Plant, R. (1985) 'The very idea of a welfare state', in P. Bean J. Ferris and D. Whynes (eds), *Independence of Welfare*. London and New York: Tavistock.

Pongsapich, A. (2001) 'Social safety nets: programmes and projects in Thailand', in OECD, *Towards Asia's Sustainable Development: The Role of Social Protection*. Paris: OECD.

Poulantzas, N. (1978) *State, Power and Socialism*. London: New Left Books.

Powell, M. (2000) 'New Labour and the third way in the British welfare state: a new and distinctive approach?' *Critical Social Policy* 20 (1): 39–60.

Powers, T. (2001) 'Blairism Brazilian style? Cardoso and the third way in Brazil'. *Political Science Quarterly* 116 (4): 611–63.

Prabhaka, R. (2003) 'Stakeholding: does it possess a stable core?'. *Journal of Political Ideologies* 8(3): 347–63

Prion, L. with A. Evans (2004) *Politics and the PRSP Approach – Synthesis Paper* Overseas Development Institute (ODI) Working Paper 237. Available at http://www.odi.org.uk/publications/working_papers/#latest.

Procacci, G. (2001) 'Poor citizens: social citizenship versus individualization of welfare', in C. Crouch, K. Eder and D. Tambini (eds), *Citizenship, Markets and the State*. Oxford: Oxford University Press.

Putnam, R. (2000) *Bowling Alone*. New York: Simon & Schuster.

Ramesh, M. (2003) 'Globalisation and social security expansion in East Asia', in L.Weiss (ed.), *States in the Global Economy: Bringing Domestic Institutions Back in*. Cambridge: Cambridge University Press.

Ramesh, M. (2004) *Social Policy in East and Southeast Asia: Education, Health, Housing and Income Maintenance*. London: Routledge.

Rawls, J. (1971) *A Theory of Justice*. Oxford: Oxford University Press.

Raz, J. (1986) *The Morality of Freedom*. Oxford: Oxford University Press.

Raz, J. (1994) *Ethics in the Public Domain: Essays in the Morality of Law and Politics*. Oxford: Oxford University Press.

Reference Group on Welfare Reform, Australia (2000) 'Participation support for a more equitable society. Final Report, Canberra.

Rhodes, M. (1992) 'The future of the social dimension of labour market regulation in post –1992 Europe'. *Journal of Common Market Studies* 30 (1): 23–51.

Rhodes, M. (1998) 'Globalisation, labour markets and welfare states: A future of competitive corporatism', in M. Rhodes, and Y. Meny (eds), *The Future of European Welfare: A New Social Contract?* London: Pinter.

Roberts, K. (1995) 'Neoliberalism and the transformation of populism in Latin America: the Peruvian case'. *World Politics* 48 (1): 82–116.

Roberts, K. (2002) 'Social inequalities without class cleavages in Latin America's neo liberal era'. *Studies in Comparative International Development* 36 (4): 3–33.

Robertson, S., X. Bonal and R. Dale (2002) 'GATS and the educational service industry: the politics of scale and global reterritorialization'. *Comparative Education Review* 46 (4): 472–96.

Robison, R. (2006) *The Neo-Liberal Revolution*. Houndsmills: Palgrave Macmillan.

Robison, R. and A. Rosser (1998) 'Contesting reform: Indonesia's New Order and the IMF'. *World Development* 26 (8): 1593–1609.

Rodan, G. and K. Hewison (2004) 'Closing the circle' *Critical Asian Studies* 36 (3): 383–404.

Rosanvallon, P. (2000) *The New Social Question: Rethinking the Welfare State*. Princeton, NJ: Princeton University Press.

Ruggie, J. (1983) 'International regimes, transactions, and change: embedded liberalism in the postwar economic order', in S. Krasner, *International Regimes*. Ithaca, NY: Cornell University Press.

Salim, M. (2001) 'The Thailand Social Investment Fund: providing social assistance and providing social capital'. *Social Innovation Update*, vol. 1 (1), September. Washington: World Bank. Available at http://www1.worldbank.org/publicsector/decentralization/sfupdate.pdf.

Samuels, R. (1987) *The Business of the Japanese State: Energy Markets in Comparative and Historical Perspective*. Ithaca, NY: Cornell University Press.

Sandel, M. (1982) *Liberalism and the Limits of Justice*. Cambridge: Cambridge University Press.

Sassoon, D. (1996) *One Hundred Years of Socialism: the West European Left in the Twentieth Century*. London: I.B. Tauris.

Scharpf, F.W. (1996) 'Negative and positive integration in the political economy of European welfare states', in G. Marks, F. Scharpf, P. Schmitter, and W. Streeck (eds), *Governance in the European Union*. London: Sage.

Schattschneider, E.E. (1960) *The Semi Sovereign People*. New York: Rinehart & Winston.

Scheuerman, W.E. (1995) *Between the Norm and the Exception: The Frankfurt School and the Rule of Law*. Cambridge, MA: MIT Press.

Schumpeter, J.A. (1943) *Capitalism, Socialism and Democracy*. London: Unwin University Books.

Sen, A. (1980) 'Equality for what?', in S.M. McMurrin (ed.), *Tanner Lectures on Human Values*. Salt Lake City: University of Utah Press.

Sen, A. (1981) *Poverty and Famines: an Essay on Entitlements and Deprivation*. Oxford: Oxford University Press.

Sen, A. (1985) *Commodities and Capabilities*. Amsterdam: North-Holland.

Sen, A. (1990) 'Individual freedom as a social commitment'. *New York Review of Books* (14 June) 49–53.

Sen, A. (1992) *Inequality Re-examined*. London: Oxford University Press.

Shearing, C. (1996) 'Reinventing policing: policing as governance', in M. Otwin (ed.), *Policing Change and Changing Police*. London: Garland Publishing.

Sherraden, M. (1997) 'Provident funds and social protection: the case of Singapore', in J. Midgley and M. Sherraden (eds), *Alternatives to Social Security*. Westport, CT: Auburn House.

Shivakumar, J. *et al.* (2000) 'Social capital and the crisis'. *Thailand Social Monitor*, Bangkok: The World Bank (January).

Simhony, A. and D. Weinstein (eds) (2001) *The New Liberalism: Reconciling Liberty and Community*. Cambridge: Cambridge University Press.

Soederberg, S. (2004) 'American empire and "excluded states" the Millennium challenge Account and the shift to pre emptive development'. *Third World Quarterly* 25 (2): 279–302.

Somers, M. (2001) 'Romancing the market, reviling the state: historicizing liberalism, privatisation and the competing claims to civil society', in C. Crouch, K. Eder and D. Tambini (eds), *Citizenship, Markets and the State*. Oxford: Oxford University Press.

Steele, J. (2001) 'Participation and deliberation in environmental law: exploring a problem-solving approach'. *Oxford Journal of Legal Studies* 21 (3): 415–42.

Stiglitz, J. (1998a) 'More instruments and broader goals: moving toward the post-Washington Consensus'. *1998 Wider Annual Lecture*, World Wide Web document. Available at http://www.worldbank.org/html/extdr/extme/js-010798/wider.htm.

Stiglitz, J. (1998b) 'Lessons of the Asian crisis'. *Financial Times* 4 December.

Teague, P. (2001) 'Deliberative governance and EU social policy'. *European Journal of Industrial Relations*, 7 (1): 7–26.

Teubner, G. (1983) 'Substantive and reflexive elements in modern law'. *Law and Society Review* 17 (2): 239–86.

Teubner, G. (1987) 'Concepts, aspects, limits, solutions', in G. Teubner (ed.), *Juridification of Social Spheres: A Comparative Analysis of Labour Corporate Government: Trust and Social Welfare Law*. New York: De Gruyter.

Thaksin Shinawatra (2001) 'Speech by His Excellency Police. Lt. Co. Thaksin Shinawatra, Prime Minister of Thailand', 24 April, Putrajaya. Available at http://www.thaigov.go.th/news/speech/Thaksin/sp25apr01.htm (accessed 12 November 2001).

Thaksin Shinawatra (2002) '"Keynote Speech" to the 2nd International Conference of Asian Political Parties, Bangkok'. Available at http://www.thaigov.go.th/news/speech/thaksin/sp23nov02-2.htm (accessed 26 November 2002).

Thomas, S., D. Hall and V. Corral (2005) *Electricity Privatisation and Restructuring in Asia Pacific* (A report commissioned by Public Services International (PSI) for its Asia-Pacific meeting in Changmai, Thailand). Available at www.world-psi.org.

Thompson, N. (1996) 'Supply side socialism: the political economy of New Labour'. *New Left Review* 216: 37–55.

Titmuss, R.M. (1950) *Essays on the Welfare State*. London: Allen & Unwin.

Titmuss, R.M. (1974) *Social Policy: An Introduction*. London: Allen & Unwin.

Van Parijs P. (2004) 'Basic income: a simple and powerful idea for the twenty first century.' *Politics and Society* 32 (1): 7–39.

Vincent, A. (2001) 'The new liberalism and citizenship', in A. Simhony and D. Weinstein (eds), *The New Liberalism: Reconciling Liberty and Community*. Cambridge: Cambridge University Press.

Wade, R. (1990) *Governing the Market: Economic Theory and Role of Government in East Asian Industrialization*. Princeton, NJ: Princeton University Press.

Wade, R. and F. Veneroso (1998) 'The Asian crisis: the high debt model versus the Wall Street–Treasury–IMF complex'. *New Left Review* March/April: 1–24.

Waligorski, C. (1997) *Liberal Economics and Democracy: Keynes, Galbraith and Thurow and Reich*. Kansas: University of Kansas Press.

Walters, W. (1997) 'The "active society": new designs for social policy'. *Policy & Politics* 25 (3): 221–34.

Walzer, M. (1983) *Spheres of Justice: A Defence of Pluralism and Justice*. New York: Basic Books.

Weber, H. (2001) 'The imposition of a global development architecture: the example of micro credit'. *CSGR Working Paper* 77/01 University of Warwick. Available at http://www.warwick.ac.uk/fac/soc/CSGR/publications.html#CSGR Working Paper.

Weber, H. (2002) 'The imposition of a global development architecture: the example of micro credit'. *Review of International Studies* 28 (3): 537–55.

Weiner, J. (2001) 'Globalisation and disciplinary neoliberal governance'. *Constellation* 8 (4): 461–79.

Weiss, L. (1998) *The Myth of the Powerless State: Governing the Economy in a Global Era*. Oxford: Polity Press.

Weiss, L. and J. Hobson (1995) *States and Economic Development: A Comparative Historical Analysis*. Oxford: Polity Press.

Weyland, K. (1996) 'Neo-populism and neo-liberalism in Latin America: unexpected Affinities'. *Studies in Comparative International Development* 32 (3): 3–31.

Weyland, K. (2004) 'Neo populism and neoliberalism in Latin America: how much affinity'. *Third World Quarterly* 24 (6): 1095–1115.

White, S. (2004) *The Civic Minimum: On the Rights and Obligations of Economic Citizenship*. Oxford: Oxford University Press.

Wong, J. (2005) *Healthy Democracies: Welfare Politics in Taiwan and South Korea*. Ithaca, NY: Cornell University Press.

Woo-Cumings, M. (ed.) (1999) *The Developmental State*. Ithaca, NY: Cornell University Press.

Worawan, C. (2003) 'Thailand's grass roots policies'. *TDRI Quarterly* 18 (2): 1–8.

World Bank (1993) *The East Asian Miracle: Economic Growth and Public Policy*. New York: Oxford University Press.

World Bank (1994) *Governance: The World Bank's Experience*. Washington, DC: World Bank. Available at http://www.worldbank.org/wbi/sourcebook/sb0405t.htm.

World Bank (1996) *The World Bank Participation Sourcebook*. Available at http://www.worldbank.org/wbi/sourcebook/sb0405t.htm.

World Bank (1997) *World Development Report 1997: The State in a Changing World*. Oxford: Oxford University Press.

World Bank (1998) *East Asia: The Road to Recovery*. Washington, DC: World Bank.

World Bank (2000) *World Development Report 2000–2001: Attacking Poverty*. Washington, DC: World Bank.

World Bank (2001) *Thailand Social Monitor*. Washington, DC: World Bank.

Yang, J. J. (2004) 'Democratic governance and bureaucratic politics: a case of pension reform in Korea'. *Policy and Politics* 32 (2): 193–206.

Yeatman, A. (1998) 'Interpreting contemporary contractualism', in M. Dean and B. Hindess (eds), *Governing Australia: Studies in Contemporary Rationalities of Government*. London: Cambridge University Press.

Yeatman, A. (2000) 'Mutual obligation: what kind of contract is this?', in P. Saunders (ed.), *Reforming the Australian Welfare State*. Melbourne: Australian Institute of Family Studies.

Yeatman, A. and K. Owler (2001) 'The role of contract in the democratisation of service delivery. *Law in Context* 18 (2): 34–57.

Yi, L. and B.H. Lee (2003) 'Changing developmental characteristics in the Korean labour market policies', UNRISD Workshop on Social Policy in a Developmental Context, Bangkok. Unpublished paper. Available at http://www.unrisd.org.

Index

189